GLENCOE LANGUAGE ARTS

Grammar and Language Workbook

GRADE 10

Glencoe
McGraw-Hill

New York, New York   Columbus, Ohio   Woodland Hills, California   Peoria, Illinois

Glencoe/McGraw-Hill

*A Division of The **McGraw·Hill** Companies*

Send all inquiries to:
Glencoe/McGraw-Hill
8787 Orion Place
Columbus, Ohio 43240-4027

ISBN 0-02-818296-0

Printed in the United States of America

21 22 23   024   09 08 07 06

Contents

*H*andbook of Definitions and Rules

PARTS OF SPEECH
Nouns

1. A **singular noun** is a word that names one person, place, thing, or idea: brother, classroom, piglet, and joy. A **plural noun** names more than one person, place, thing, or idea: brothers, classrooms, piglets, and joys.

2. To help you determine whether a word in a sentence is a noun, try adding it to the following sentences. Nouns will fit in at least one of these sentences:

   I know something about _____.   I know something about a(n) _____.
   I know something about **brothers**.   I know something about a **classroom**.

3. A **collective noun** names a group. When the collective noun refers to the group as a whole, it is singular. When it refers to the individual group members, the collective noun is plural.
   The class meets two days a week. (singular)
   The board of trustees come from all walks of life. (plural)

4. A **common noun** names a general class of people, places, things, or ideas: soldier, country, month, or theory. A **proper noun** specifies a particular person, place, thing, event, or idea. Proper nouns are always capitalized: **General Schwartzkopf, America, July,** or **Big Bang.**

5. A **concrete noun** names an object that occupies space or that can be recognized by any of the senses: tuba, music, potato, and aroma. An **abstract noun** names an idea, a quality, or a characteristic: courage, sanity, power, and memory.

6. A **possessive noun** shows possession, ownership, or the relationship between two nouns: Raul's house, the cat's fur, and the girls' soccer ball.

Pronouns

1. A **pronoun** takes the place of a noun, a group of words acting as a noun, or another pronoun.

2. A **personal pronoun** refers to a specific person or thing. **First person** personal pronouns refer to the speaker, **second person** pronouns refer to the one spoken to, and **third person** pronouns refer to the one spoken about.

	Nominative Case	Possessive Case	Objective Case
First Person, Singular	I	my, mine	me
First Person, Plural	we	our, ours	us
Second Person, Singular	you	your, yours	you
Second Person, Plural	you	your, yours	you
Third Person, Singular	he, she, it	his, her, hers, its	him, her, it
Third Person, Plural	they	their, theirs	them

3. A **reflexive pronoun** refers to the subject of the sentence. An **intensive pronoun** adds emphasis to a noun or another pronoun. A **demonstrative pronoun** points out specific persons, places, things, or ideas.
   Reflexive: **They** psyched **themselves** up for the football game.
   Intensive: **Freddie himself** asked Julie out.
   Demonstrative: **That** is a good idea!   **Those** are my friends.

4. An **interrogative pronoun** is used to form questions. A **relative pronoun** is used to introduce a subordinate clause. An **indefinite pronoun** refers to persons, places, or things in a more general way than a noun does.
   Interrogative: **Which** is your choice?   With **whom** were you playing video games?

Relative: The cake **that** we baked was delicious.
Indefinite: **Everyone** has already voted.   **No one** should enter without knocking.

5. The **antecedent** of a pronoun is the word or group of words referred to by the pronoun.
Ben rode **his** bike to school. (*Ben* is the antecedent of *his.*)

Verbs

1. A **verb** is a word that expresses action or a state of being and is necessary to make a statement. Most verbs will fit one or more of these sentences:

We _____ .   We _____ loyal.   We _____ it.   It _____ .
We **sleep**.   We **remain** loyal.   We **love** it!   It **snowed**.

2. An **action verb** tells what someone or something does. The two types of action verbs are transitive and intransitive. A **transitive verb** is followed by a word or words that answer the question *what?* or *whom?* An **intransitive verb** is not followed by a word that answers *what?* or *whom?*

Transitive: Children **trust** their parents.   The puppy **carried** the bone away.
Intransitive: The team **played** poorly.   The light **burned** brightly.

3. A **linking verb** links, or joins, the subject of a sentence with an adjective, a noun, or a pronoun.
The concert **was** loud. (adjective)   I **am** a good card player. (noun)

4. A **verb phrase** consists of a main verb and all its **auxiliary**, or helping, verbs.
My stomach **has been growling** all morning.   I **am waiting** for a letter.

5. Verbs have four **principle parts** or forms: base, past, present participle, and past participle.
Base: I eat.   Present Participle: I am eating.
Past: I ate.   Past Participle: I have eaten.

6. The principle parts are used to form six verb tenses. The **tense** of a verb expresses time.

Simple Tenses

Present Tense: She **eats**. (present or habitual action)
Past Tense: She **ate**. (action completed in the past)
Future Tense: She **will eat**. (action to be done in the future)

Perfect Tenses

Present Perfect Tense: She **has eaten**. (action done at some indefinite time or still in effect)
Past Perfect Tense: She **had eaten**. (action completed before some other past action)
Future Perfect Tense: She **will have eaten**. (action to be completed before some future time)

7. **Irregular verbs** form their past and past participle without adding *-ed* to the base form.

PRINCIPAL PARTS OF IRREGULAR VERBS

Base Form	Past Form	Past Participle	Base Form	Past Form	Past Participle
be	was, were	been	catch	caught	caught
beat	beat	beaten	choose	chose	chosen
become	became	become	come	came	come
begin	began	begun	do	did	done
bite	bit	bitten *or* bit	draw	drew	drawn
blow	blew	blown	drink	drank	drunk
break	broke	broken	drive	drove	driven
bring	brought	brought	eat	ate	eaten

Base Form	Past Form	Past Participle	Base Form	Past Form	Past Participle
fall	fell	fallen	run	ran	run
feel	felt	felt	say	said	said
find	found	found	see	saw	seen
fly	flew	flown	set	set	set
freeze	froze	frozen	shrink	shrank *or* shrunk	shrunk *or* shrunken
get	got	got *or* gotten	sing	sang	sung
give	gave	given	sit	sat	sat
go	went	gone	speak	spoke	spoken
grow	grew	grown	spring	sprang *or* sprung	sprung
hang	hung *or* hanged	hung *or* hanged	steal	stole	stolen
have	had	had	swim	swam	swum
know	knew	known	take	took	taken
lay	laid	laid	tear	tore	torn
lead	led	led	tell	told	told
lend	lent	lent	think	thought	thought
lie	lay	lain	throw	threw	thrown
lose	lost	lost	wear	wore	worn
put	put	put	win	won	won
ride	rode	ridden	write	wrote	written
ring	rang	rung			
rise	rose	risen			

8. **Progressive forms** of verbs, combined with a form of *be,* express a continuing action. **Emphatic forms**, combined with a form of *do,* add emphasis or form questions.
   Kari **is scratching** the cat.   Loni **has been washing** the walls.
   We **do support** our hometown heroes. (present)   He **did want** that dinner. (past)

9. The **voice** of a verb shows whether the subject performs the action or receives the action of the verb. The **active voice** occurs when the subject performs the action. The **passive voice** occurs when the action of the verb is performed on the subject.
   The owl **swooped** upon its prey. (active)   The ice cream **was scooped** by the cashier. (passive)

10. A verb can express one of three moods. The **indicative mood** makes a statement or asks a question. The **imperative mood** expresses a command or request. The **subjunctive mood** indirectly expresses a demand, recommendation, suggestion, statement of necessity, or a condition contrary to fact.
    I **am** overjoyed. (indicative)   **Stop** the car. (imperative)
    If I **were** angry, I would not have let you in. (subjunctive)

Adjectives

1. An **adjective** modifies a noun or pronoun by giving a descriptive or specific detail. Adjectives can usually show comparisons. (See Using Modifiers Correctly on pages 9 and 10.)
   cold winter   **colder** winter   **coldest** winter

2. Most adjectives will fit this sentence:
   The _____ one looks very _____.
   The **dusty** one looks very **old**.

3. Articles are the adjectives *a, an,* and *the.* Articles do not meet the above test for adjectives.

4. A **proper adjective** is formed from a proper noun and begins with a capital letter.
   Marijka wore a **Ukrainian** costume.   He was a **Danish** prince.

5. An adjective used as an **object complement** follows and describes a direct object.
   My aunt considers me **funny.**

Adverbs

1. An **adverb** modifies a verb, an adjective, or another adverb. Most adverbs can show comparisons. (See Using Modifiers Correctly on pages 9 and 10.)

   a. Adverbs that tell how, where, when, or to what degree modify verbs or verbals.
   The band stepped **lively.** (how)   Maria writes **frequently.** (when)
   Put the piano **here.** (where)   We were **thoroughly** entertained. (to what degree)

   b. Adverbs of degree strengthen or weaken the adjectives or other adverbs that they modify.
   A **very** happy fan cheered. (modifies adjective)   She spoke **too** fast. (modifies adverb)

2. Many adverbs fit these sentences:
   She thinks _____.   She thinks _____ fast.   She _____ thinks fast.
   She thinks **quickly.**   She thinks **unusually** fast.   She **seldom** thinks fast.

Prepositions, Conjunctions, and Interjections

1. A **preposition** shows the relationship of a noun or a pronoun to some other word. A **compound preposition** is made up of more than one word.
   The first group **of** students arrived.   They skated **in spite of** the cold weather.

2. Some common prepositions include these: *about, above, across, after, against, along, among, around, at, before, behind, below, beneath, beside, besides, between, beyond, but, by, concerning, down, during, except, for, from, into, like, near, of, off, on, out, outside, over, past, round, since, through, till, to, toward, under, underneath, until, up, upon, with, within, without.*

3. A **conjunction** is a word that joins single words or groups of words. A **coordinating conjunction** joins words or groups of words that have equal grammatical weight. **Correlative conjunctions** work in pairs to join words and groups of words of equal weight. A **subordinating conjunction** joins two clauses in such a way as to make one grammatically dependent on the other.
   Coordinating conjunction: He **and** I talked for hours.
   Correlative conjunctions: Russ wants **either** a cat **or** a dog.
   Subordinating conjunction: We ate lunch **when** it was ready.

4. A **conjunctive adverb** clarifies a relationship.
   He did not like cold weather; **nevertheless,** he shoveled the snow.

5. An **interjection** is an unrelated word or phrase that expresses emotion or exclamation.
   Wow, that was cool!   **Aha!** You fell right into my trap!

PARTS OF THE SENTENCE

Subjects and Predicates

1. The **simple subject** is the key noun or pronoun that tells what the sentence is about. A **compound subject** is made up of two or more simple subjects that are joined by a conjunction and have the same verb.
   My **father** snores.   My **mother** and **I** can't sleep.

2. The **simple predicate** is the verb or verb phrase that expresses the essential thought about the subject of the sentence. A **compound predicate** is made up of two or more verbs or verb phrases that are joined by a conjunction and have the same subject.

The night **was** cold.   The elves **sang** and **danced** in the flower garden.

3. The **complete subject** consists of the simple subject and all the words that modify it.

The bright lights of the city burned intensely.   **The warm, soothing fire** kept us warm.

4. The **complete predicate** consists of the simple predicate and all the words that modify it or complete its meaning.

Dinosaurs **died out 65 million years ago.**   The sun **provides heat for the earth.**

5. Usually the subject comes before the predicate in a sentence. In inverted sentences, all or part of the predicate precedes the subject.

There **are** two **muffins** on the plate   Over the field **soared** the **glider.**

Complements

1. A **complement** is a word or a group of words that complete the meaning of the verb. There are four kinds of complements: direct objects, indirect objects, object complements, and subject complements.

2. A **direct object** answers *what?* or *whom?* after an action verb.
Sammi ate the **turkey.** (Sammi ate what?)
Carlos watched his **sister** in the school play. (Carlos watched whom?)

3. An **indirect object** receives what the direct object names.
Marie wrote **June** a letter.   George Washington gave his **troops** orders.

4. A **subject complement** follows a subject and a linking verb and identifies or describes the subject. A **predicate nominative** is a noun or a pronoun that follows a linking verb and further identifies the subject. A **predicate adjective** follows a linking verb and further describes the subject.
Predicate Nominative: The best football player is **Jacob.**
Predicate Adjective: The people have been very **patient.**

5. An **object complement** describes or renames a direct object.
Object Complement: Ami found the man **handsome.**
Object Complement: Carlo thought the woman a **genius.**

PHRASES

1. A **phrase** is a group of words that acts in a sentence as a single part of speech.

2. A **prepositional phrase** is a group of words that begins with a preposition and usually ends with a noun or a pronoun called the **object of the preposition**. A prepositional phrase can modify a noun or a pronoun, a verb, an adjective, or an adverb.
One of my favorite meals is pigs **in a blanket.** (modifies the noun *pigs*)
The supersonic jet soared **into the sky.** (modifies the verb *soared*)
The love of a household pet can be valuable **for a family.** (modifies the adjective *valuable*)
The child reads well **for a six-year-old.** (modifies the adverb *well*)

3. An **appositive** is a noun or a pronoun that is placed next to another noun or pronoun to identify it or give more information about it. An **appositive phrase** is an appositive plus its modifiers.
My grandfather **Géza** takes me fishing.   C.S. Lewis, **my favorite author,** lived in England.

4. A **verbal** is a verb form that functions in a sentence as a noun, an adjective, or an adverb. A **verbal phrase** is a verbal plus any complements and modifiers.

a. A **participle** is a verbal that functions as an adjective: Gary comforted the **crying** baby.

b. A **participial phrase** contains a participle plus any complements or modifiers: **Thanking everyone,** my uncle began to carve the turkey.

c. A **gerund** is a verbal that ends with -*ing.* It is used in the same way a noun is used: **Skiing** is a popular sport.

d. A **gerund phrase** is a gerund plus any complements or modifiers: **Singing the national anthem** is traditional at many sports events.

e. An **infinitive** is a verbal that is usually preceded by the word *to.* It is used as a noun, an adjective, or an adverb: I never learned **to dance.** (noun) She has an errand **to run.** (adjective) I will be happy **to help.** (adverb)

f. An **infinitive phrase** contains an infinitive plus any complements or modifiers: My father woke up **to watch the news on television.**

5. An **absolute phrase** consists of a noun or a pronoun that is modified by a participle or a participial phrase but has no grammatical relation to the sentence. **His legs terribly tired,** Honori sat down.

CLAUSES AND SENTENCE STRUCTURE

1. A **clause** is a group of words that has a subject and a predicate and is used as a sentence or part of a sentence. There are two types of clauses: main and subordinate. A **main clause** has a subject and a predicate and can stand alone as a sentence. A **subordinate clause** has a subject and a predicate, but it cannot stand alone as a sentence.

     main   sub.
The book bored me, until I read Chapter 5.

2. There are three types of subordinate clauses: adjective, adverb, and noun.

a. An **adjective clause** is a subordinate clause that modifies a noun or a pronoun.
The students **who stayed after school for help** did well on the test.

b. An **adverb clause** is a subordinate clause that modifies a verb, an adjective, or an adverb. It tells *when, where, how, why, to what extent,* or *under what conditions.*
When the sun set, everyone watched from the window. (modifies a verb)
Today is warmer **than yesterday was.** (modifies an adjective)

c. A **noun clause** is a subordinate clause used as a noun.
Who will become president has been declared.   I now remember **what I need to buy.**

3. Main and subordinate clauses can form four types of sentences. A **simple sentence** has only one main clause and no subordinate clauses. A **compound sentence** has two or more main clauses. A **complex sentence** has one main clause and one or more subordinate clauses. A **compound-complex sentence** has more than one main clause and at least one subordinate clause.

                              main
Simple: The stars fill the sky.
                         main   main
Compound: The plane landed,   and the passengers left.
                        sub.   main
Complex: Although the children found the letter,   they couldn't read it.
                    main   main   sub.
Compound-Complex: The earth is bountiful; we may destroy it   if we abuse it.

4. A sentence that makes a statement is classified as a **declarative sentence**: The Cleveland Browns are my favorite team. An **imperative sentence** gives a command or makes a request: Please go to the dance with me. An **interrogative sentence** asks a question: Who would abandon a family pet? An **exclamatory sentence** expresses strong emotion: Look out!

SUBJECT-VERB AGREEMENT

1. A verb must agree with its subject in person and number.
   Doli **runs**. (singular)   Doli and Abay **run**. (plural)
   He **is** singing. (singular) They **are** singing. (plural)

2. In **inverted sentences** the subject follows the verb. The sentence may begin with a prepositional phrase, the words *there* or *here*, or the verb form of *do*.
   Out of the bushes **sprang** the *leopard*.   There **is** never enough *time*.
   Do those *pigs* **eat** leftover food?

3. Do not mistake a word in a prepositional phrase for the subject.
   The **boss** of the employees **works** very hard. (The verb *works* tells the action of the boss.)

4. Make the verb in a sentence agree with the subject, not with the predicate nominative.
   Her problem **was** the twins.   The twins **were** her problem.

5. A title is always singular, even if nouns in the title are plural.
   ***The War of the Worlds* was** a radio broadcast that caused widespread panic.

6. Subjects combined with *and* or *both* use plural verbs unless the parts are of a whole unit. When compound subjects are joined with *or* or *nor*, the verb agrees with the subject listed last.
   Chocolate, strawberry, and vanilla are common ice cream flavors.
   Peanut butter and jelly is a good snack.   Neither **books nor a briefcase is** needed.

7. Use a singular verb if the compound subject is preceded by the words *many a*, *every*, or *each*.
   Every **dog and cat** needs to be cared for.   Many a **young man** has stood here.

8. A subject remains singular or plural regardless of any intervening expressions.
   Gloria, as well as the rest of her family, **was** late.
   The **players,** accompanied by the coach, **enter** the field.

9. A verb must agree in number with an indefinite pronoun subject.
   Always singular: *each, either, neither, one, everyone, everybody, everything, no one, nobody, nothing, anyone, anybody, anything, someone, somebody,* and *something.*
   Always plural: *several, few, both,* and *many.*
   Either singular or plural: *some, all, any, most,* and *none.*
   Is any of the **lemonade** left?   **Are** any of the **biscuits** burnt?

10. When the subject of an adjective clause is a relative pronoun, the verb in the clause must agree with the antecedent of the relative pronoun.
    He is one of the singers who dance. (The antecedent of *who* is *singers,* plural: singers dance.)

USING PRONOUNS CORRECTLY

1. Use the **nominative case** when the pronoun is a subject or a predicate nominative.
   She eats cake.   Is **he** here?   That is **I.** (predicate nominative)

2. Use the **objective case** when the pronoun is an object.
   Clarence invited **us.** (direct object)   Chapa gave **me** a gift. (indirect object)
   Spot! Don't run around **me**! (object of preposition)

3. Use the **possessive case** to replace possessive nouns and precede gerunds. Never use an apostrophe in a possessive pronoun.
   That new car is **hers.**   They were thrilled at **his** playing the violin.

4. Use the **nominative case** when the pronoun is a subject or a predicate nominative.
   We three—Marijian, his sister, and I—went to camp.

5. Use the **objective case** to rename an object.
   The teacher acknowledged **us,** Burny and **me.**

6. When a pronoun is followed by an appositive, choose the case of the pronoun that would be correct if the appositive were omitted.
   We the jury find the defendant guilty.   That building was erected by **us** workers.

7. In elliptical adverb clauses using *than* and *as*, choose the case of the pronoun that you would use if the missing words were fully expressed.
   Kareem is a better sprinter than **I.** (I am)   It helped you more than **me.** (it helped me)

8. Use a **reflexive pronoun** when it refers to the person who is the subject of the sentence. Avoid using *hisself* or *theirselves.*
   Jerry found **himself** in a mess.   The candidates questioned **themselves** about their tactics.

9. In questions, use *who* for subjects and *whom* for objects. Use *who* and *whoever* for subjects and predicate nominatives in subordinate clauses. Use the objective pronouns *whom* and *whomever* for objects of subordinate clauses.
   Who roasted these marshmallows?   **Whom** will you hire next?
   This medal is for **whoever** finishes first.
   The newspaper will interview **whomever** the editor chooses.

10. An **antecedent** is the word or group of words to which a pronoun refers or that a pronoun replaces. All pronouns must agree with their antecedents in number, gender, and person.
    Colleen's **friends** gave up **their** free time to help.   The **Senate** passed **its** first bill of the year.

11. Make sure that the antecedent of a pronoun is clearly stated.
    VAGUE: The people who lost their dogs stayed in their yards, hoping **they** would return.
    CLEAR: The people who lost their dogs stayed in their yards, hoping **the dogs** would return.

    INDEFINITE: If you park the car under the sign **it** will be towed away.
    CLEAR: If you park the car under the sign **the car** will be towed away.

USING MODIFIERS CORRECTLY

1. Most adjectives and adverbs have three **degrees of form**. The **positive form** of a modifier cannot be used to make a comparison. The **comparative form** of a modifier shows two things being compared. The **superlative form** of a modifier shows three or more things being compared.
   The year went by **fast.**   This year went by **faster** than last year.
   I expect next year to go by the **fastest** of all.

2. One- and two-syllable adjectives add *-er* to form comparative and *-est* to form superlative.
   POSITIVE: bold   happy   strong
   COMPARATIVE: bolder   happier   stronger
   SUPERLATIVE: boldest   happiest   strongest

3. For adverbs ending in *-ly* and modifiers with three or more syllables, use *more* and *most* or *less* and *least* to form the comparative and superlative degrees.
   He was the **least** exhausted of the group.   She spoke **more** caringly than some others.

4. Some modifiers have irregular forms.
   POSITIVE: good, well   badly, ill   far   many, much   little
   COMPARATIVE: better   worse   farther   more   less
   SUPERLATIVE: best   worst   farthest   most   least

5. Do not make a double comparison using both *-er* or *-est* and *more* or *most*.
   INCORRECT: That musical was the **most funniest** I have ever seen.
   CORRECT: That musical was the **funniest** I have ever seen.

6. Do not make an incomplete or unclear comparison by omitting *other* or *else* when you compare one member of a group with another.
   UNCLEAR: Joey has missed more school than any kid in the ninth grade.
   CLEAR: Joey has missed more school than any **other** kid in the ninth grade.

7. Avoid **double negatives**, which are two negative words in the same clause.
   INCORRECT: I have **not** seen **no** stray cats.
   CORRECT: I have **not** seen **any** stray cats.

8. For clarity, place modifiers as close as possible to the words they modify.

   MISPLACED: The fire was snuffed out by the storm **that we accidentally started**.

   CLEAR: The fire **that we accidentally started** was snuffed out by the storm.

   DANGLING: **To avoid the long walk,** a friend drove us.

   CLEAR: **To avoid the long walk,** we were driven by a friend.

9. Place the adverb *only* immediately before the word or group of words it modifies.
   Only Afi wants choir rehearsal next week. (No one but Afi wants rehearsal.)
   Afi wants **only** choir rehearsal next week. (She wants no other rehearsal.)
   Afi wants choir rehearsal **only** next week. (She does not want rehearsal any other week.)

USAGE GLOSSARY

a, an Use the article *a* when the following word begins with a consonant sound. Use *an* when the following word begins with a vowel sound.
   a house   **an** understudy   **an** hour   **a** united front

a lot, alot Always write this expression, meaning "a large amount," as two words.
   With his help, we will learn **a lot** about photography.

a while, awhile *In* or *for* often precedes *a while*, forming a prepositional phrase. *Awhile* is used only as an adverb.
   Let us listen to the forest for **a while**.   The students listened **awhile**.

accept, except *Accept,* a verb, means "to receive" or "to agree to." *Except* may be a preposition or a verb. As a preposition it means "but." As a verb it means "to leave out."
I will **accept** all of your terms **except** the last one.

adapt, adopt *Adapt* means "to adjust." *Adopt* means "to take something for one's own."
Species survive because they **adapt** to new situations. My church will **adopt** a needy family.

advice, advise *Advice,* a noun, means "helpful opinion." *Advise,* a verb, means "to give advice."
I must **advise** you to never take Jakel's **advice.**

affect, effect *Affect,* a verb, means "to cause a change in, to influence." *Effect* may be a noun or a verb. As a noun it means "result." As a verb it means "to bring about."
Is it true that the observer can **affect** the results? (verb)
I have no idea what **effect** that may have. (noun)
How can the president **effect** a good approval rating? (verb)

ain't *Ain't* is unacceptable in speaking and writing. Use only in exact quotations.

all ready, already *All ready* means "completely ready." *Already* means "before or by this time."
We had **already** purchased our plane tickets, and we were **all ready** to board.

all right, alright Always write this expression as two words. *Alright* is unacceptable.
Because she is your friend, she is **all right** with me.

all together, altogether The two words *all together* mean "in a group." The single word *altogether* is an adverb meaning "completely" or "on the whole."
The hikers gathered **all together** for lunch, and they were **altogether** exhausted.

allusion, illusion *Allusion* means "an indirect reference." *Illusion* refers to something false.
Mr. Lee made an **allusion** to *The Grapes of Wrath.*   The magician performed **illusions.**

anyways, anywheres, everywheres, somewheres Write these words and others like them without a final *-s: anyway, anywhere, everywhere, somewhere.*

bad, badly Use *bad* as an adjective and *badly* as an adverb.
We watched a **bad** movie.   He sang the national anthem quite **badly.**

being as, being that Use these only informally. In formal writing and speech, use *because* or *since.*

beside, besides *Beside* means "next to." *Besides* means "moreover" or "in addition to."
Who, **besides** Antonio, will offer to sit **beside** the window?

between, among Use *between* to refer to or to compare two separate nouns. Use *among* to show a relationship in a group.
I could not choose **between** Harvard and Princeton.   Who **among** the class knows me?

borrow, lend, loan *Borrow* is a verb meaning "to take something that must be returned." *Lend* is a verb meaning "to give something that must be returned." *Loan* is a noun.
People **borrow** money from banks.   Banks will **lend** money to approved customers.
People always must apply for a **loan.**

bring, take Use *bring* to show movement from a distant place to a closer one. Use *take* to show movement from a nearby place to a more distant one.
Bring in the paper, and **take** out the trash.

can, may *Can* indicates the ability to do something. *May* indicates permission to do something.
Anyone **can** use a credit card, but only the cardholder **may** authorize it.

can't hardly, can't scarcely These terms are considered double negatives. Do not use them. Use *can hardly* and *can scarcely.*

continual, continuous *Continual* describes repetitive action with pauses between occurrences. *Continuous* describes an action that continues with no interruption in space or time.

We make **continual** trips to the grocery.   **Continuous** energy from our sun lights the sky.

could of, might of, must of, should of, would of Do not use *of* after *could, might, must, should,* or *would.* Instead, use the helping verb *have.*

That **must have been** the longest play ever!

different from, different than The expression *different from* is preferred to *different than.*

Baseball is **different from** the English sport of cricket.

doesn't, don't *Doesn't* is the contraction of *does not* and should be used with all singular nouns. *Don't* is the contraction of *do not* and should be used with *I, you,* and all plural nouns.

My dog **doesn't** like the mail carrier.   Bobsled riders **don't** take their job lightly.

emigrate, immigrate Use *emigrate* to mean "to move from one country to another." Use *immigrate* to mean "to enter a country to settle there." Use *from* with *emigrate* and *to* with *immigrate.*

Refugees **emigrate** from war-torn countries.   My great-grandfather **immigrated** to America.

farther, further *Farther* refers to physical distance. *Further* refers to time or degree.

Traveling **farther** from your home may **further** your understanding of different places.

fewer, less Use *fewer* to refer to nouns that can be counted. Use *less* to refer to nouns that cannot be counted. Also use *less* to refer to figures used as a single amount or quantity.

If **fewer** crimes were committed, there would be **less** misery in the world.

The box measured **less** than 100 cm².

good, well *Good* is an adjective, and *well* is an adverb.

That spot is a **good** place for a picnic.   We dined **well** that day.

had of Do not use *of* between *had* and a past participle.

I wish I **had eaten** my sundae when I had the chance.

hanged, hung Use *hanged* to mean "put to death by hanging." Use *hung* in all other cases.

In the Old West, many were convicted and **hanged**.   I **hung** my coat on the hook.

in, into, in to Use *in* to mean "inside" or "within" and *into* to indicate movement or direction from outside to a point within. *In to* is made up of an adverb *(in)* followed by a preposition *(to).*

The fish swim **in** the sea.   We moved **into** a new house last year.

The student walked **in to** see the principal for a meeting.

irregardless, regardless Always use *regardless. Irregardless* is a double negative.

Root beer tastes great **regardless** of the brand.

this kind, these kinds Because *kind* is singular, it is modified by the singular form *this* or *that.* Because *kinds* is plural, it is modified by the plural form *these* or *those.*

I love **these kinds** of desserts!   I do not feel comfortable with **this kind** of situation.

lay, lie *Lay* means "to put" or "to place," and it takes a direct object. *Lie* means "to recline" or "to be positioned," and it never takes an object.

I taught my dog to **lay** the paper at my feet and then **lie** on the ground.

learn, teach *Learn* means "to receive knowledge." *Teach* means "to impart knowledge."

I want to **learn** a new language and later **teach** it to others.

leave, let *Leave* means "to go away." *Let* means "to allow" or "to permit."

My guest had to **leave** because his parents do not **let** him stay up too late.

like, as *Like* is a preposition and introduces a prepositional phrase. *As* and *as if* are subordinating conjunctions and introduce subordinate clauses. Never use *like* before a clause.

I felt **like** a stuffed crab after the feast.   The pigeons flew away, **as** they always do when scared.

loose, lose Use *loose* to mean "not firmly attached" and *lose* to mean "to misplace" or "to fail to win."

You don't want to **lose** your nice pair of **loose** jeans.

passed, past *Passed* is the past tense and the past participle of the verb *to pass. Past* can be an adjective, a preposition, an adverb, or a noun.

He **passed** the exit ramp because he could not see the sign **past** the bushes.

precede, proceed *Precede* means "to go or come before." *Proceed* means "to continue."

We can **proceed** with the plans.   From a distance, lightning appears to **precede** thunder.

raise, rise *Raise* means "to cause to move upward," and it always takes an object. *Rise* means "to get up"; it is intransitive and never takes an object.

Raise the drawbridge!   For some, it is difficult to **rise** in the morning.

reason is because Use either *reason is that* or *because.*

The **reason** he left **is that** he was bored. He left **because** he was bored.

respectfully, respectively *Respectfully* means "with respect." *Respectively* means "in the order named."

We **respectfully** bowed to the audience.

Abla, Héctor, and Shelly, **respectively,** play first, second, and third base.

says, said *Says* is the third-person singular of *say. Said* is the past tense of *say.*

Listen carefully to what she **says.**   I love what the keynote speaker **said.**

sit, set *Sit* means "to place oneself in a sitting position." It rarely takes an object. *Set* means "to place" or "to put" and usually takes an object. *Set* can also refer to the sun's going down."

Sit anywhere you would like.   **Set** the nozzle back in its slot before paying for the gas.
                                    Today the sun will **set** at seven o'clock.

than, then *Than* is a conjunction that is used to introduce the second element in a comparison; it also shows exception. *Then* is an adverb.

Julio hit more home runs **than** Jacob this year.   Call for help first, and **then** start CPR.

this here, that there Avoid using *here* and *there* after *this* and *that.*

This bunk is yours.

who, whom *Who* is a subject, and *whom* is an object.

Who first sang the song "Memories"?   To **whom** should I throw the ball now?

CAPITALIZATION

1. Capitalize the first word in a sentence, including direct quotes and sentences in parentheses unless they are contained within another sentence.

   Shakespeare asked, "**What's** in a name?" (**This** is from *Romeo and Juliet.*)

2. Always capitalize the pronoun *I* no matter where it appears in a sentence.

   Because **I** woke up late, **I** had to race to school.

3. Capitalize the following proper nouns.

   a. Names of individuals, titles used in direct address or preceding a name, and titles describing a family relationship used with a name or in place of a name

   President Nixon   **George Burns**   **Sis**   **Sir Anthony Hopkins**   **Uncle Jay**

b. Names of ethnic groups, national groups, political parties and their members, and languages

African Americans   **Mexicans**   **Republican party**   **Hebrew**

c. Names of organizations, institutions, firms, monuments, bridges, buildings, and other structures

National Honor Society   **Vietnam War Memorial**   **Brooklyn Bridge**   **Parliament**

d. Trade names and names of documents, awards, and laws

Kleenex tissues   **Declaration of Independence**   **Academy Award**   **Bill of Rights**

e. Geographical terms and regions or localities

North Carolina   **Arctic Ocean**   **Nile River**   **West Street**   the **South**   **Central Park**

f. Names of planets and other heavenly bodies

Jupiter   **Horsehead Nebula**   the **Milky Way**

g. Names of ships, planes, trains, and spacecraft

Challenger   *Spirit of St. Louis*   **USS** *George Washington*

h. Names of most historical events, eras, calendar items, and religions terms

Fourth of July   **Jurassic**   **Gulf War**   **Friday**   **Yom Kippur**   **Protestant**

i. Titles of literary works, works of art, and musical compositions

"The Road Less Traveled" (poem)   *The Old Man and the Sea* (book)
Venus de Milo (statue)   *The Magic Flute* (opera)

4. Capitalize proper adjectives (adjectives formed from proper nouns).

Socratic method   **Jungian theory**   **Chinese food**   **Georgia clay**   **Colombian coffee**

PUNCTUATION, ABBREVIATIONS, AND NUMBERS

1. Use a period at the end of a declarative sentence and at the end of a polite command.
   Robin Hood was a medieval hero.   Pass the papers to the front.

2. Use an exclamation point to show strong feeling or to give a forceful command.
   What a surprise that is!   Watch out!   That's just what I need!

3. Use a question mark to indicate a direct question. Use a period to indicate an indirect question.
   DIRECT: Who ruled France in 1821?
   INDIRECT: Gamal wanted to know how much time was left before lunch.

4. Use a colon to introduce a list or to illustrate or restate previous material.
   For my team, I choose the following people: Zina, Ming, and Sue.
   In light of the data, the conclusion was not hard to obtain: Earth is not flat.

5. Use a colon for precise time measurements, biblical chapter and verse references, and business letter salutations.
   10:02 A.M.   John 3:16   Dear Ms. Delgado:

6. Use a semicolon in the following situations:

   a. To separate main clauses not joined by a coordinating conjunction
      My computer isn't working; perhaps I need to call a technician.

   b. To separate main clauses joined by a conjunctive adverb or by *for example* or *that is*
      Cancer is a serious disease; however, heart disease kills more people.

   c. To separate items in a series when those items contain commas
      I have done oral reports on Maya Angelou, a poet; Billy Joel, a singer; and Mario van Peebles, a director and actor.

d. To separate two main clauses joined by a coordinating conjunction when such clauses already contain several commas
According to Bruce, he spent his vacation in Naples, Florida; but he said it was a business, not a pleasure, trip.

7. Use a comma in the following situations:

a. To separate the main clauses of compound sentences
She was a slow eater, but she always finished her meal first.

b. To separate three or more words, phrases, or clauses in a series
Apples, oranges, grapefruit, and cherries are delicious.

c. To separate coordinate modifiers
The prom was a happy, exciting occasion.

d. To set off parenthetical expressions
He will, of course, stay for dinner.   Mary, on the other hand, is very pleasant.

e. To set off nonessential clauses and phrases; to set off introductory adverbial clauses, participial phrases, and long prepositional phrases.

Adjective clause: The bride, who is a chemist, looked lovely.
Appositive phrase: The parade, the longest I've ever seen, featured twelve bands.
Adverbial clause: After we had eaten, I realized my wallet was still in the car.
Participial phrase: Laughing heartily, Milan quickly left the room.
Prepositional phrase: At the sound of the final buzzer, the ball slid through the hoop.

f. To separate parts of an address, a geographical term, or a date
1640 Chartwell Avenue, Edina, Minnesota   September 11, 1982

g. To set off parts of a reference
Read *Slaughterhouse-Five*, pages 15–20.   Perform a scene from *Hamlet*, Act II.

h. To set off words or phrases of direct address and tag questions
Sherri, please pass the butter.   How are you, my friend?   We try hard, don't we?

i. After the salutation and close of a friendly letter and after the close of a business letter
Dear Richard,   Sincerely,   Yours,   Dear Mother,

8. Use dashes to signal a change in thought or to emphasize parenthetical matter.
"Remember to turn off the alarm—oh, don't touch that!"

9. Use parentheses to set off supplemental material. Punctuate within the parentheses only if the punctuation is part of the parenthetical expression.
I saw Bill Cosby (he is my favorite comedian) last night.

10. Use brackets to enclose information inserted by someone besides the original writer.
The paper continues, "The company knows he [Watson] is impressed."

11. Ellipsis points, a series of three spaced points, indicate an omission of material.
The film critic said, "The show was great . . . a must see!"

12. Use quotation marks to enclose a direct quotation. When a quotation is interrupted, use two sets of quotation marks. Use single quotation marks for a quotation within a quotation.
"This day," the general said, "will live on in infamy."
"Yes," the commander replied. "The headlines today read, 'Allies Retreat.'"

13. Use quotation marks to indicate titles of short works, unusual expressions, and definitions.
"The Gift of the Magi" (short story)   "Ave Maria" (song)
Large speakers are called "woofers," and small speakers are called "tweeters."

14. Always place commas and periods *inside* closing quotation marks. Place colons and semicolons *outside* closing quotation marks. Place question marks and exclamation points *inside* closing quotation marks only when those marks are part of the quotation.

"Rafi told me," John said, "that he could not go."

Let me tell you about "Piano Man": it is a narrative song.

He yelled, "Who are you?"

Did she say "Wait for me"?

15. Italicize (underline) titles of books, lengthy poems, plays, films, television series, paintings and sculptures, long musical compositions, court cases, names of newspapers and magazines, ships, trains, airplanes, and spacecraft.

The Last Supper (painting)   *Bang the Drum Slowly* (film)   *Roe* v. *Wade* (court case)

Titanic (ship)   *Time* (magazine)   *The Boston Globe* (newspaper)

16. Italicize (underline) foreign words and expressions that are not used frequently in English and words, letters, and numerals used to represent themselves.

Please discuss the phrase *caveat emptor.*

Today, *Sesame Street* was sponsored by the letters *t* and *m* and the number **6.**

17. Add an apostrophe and *-s* to all singular indefinite pronouns, singular nouns, plural nouns not ending in *-s,* and compound nouns to make them possessive. Add only an apostrophe to plural nouns ending in *-s* to make them possessive.

anyone**'s** guess   the dog**'s** leash   the women**'s** club

students**'** teacher   singers**'** microphones   runners**'** shoes

18. If two or more people possess something jointly, use the possessive form for the last person's name. If they possess things individually, use the possessive form for both names.

mom and dad**'s** checkbook   Carmen**'s** and Sumil**'s** projects

19. Use a possessive form to express amounts of money or time that modify a noun.

a day**'s** pay   fifty dollars**'** worth   a block**'s** walk

20. Use an apostrophe in place of omitted letters or numerals. Use an apostrophe and *-s* to form the plural of letters, numerals, and symbols.

cannot is *can't*   *do not* is *don't*   *1978* is *'78*

Mind your **p's** and **q's.**

21. Use a hyphen after any prefix joined to a proper noun or a proper adjective. Use a hyphen after the prefixes *all-, ex-,* and *self-* joined to a noun or an adjective, the prefix *anti-* joined to a word beginning with *i-,* the prefix *vice-* (except in *vice president*), and the *prefix re-* to avoid confusion between words tthat are spelled the same but have different meanings.

all-inclusive   ex-wife   self-reliance

anti-immigrant   vice-principal   re-call *instead of* recall

22. Use a hyphen in a compound adjective that precedes a noun. Use a hyphen in compound numbers and in fractions used as adjectives.

a green-yellow jersey   a red-hot poker   jet-black hair

ninety-nine   one-fifth cup of sugar

23. Use a hyphen to divide words at the end of a line.

daz-zle   terri-tory   Mediter-ranean

24. Use one period at the end of an abbreviation. If punctuation other than a period ends the sentence, use both the period and the other punctuation.

Bring me the books, papers, pencils, etc.   Could you be ready at 2:00 P.M.?

25. Capitalize the abbreviations of proper nouns and some personal titles.
    U.K.   C.E.O.   R. F. Kennedy   B.C.   A.D.   Ph.D.

26. Abbreviate numerical measurements in scientific writing but not in ordinary prose.
    Measure 89 g into the crucible.   Jim ran ten yards when he heard that dog barking!

27. Spell out cardinal and ordinal numbers that can be written in one or two words and those that
    appear at the beginning of a sentence.
    Five hundred people attended.   I look forward to my **eighteenth** birthday.

28. Use numerals for dates; for decimals; for house, apartment, and room numbers; for street and
    avenue numbers greater than ten; for sums of money involving both dollars and cents; and to
    emphasize the exact time of day and with A.M. and P.M.
    April **1, 1996**   Room **251**   **$2.51**   **2:51** P.M.

29. Express all related numbers in a sentence as numerals if any one should be a numeral.
    The subscriptions gradually rose from **10 to 116**.

30. Spell out numbers that express decades, amounts of money that can be written in one or two
    words, steets and avenues less than ten, and the approximate time of day.
    the **seventies**   **fifty** cents   **Fifth** Avenue   half past **five**

VOCABULARY AND SPELLING

1. Clues to the meaning of an unfamiliar word can be found in its **context**. Context clues include
   definition, the meaning stated; **example**, the meaning explained through one familiar case;
   comparison, similarity to a familiar word; **contrast**, opposite of a familiar word; and **cause and
   effect**, a cause described by its effects.

2. Clues to the meaning of a word can be obtained from its **base word**, its **prefix**, or its **suffix**.
   telegram **gram** = writing   psychology **psych** = soul, mind
   antibacterial **anti** = against   biology **-logy** = study

3. The *i* comes before the *e*, except when both letters follow a *c* or when both letters are
   pronounced together as an $\bar{a}$ sound. However, many exceptions exist to this rule.
   f**ie**ld (*i* before *e*)   dec**ei**ve (*ei* after *c*)   r**ei**gn ($\bar{a}$ sound)   **wei**rd (exception)

4. Most word endings prounounced *sēd* are spelled *-cede*. In one word, *supersede*, the ending is
   spelled *-sede*. In *proceed*, *exceed*, and *succeed*, the ending is spelled *-ceed*.
   pre**cede**   re**cede**   con**cede**

5. An unstressed vowel sound is not emphasized when a word is pronounced. Determine the
   spelling of this sound by comparing it to a known word.
   hesitant (Compare to *hesitate*.)   *fantasy* (Compare to *fantastic*.)

6. When adding a suffix that begins with a consonant to a word that ends in silent *e*, generally
   keep the *e*. If the suffix begins with a vowel or *y*, generally drop the *e*. If the suffix begins with
   a or *o* and the word ends in *ce* or *ge*, keep the *e*. If the suffix begins with a vowel and the word
   ends in *ee*, or *oe*, keep the *e*.
   encourag**ement**   scary   chang**eable**   flee**ing**

7. When adding a suffix to a word ending in a consonant +*y*, change the *y* to *i* unless the suffix
   begins with *i*. If the word ends in a vowel +*y*, keep the *y*.
   heart**iness**   read**iness**   spy**ing**   stray**ing**

8. Double the final consonant before adding a suffix that begins with a vowel to a word that ends in a single consonant preceded by a single vowel if the accent is on the root's last syllable.

   plan**ned**   fin**ned**   misfit**ted**

9. When adding *-ly* to a word that ends in a single *l*, keep the *l*. If it ends in a double *l*, drop one *l*. If it ends in a consonant *+le*, drop the *le*.

   real becomes real**ly**   dull becomes dul**ly**   inexplicable becomes inexplica**bly**

10. When adding *-ness* to a word that ends in *n*, keep the *n*.

    lean**ness**   mean**ness**   green**ness**

11. When joining a word or prefix that ends in a consonant to a suffix or word that begins with a consonant, keep both consonants.

    quiet**ness**   great**ly**   red**ness**

12. Most nouns form their plurals by adding *-s*. However, nouns that end in *-ch, -s, -sh, -x,* or *-z* form plurals by adding *-es*. If the noun ends in a consonant *+y*, change *y* to *i* and add *-es*. If the noun ends in *-lf*, change *f* to *v* and add *-es*. If the noun ends in *-fe*, change *f* to *v* and add *-s*.

    can**s**   chur**ches**   fa**xes**   sp**ies**   hal**ves**   loa**ves**

13. To form the plural of proper names and one-word compound nouns, follow the general rules for plurals. To form the plural of hyphenated compound nouns or compound nouns of more than one word, make the most important word plural.

    Shatner**s**   Stockholder**s**   brother**s**-in-law   Master Sergeant**s**

14. Some nouns have the same singular and plural forms.

    sheep   species

COMPOSITION

Writing Themes and Paragraphs

1. Use **prewriting** to find ideas to write about. One form of prewriting, **freewriting**, starts with a subject or topic and branches off into related ideas. Another way to find a topic is to ask and answer questions about your starting subject, helping you to gain a deeper understanding of your chosen topic. Also part of the prewriting stage is determining who your readers or **audience** will be and deciding your **purpose** for writing. Your purpose—as varied as writing to persuade, to explain, to describe something, or to narrate—is partially shaped by who your audience will be, and vice versa.

2. To complete your first **draft**, organize your prewriting into an introduction, body, and conclusion. Concentrate on unity and coherence of the overall piece. Experiment with different paragraph orders: **chronological order** places events in the order in which they happened; **spatial order** places objects in the order in which they appear; and **compare/contrast order** shows similarities and differences in objects or events.

3. **Revise** your composition if necessary. Read through your draft, looking for places to improve content and structure. Remember that varying your sentence patterns and lengths will make your writing easier and more enjoyable to read.

4. In the **editing** stage, check your grammar, spelling, and punctuation. Focus on expressing your ideas clearly and concisely.

5. Finally, prepare your writing for **presentation**. Sharing your composition, or ideas, with others may take many forms: printed, oral, or graphic.

Outlining

1. The two common forms of outlines are **sentence outlines** and **topic outlines**. Choose one type of outline and keep it uniform throughout.

2. A period follows the number or letter of each division. Each point in a sentence outline ends with a period; the points in a topic outline do not.

3. Each point begins with a capital letter.

4. A point may have no fewer than two subpoints.

SENTENCE OUTLINE
I. This is the main point.
  A. This is a subpoint of *I*.
    1. This is a detail of *A*.
      a. This is a detail of *1*.
      b. This is a detail of *1*.
    2. This is a detail of *A*.
  B. This is a subpoint of *I*.
II. This is another main point.

TOPIC OUTLINE
I. Main point
  A. Subpoint of *I*
    1. Detail of *A*
      a. Detail of *1*
      b. Detail of *1*
    2. Detail of *A*
  B. Subpoint of *I*
II. Main point

Writing letters

1. **Personal letters** are usually handwritten in indented form (the first line of paragraphs, each line of the heading, the complimentary close, and the signature are indented). **Business letters** are usually typewritten in block or semiblock form. Block form contains no indents; semiblock form indents the heading, the complimentary close, and the signature.

2. The five parts of a personal letter are the heading (the writer's address and the date), the salutation (greeting), the body (message), the complimentary close (such as "Yours truly"), and the signature (the writer's name). The business letter has the same parts and also includes an inside address (the recipient's address).

PERSONAL LETTER

Heading

Salutation

Body

Complimentary Close
Signature

BUSINESS LETTER

Heading

Inside Address

Salutation

Body

Complimentary Close
Signature

3. Reveal your personality and imagination in colorful personal letters. Keep business letters brief, clear, and courteous.

4. **Personal letters** include letters to friends and family members. **Thank-you notes** and **invitations** are personal letters that may be either formal or informal in style.

5. Use a **letter of complaint** to convey a concern. Begin the letter by telling what happened. Then use supporting details as evidence. Complete the letter by explaining what you want done. Avoid insults and threats, and make reasonable requests. Use a **letter of request** to ask for information or to place an order of purchase. Be concise, yet give all the details necessary for your request to be fulfilled. Keep the tone of your letter courteous and be generous in allotting time for a response.

6. Use an **opinion letter** to take a firm stand on an issue. Make the letter clear, firm, rational, and purposeful. Be aware of your audience, their attitude, how informed they are, and their possible reactions to your opinion. Support your statements of opinion with facts.

7. Use a **résumé** to summarize your work experience, school experience, talents, and interests. Be clear, concise, and expressive. Use a consistent form. You do not need to write in complete sentences, but use as many action verbs as possible.

8. Use a **cover letter** as a brief introduction accompanying your résumé.

*T*roubleshooter

Sentence Fragments

PROBLEM 1

Fragment that lacks a subject

frag	Ali baked a chocolate cake. (Took it to the party.)
frag	Maria thought the comedian was funny. (Laughed at his jokes.)

SOLUTION

Ali baked a chocolate cake. He took it to the party.
Maria thought the comedian was funny. She laughed at his jokes.

Make a complete sentence by adding a subject to the fragment.

PROBLEM 2

Fragment that lacks a complete verb

frag	Helen is a photographer. (She becoming well-known for her work.)
frag	Alicia has a new computer. (It very powerful.)

SOLUTION A

Helen is a photographer. She is becoming well-known for her work.
Alicia has a new computer. It is very powerful.

Make a complete sentence by adding a complete verb or a helping verb.

SOLUTION B

Helen is a photographer and is becoming well-known for her work.
Alicia has a new computer, which is very powerful.

Combine the fragment with another sentence.

PROBLEM 3

Fragment that is a subordinate clause

frag   Akira repaired the old boat. Because it was beautiful.

frag   Jennifer has two race car magazines. Which she bought at the store.

SOLUTION A

Akira repaired the old boat because it was beautiful.

Jennifer has two race car magazines, which she bought at the store.

Combine the fragment with another sentence.

SOLUTION B

Akira repaired the old boat. He thought it was beautiful.

Jennifer has two race car magazines. She bought them at the store.

Make the fragment a complete sentence by removing the subordinating conjunction or the relative pronoun and adding a subject or other words necessary to make a complete thought.

PROBLEM 4

Fragment that lacks both subject and verb

frag   The soft rustle of the trees makes me sleepy. In the afternoon.

frag   The next morning. We talked about our adventure.

SOLUTION

The soft rustle of the trees makes me sleepy in the afternoon.

The next morning, we talked about our adventure.

Make the fragment part of a sentence.

More help in avoiding sentence fragments is available in Lesson 31.

Run-on Sentences

PROBLEM 1

Comma splice—two main clauses separated only by a comma

run-on I don't know where the oil paints are, they were over by the easel.

SOLUTION A

I don't know where the oil paints are. They were over by the easel.

Make two sentences by separating the first clause from the second with end punctuation, such as a period or a question mark, and start the second sentence with a capital letter.

SOLUTION B

I don't know where the oil paints are; they were over by the easel.

Place a semicolon between the main clauses of the sentence.

SOLUTION C

I don't know where the oil paints are, but they were over by the easel.

Add a coordinating conjunction after the comma.

PROBLEM 2

No punctuation between two main clauses

run-on Deelra ran the hurdles in record time Shawna placed second.

SOLUTION A

Deelra ran the hurdles in record time. Shawna placed second.

Make two sentences out of the run-on sentence.

SOLUTION B

Deelra ran the hurdles in record time; Shawna placed second.

Separate the main clauses with a semicolon.

SOLUTION C

Deelra ran the hurdles in record time, but Shawna placed second.

Add a comma and a coordinating conjunction between the main clauses.

PROBLEM 3

Two main clauses without a comma before the coordinating conjunction

run-on The robins usually arrive in the spring and they start building nests at once.

run-on Emily won the scholarship last year but she decided not to accept it.

SOLUTION

The robins usually arrive in the spring, and they start building nests at once.

Emily won the scholarship last year, but she decided not to accept it.

Separate the main clauses by adding a comma before the coordinating conjunction.

Need More Help? *More help in avoiding run-on sentences is available in Lesson 32.*

PROBLEM 1

A prepositional phrase between a subject and its verb

agr	The arrangement of those colorful pictures (make) a vivid, exciting combination.
agr	One of those big, gray sea gulls (have perched) on the roof.

SOLUTION

The arrangement of those colorful pictures makes a vivid, exciting combination.

One of those big, gray sea gulls has perched on the roof.

Make the verb agree with the subject, not with the object of the preposition.

PROBLEM 2

A predicate nominative differing in number from the subject

agr	Fast-paced adventure movies (was) always Jenny's choice.

SOLUTION

Fast-paced adventure movies were always Jenny's choice.

Make the verb agree with the subject, not with the predicate nominative.

PROBLEM 3

A subject following the verb

agr	On the sun deck there (was) several chairs and a table.
agr	Here (comes) the rain clouds and the heavy, slanting rain.

SOLUTION

On the sun deck there were several chairs and a table.
Here come the rain clouds and the heavy, slanting rain.

Look for the subject after the verb in an inverted sentence. Make sure that the verb agrees with the subject.

PROBLEM 4

Collective nouns as subjects

agr   The crowd really (like) the music, doesn't it?

agr   Margaret's company (arrives) tomorrow by bus and by train.

SOLUTION A

The crowd really likes the music, doesn't it?

Use a singular verb if the collective noun refers to a group as a whole.

SOLUTION B

Margaret's company arrive tomorrow by bus and by train.

Use a plural verb if the collective noun refers to each member of a group individually.

PROBLEM 5

A noun of amount as the subject

agr   The past two days (seems) like a week.

agr   One thousand millimeters (equal) a meter.

SOLUTION

The past two days seem like a week.
One thousand millimeters equals a meter.

A noun of amount that refers to one unit is singular. A noun of amount that refers to a number of individual units is plural.

PROBLEM 6

Compound subject joined by and

agr	A clear day and a light breeze (brightens) a summer afternoon.
agr	Pop and pizza (are) a common meal.

SOLUTION A

A clear day and a light breeze brighten a summer afternoon.

Use a plural verb if the parts of the compound subject do not belong to one unit or if they refer to different people or things.

SOLUTION B

Pop and pizza is a common meal.

Use a singular verb if the parts of the compound subject belong to one unit or if they refer to the same person or thing.

PROBLEM 7

Compound subject joined by or or nor

agr	Neither Yuri nor Sarah (like) the menu.

SOLUTION

Neither Yuri nor Sarah likes the menu.

Make your verb agree with the subject closer to it.

PROBLEM 8

Compound subject preceded by many a, every, or each

agr	Many a brush and tube of paint (were scattered) around the studio.

> ### SOLUTION
>
> **Many a brush and tube of paint was scattered around the studio.**
>
> The subject is considered singular when *many a, each,* or *every* precedes a compound subject.

PROBLEM 9

Subjects separated from the verb by an intervening expression

> agr   Jamal's new sculpture, in addition to his other recent works, (reflect) his abiding love of nature.

> ### SOLUTION
>
> **Jamal's new sculpture, in addition to his other recent works, reflects his abiding love of nature.**
>
> Expressions that begin with *as well as, in addition to,* and *together with,* do not change the number of the subject. Make the verb agree with its subject, not with the intervening expression.

PROBLEM 10

Indefinite pronouns as subjects

> agr   Each of the trees along the old canal (have) different colors in the fall.

> ### SOLUTION
>
> **Each of the trees along the old canal has different colors in the fall.**
>
> Some indefinite pronouns are singular, some are plural, and some can be either singular or plural depending on the noun they refer to. (A list of indefinite pronouns is on page 54.)

More help with subject-verb agreement is available in Lessons 44–51.

Lack of Agreement Between Pronoun and Antecedent

PROBLEM 1

A singular antecedent that can be either male or female

ant   A great coach inspires (his) athletes to be their best on or off the field.

Traditionally, masculine pronouns referred to antecedents that might have been either male or female.

SOLUTION A

A great coach inspires his or her athletes to be their best on or off the field.

Use *he or she, him or her,* and so on, to reword the sentence.

SOLUTION B

Great coaches inspire their athletes to be their best on or off the field.

Make both the antecedent and the pronoun plural.

SOLUTION C

Great coaches inspire athletes to be their best on or off the field.

Eliminate the pronoun.

PROBLEM 2

A second-person pronoun that refers to a third-person antecedent

ant   Mary and Jodi prefer the new bridle trail because (you) get long stretches for galloping.

Do not use the second-person pronoun *you* to refer to an antecedent in the third person.

SOLUTION A

Mary and Jodi prefer the new bridle trail because they get long stretches for galloping.

Replace *you* with the appropriate third-person pronoun.

SOLUTION B

Mary and Jodi prefer the new bridle trail because the horses have long stretches for galloping.

Replace *you* with an appropriate noun.

PROBLEM 3

Singular indefinite pronouns as antecedents

ant   Each of the women in the boat received a rowing medal for (their) victory.

SOLUTION

Each of the women in the boat received a rowing medal for her victory.

Determine whether the antecedent is singular or plural, and make the personal pronoun agree with it.

More help with pronoun-antecedent agreement is available in Lessons 55–57.

PROBLEM 1

Unclear antecedent

ref	The wind was fair and the water calm, and (that) made sailing across the bay an absolute pleasure.
ref	The traffic was snarled, (which) was caused by an accident.

SOLUTION A

The wind was fair and the water calm, and those conditions made sailing across the bay an absolute pleasure.

Substitute a noun for the pronoun.

SOLUTION B

The traffic was snarled in a massive tie-up, which was caused by an accident.

Rewrite the sentence, adding a clear antecedent for the pronoun.

PROBLEM 2

A pronoun that refers to more than one antecedent

ref	The team captain told Karen to take (her) guard position.
ref	The buses came early for the students, but (they) were not ready.

SOLUTION A

The team captain told Karen to take the captain's guard position.

Substitute a noun for the pronoun.

SOLUTION B

Because the buses came early, the students were not ready.

Rewrite the sentence, eliminating the pronoun.

PROBLEM 3

Indefinite uses of you *or* they

ref	In those hills (you) rarely see mountain lions.
ref	In some movies (they) have too much violence.

SOLUTION A

In those hills hikers rarely see mountain lions.

Substitute a noun for the pronoun.

SOLUTION B

Some movies have too much violence.

Eliminate the pronoun entirely.

More help in making clear pronoun references is available in Lesson 58.

Troubleshooter

PROBLEM 1

Incorrect shift in person between two pronouns

pro	They went to the stadium for the game, but (you) could not find a place to park.
pro	One needs to remember to always keep (their) study time free from other commitments.
pro	We were on the hill at dawn, and (you) could see the most wondrous sunrise.

Incorrect pronoun shifts occur when a writer or speaker uses a pronoun in one person and then illogically shifts to a pronoun in another person.

SOLUTION A

They went to the stadium for the game, but they could not find a place to park.

One needs to remember to always keep one's study time free from other commitments.

Replace the incorrect pronoun with a pronoun that agrees with its antecedent.

SOLUTION B

We were on the hill at dawn, and Mary and I could see the most wondrous sunrise.

Replace the incorrect pronoun with an appropriate noun.

Need More Help?

More help in eliminating incorrect pronoun shifts is available in Lessons 52–58.

Shift in Verb Tenses

PROBLEM 1

Unnecessary shifts in tense

> shift t   Akira waits for the bus and (worked) on the computer.
>
> shift t   Jenny hit the home run and (runs) around the bases.

       Two or more events occurring at the same time must have the same verb tense.

> **SOLUTION**
>
> **Akira waits for the bus and works on the computer.**
> **Jenny hit the home run and ran around the bases.**
>
> Use the same tense for both verbs.

PROBLEM 2

Tenses do not indicate that one event precedes or succeeds another

> shift t   By the time the movie finally started, we (waited) impatiently
> through ten minutes of commercials.

       If events being described occurred at different times, shift tenses to show that one event precedes or follows another.

> **SOLUTION**
>
> **By the time the movie finally started, we had waited impatiently**
> **through ten minutes of commercials.**
>
> Use the past perfect tense for the earlier of two actions to indicate that one action began and ended before another action began.

**More help with shifts in
verb tenses is available in
Lessons 38–40 and 42.**

Incorrect Verb Tenses or Forms

PROBLEM 1

Incorrect or missing verb endings

> tense   Ricardo said it (snow) last night.
>
> tense   Karen and her family (travel) to Costa Rica last year.

> **SOLUTION**
>
> **Ricardo said it snowed last night.**
>
> **Karen and her family traveled to Costa Rica last year.**
>
> Regular verbs form the past tense and the past participle by adding *-ed*.

PROBLEM 2

Improper formation of irregular verbs

> tense   The sun (rised) out of scarlet clouds into a clear, blue sky.

> **SOLUTION**
>
> **The sun rose out of scarlet clouds into a clear, blue sky.**
>
> An irregular verb forms its past tense and past particple in some way other than by adding *-ed*.

PROBLEM 3

Confusion between the past form of the verb and the past participle

> tense   The horses (have ate) their feed already.
>
> tense   The coach (has wore) the old team jacket to every graduation.

SOLUTION

The horses have eaten their feed already.

The coach has worn the old team jacket to every graduation.

When you use the auxiliary verb *have,* use the past participle form of an irregular verb, not its simple past form.

PROBLEM 4

Improper use of the past participle

| tense | Deemee (drawn) the winning ticket for the door prize at the dance. |
| tense | The old rowboat (sunk) just below the surface of the lake. |

Past participles of irregular verbs cannot stand alone as verbs. They must be used in conjunction with a form of the auxiliary verb *have.*

SOLUTION A

Deemee had drawn the winning ticket for the door prize at the dance.

The old rowboat had sunk just below the surface of the lake.

Form a complete verb by adding a form of the auxiliary verb *have* to the past participle.

SOLUTION B

Deemee drew the winning ticket for the door prize at the dance.

The old rowboat sank just below the surface of the lake.

Use the simple past form of the verb instead of the past participle.

More help with correct verb forms is available in Lessons 36, 37, and 41.

Misplaced or Dangling Modifiers

PROBLEM 1

Misplaced modifier

mod   (Untended and overgrown since last summer,) Marlene helped Keshia in her garden.

mod   Sarah won the jumping contest with her mother's horse, (wearing western riding gear.)

A misplaced modifier appears to modify the wrong word or group of words.

SOLUTION

Marlene helped Keshia in her garden, untended and overgrown since last summer.

Wearing western riding gear, Sarah won the jumping contest with her mother's horse.

Place the modifying phrase as close as possible to the word or words it modifies.

PROBLEM 2

Misplacing the adverb only

mod   Akiko (only) runs hurdles in track.

SOLUTION

Only Akiko runs hurdles in track.

Akiko runs only hurdles in track.

Akiko runs hurdles only in track.

Each time *only* is moved in the sentence, the meaning of the sentence changes. Place the adverb immediately before the word or group of words it is to modify.

PROBLEM 3

Dangling modifiers

mod   (Branches swaying in the breeze,) we rested in the shade.

mod   (Trying out the new exercise equipment,) the new gym is a great improvement over the old one.

A dangling modifier does not modify any word in the sentence.

SOLUTION

Branches swaying in the breeze, the tree provided us with shade.

Trying out the new exercise equipment, Mary said the new gym is a great improvement over the old one.

Add a noun to which the dangling phrase clearly refers. You might have to add or change other words, as well.

More help with misplaced or dangling modifiers is available in Lesson 64.

Misplaced or Missing Possessive Apostrophes

PROBLEM 1

Singular nouns

poss   (Charles)car is the white one, but(Jamals)is the red convertible.

SOLUTION

Charles's car is the white one, but Jamal's is the red convertible.

To form the possessive of a singular noun, even one that ends in -*s*, use an apostrophe and an -*s* at the end of the word.

PROBLEM 2

Plural nouns that end in -s

poss   The seven maple (trees)cool, delicious shade is the best in the park.

SOLUTION

The seven maple trees' cool, delicious shade is the best in the park.

To form the possessive of a plural noun that ends in -*s*, use an apostrophe by itself after the final -*s*.

PROBLEM 3

Plural nouns that do not end in -s

poss   The (childrens)movies are on that rack next to the nature films.

SOLUTION

The children's movies are on that rack next to the nature films.

Form the possessive of a plural noun that does not end in -*s* by using an apostrophe and -*s* at the end of the word.

PROBLEM 4

Pronouns

poss   That painting cannot be just (anybodys) work.

poss   (Their's) is the trophy in the center of the display case.

SOLUTION A

That painting cannot be just anybody's work.

Form the possessive of a singular indefinite pronoun by adding an apostrophe and *-s* to it.

SOLUTION B

Theirs is the trophy in the center of the display case.

With any of the possessive personal pronouns, do not use an apostrophe.

PROBLEM 5

Confusing its *with* it's

poss   The computer is booting up; I see (it's) power light blinking.

poss   (Its) going to be a great victory party.

SOLUTION

The computer is booting up; I see its power light blinking.
It's going to be a great victory party.

It's is the contraction of *it is*, not the possessive of *it*.

More help with apostrophes and possessives is available in Lessons 3 and 89.

Missing Commas with Nonessential Elements

PROBLEM 1

Missing commas with nonessential participles, infinitives, and their phrases

com	Lois scowling fiercely turned her back on Clark.
com	The dectective mystified by the fresh clue scratched his head in bewilderment.
com	Television to tell the truth just doesn't interest me.

SOLUTION

Lois, scowling fiercely, turned her back on Clark.

The detective, mystified by the fresh clue, scratched his head in bewilderment.

Television, to tell the truth, just doesn't interest me.

If the participle, infinitive, or phrase is not essential to the meaning of the sentence, set off the phrase with commas.

PROBLEM 2

Missing commas with nonessential adjective clauses

com	The sailboat which looked like a toy in the storm rounded the point into the breakwater.

SOLUTION

The sailboat, which looked like a toy in the storm, rounded the point into the breakwater.

If the clause is not essential to the meaning of the sentence, set it off with commas.

PROBLEM 3

Missing commas with nonessential appositives

> com   The palomino a beautiful horse with almost golden hair is often
>   seen in parades.

SOLUTION

**The palomino, a beautiful horse with almost golden hair, is often
seen in parades.**

If the appositive is not essential to the meaning of the sentence, set it off
with commas.

PROBLEM 4

Missing commas with interjections and parenthetical expressions

> com   Wow did you see that falling star?
> com   I would have told you by the way but you weren't home.

SOLUTION

Wow, did you see that falling star?
I would have told you, by the way, but you weren't home.

Set off the interjection or parenthetical expression with commas.

**More help with commas and
nonessential elements is
available in Lesson 78.**

Missing Commas in a Series

PROBLEM 1

Commas missing in a series of words, phrases, or clauses

> *s com*   Mona said that Amy Tan James Baldwin and Charles Dickens were her favorite authors.
>
> *s com*   Sailing on the Great Lakes can be as challenging adventurous and rewarding as sailing on the ocean.
>
> *s com*   Our forensic team practiced hard did their research and used all their wit and intelligence to win the championship.
>
> *s com*   The wind shifted the clouds parted and the sunlight streamed down.

SOLUTION

Mona said that Amy Tan, James Baldwin, and Charles Dickens were her favorite authors.

Sailing on the Great Lakes can be as challenging, adventurous, and rewarding as sailing on the ocean.

Our forensic team practiced hard, did their research, and used all their wit and intelligence to win the championship.

The wind shifted, the clouds parted, and the sunlight streamed down.

Use a comma after each item in a series except the last.

More help with commas is available in Lessons 76–82.

Grammar

Unit 1: Parts of Speech

Lesson 1
Nouns: Concrete, Abstract, and Collective

A **noun** is a word that names a person, place, thing, or idea. A **singular noun** names one person, place, thing, or idea, and a **plural noun** names more than one.

	SINGULAR	PLURAL
Person:	friend	friends
Place:	field	fields
Thing:	melody	melodies
Idea:	freedom	freedoms

A **collective noun** names a group. A collective noun is singular when it refers to the group as a whole. A collective noun is plural when it refers to the individual members of a group.

The **committee** is studying the issue. (singular)
The **committee** have gone to lunch. (plural)

▶ **Exercise 1** Write *S* above each singular noun and *pl.* above each plural noun.

     pl.   **pl.**
The staff voted to rearrange their schedules.

1. Our group is planning a trip to New York.

2. The fountain in Grant Park is lovely at night.

3. A crowd had formed outside the department store.

4. The class donated their time to the senior citizens' center.

5. A company of actors entertained the children.

6. Sheep grazed on the grassy plain while tourists took pictures.

7. The soccer team will practice after the softball team.

8. The greenhouse was filled with orchids and irises.

9. This road follows the shoreline for five miles.

10. We saw surreys, covered wagons, and streetcars at the transportation museum.

11. The art league sponsored a competition for high school students.

12. Natalie and Suzanne often watch the evening news.

13. Geese wandered into our pond and stayed for nearly a week.

14. A vacant mansion was hidden behind the overgrown trees.

15. The show choir left their costumes in the auditorium.

A **concrete noun** names an object that occupies space or can be recognized by any of the senses.

| grass | apple | odor | stars | actor |

An **abstract noun** names an idea, a quality, or a characteristic.

| beauty | splendor | poverty | anger | success |

▶ **Exercise 2** Write *con.* above each concrete noun and *abst.* above each abstract noun.

con.   abst.
The flowers were a complete surprise.

1. His honesty impressed the members of the jury.

2. Carolyn is seeking compensation for her invention.

3. My diary contains no secrets.

4. People gathered around the stage in amazement.

5. We have plans to celebrate the victory.

6. Rita's notion of fairness is based on principle.

7. Mrs. Sanchez built a generator just for this experiment.

8. Freida made every effort to win the race.

9. Sherry can speak French, but Alicia knows both French and Spanish.

10. I finally understand the meaning of that song.

11. Juan has written an intriguing short story.

12. Talia listens to her favorite rock music on the radio.

13. Earl expressed curiosity about the plot of the novel.

14. With a little luck, Stan will get loge tickets to the concert.

15. Dwayne received an award for his devotion to this cause.

48 *Grammar and Language Workbook, Grade 10*

Lesson 2
Nouns: Proper and Common

we are going to her house

A **proper noun** is the name of a specific person, place, or thing. Proper nouns are capitalized. A **common noun** refers to persons, places, or things in general.

PROPER NOUNS	COMMON NOUNS
Person: George Washington	president
Place: Sahara	desert
Thing: Iguanodon	dinosaur
Idea: Renaissance	thought

▶ **Exercise 1** Write *prop.* above each proper noun and *com.* above each common noun.

    prop.   prop.   com.
Europeans came to America in ships.

1. The vast Atlantic separates Europe from America.

2. After the Revolution, the United States attracted more and more people.

3. Most of the new arrivals settled in New England.

4. Many people chose to live near the water.

5. Area merchants knew that money was to be made in trade.

6. Residents of seaports, such as Salem, Massachusetts, built many ships.

7. Americans built their sailing craft with pride.

8. Designers created many new ships.

9. These new ships could sail as far as China.

10. Young people were attracted to the adventure of the oceans.

11. Nathaniel Brown Palmer was born in the late eighteenth century.

12. His father designed and built ships.

13. Young Nat grew up with knowledge of the sea.

14. He became a captain at the age of eighteen.

15. Three years later he made a discovery.

16. He was the first person to sight Antarctica.

17. Later, he supplied weapons to Simón Bolívar.

18. Bolívar is known as the liberator of South America.

19. Nat Palmer then became captain of a packet ship.

20. Packet ships were forerunners of the clippers.

21. Clippers are the most famous type of sailing ships.

22. Nat Palmer designed better and better packet ships.

23. Palmer sailed these ships to Europe and back.

24. His business partner was Edward Knight Collins.

25. Collins designed flat-bottomed sailing ships.

26. The new models carried larger cargoes.

27. Profits rose for Collins and Palmer.

28. Other merchants started copying the new ships.

29. Abbot Low and his brothers opened trade routes to China.

30. The Americans and the Chinese were trading partners for a century.

▶ **Writing Link** Write a paragraph about the plot of your favorite movie. Use proper and common nouns.

_____

_____

_____

_____

_____

_____

_____

_____

_____

Lesson 3
Pronouns: Personal and Possessive; Reflexive and Intensive

A **pronoun** is a word that takes the place of a noun, a group of words acting as a noun, or another pronoun. A **personal pronoun** refers to a specific person or thing by indicating the person speaking (the first person), the person being addressed (the second person), or any other person or thing being discussed (the third person).

	SINGULAR	PLURAL
First person	I, me	we, us
Second person	you	you
Third person	he, him, she, her, it	they, them

A **possessive pronoun** shows possession or control. It takes the place of a possessive noun.

	SINGULAR	PLURAL
First person	my, mine	our, ours
Second person	your, yours	your, yours
Third person	his, her, hers, its	their, theirs

▶ **Exercise 1** Underline each personal pronoun and circle each possessive pronoun.

I told her that it was yours.

1. Carlos read the story to his younger brother.

2. She brought them to the skating rink yesterday.

3. They swim in their pool each day during the summer.

4. Your dog is begging you to feed him.

5. I lost their video somewhere between the library and my house.

6. She granted us the time we needed to complete the assignment.

7. You first organized the recycling campaign with their assistance.

8. Can we ask her to join us for lunch?

9. He played Felix in our production of *The Odd Couple.*

10. Candice called them before they left for the airport.

11. The snow covered the windshield of his car.

12. Did you enjoy their convention as much as we did?

13. Our wagon creaked under the pressure of its weight.

14. We studied their arguments carefully before making our final decision.

15. Carl wrote <u>them</u> a letter of recommendation about (her.)

16. <u>You</u> could be mistaken about <u>him</u>.

17. If (you) don't like (yours,) <u>you</u> can have some of (mine.)

18. <u>They</u> returned to the football game before <u>it</u> was over.

19. <u>I</u> cannot decide which book <u>she</u> would prefer.

20. He owes <u>her</u> an apology for (his) inconsiderate remark.

A **reflexive pronoun** refers to a noun or another pronoun and indicates that the same person or thing is involved. An **intensive pronoun** adds emphasis to a noun or another pronoun.

He surprised **himself** by breaking the home-run record. (reflexive)
Leo **himself** prepared the main course. (intensive)

	SINGULAR	PLURAL
First person	myself	ourselves
Second person	yourself	yourselves
Third person	himself, herself, itself	themselves

▶ **Exercise 2** Underline each reflexive pronoun and circle each intensive pronoun.

She helped <u>herself</u> by finishing her homework early.

1. The puppy scared <u>itself</u> by watching its shadow.

2. You (yourselves) can lead the singing tonight.

3. He bought <u>himself</u> a computer at the garage sale.

4. I (myself) forgot to bring the luggage.

5. They voted for the unknown candidate (themselves.)

6. You let <u>yourself</u> eat too much chocolate.

7. Bonita composed the music playing in the background (herself.)

8. We will learn the new dance (ourselves)

9. Did you (yourself) advance in the standings after the first round of play?

10. They allowed <u>themselves</u> plenty of time to reach the arena.

11. He (himself) assured us it would not rain on our picnic.

12. The train (itself) seemed to stop suddenly.

13. We promised (ourselves) we would see that movie Friday night.

14. You have visited Virginia many times (yourself.)

Lesson 4

Pronouns: Interrogative and Relative; Demonstrative and Indefinite

Grammar

An **interrogative pronoun** is used to form questions. Interrogative pronouns are *who, whom, whose, what,* and *which.* Other forms of the interrogative pronouns are *whoever, whomever, whosoever, whatever,* and *whichever.*

Who is planning to attend the silent auction?
Whatever are the Wilsons going to do with the leftover potato salad?

A **relative pronoun** is used to begin a special subject-verb word group called a subordinate clause (see Lesson 24).

The tour guide says this is the invention **that** changed history.

RELATIVE PRONOUNS

who	whom	what	which	that
whoever	whomever	whatever	whichever	whose

▶ **Exercise 1** Underline each interrogative pronoun and circle each relative pronoun.

Which of these schedules lists the time (that) the bus to Topeka leaves?

1. The caterer (who) furnished this meal did an excellent job.

2. Whatever happened to common courtesy?

3. We will see (whichever) of the Broadway plays you like.

4. The pianist (who) played last night gave a magnificent performance.

5. Who is the passenger (whose) briefcase was lost?

6. Sadie will give the package to (whoever) answers the door.

7. Father's car, (which) is bright red, is parked across the street.

8. Whom did you say the biography was about?

9. What crawled up your arm?

10. Whichever are we hoping to locate?

11. Whose scuplture did Terence admire at the art exhibit?

12. The quilt (that) Derek and Denise made is an anniversary gift for their parents. NO E

13. Aunt Tina purchased the blue silk dress (that) was displayed in the window. NO E

14. What was decided about the park (that) borders Silver Lake?

15. Give me (whatever) needs to be repaired.

A **demonstrative pronoun** points out specific persons, places, things, or ideas.

This was signed by the entire class.

SINGULAR	PLURAL
this	these
that	those

An **indefinite pronoun** refers to persons, places, or things in a more general way than a noun does.

Someone decorated the dining room for Corinne's birthday.

INDEFINITE PRONOUNS

all	both	everything	none	some
another	each	few	nothing	somebody
any	either	many	one	someone
anybody	enough	most	other	something
anyone	everybody	neither	others	
anything	everyone	nobody	several	

▶ **Exercise 2 Draw a line under each indefinite pronoun and circle each demonstrative pronoun.**

(That) appears to be a game anyone can win.

1. These belong on the shelf next to the mystery novels.

2. Neither gave the public a reason to rejoice.

3. Everybody wants a copy of Taylor Joyce's newest novel.

4. This is the key to unlocking the secrets of Ms. Dupont's success.

5. Those provoked quite an argument at the meeting last night.

6. Many attempt to win the contest, but few actually claim first prize.

7. The instructor gave others an opportunity to voice their opinions.

8. Joseph demonstrated that yesterday when he received his first traffic ticket.

9. Of all the directors, one achieved true greatness with his documentary.

10. Somebody made signs to show us the way to the tournament.

11. Take these to the laboratory on Clifford Street.

12. This certainly tastes delicious on top of a bed of lettuce.

13. Most of Gary's time was spent researching the issue.

14. Both captured our attention as we waited in the incredibly long line.

15. Everyone wishes those would last forever.

Lesson 5
Action Verbs: Transitive and Intransitive

A **verb** is a word that expresses action or a state of being and is necessary to make a statement. An **action verb** tells what someone or something does. Action verbs can express either physical or mental action. A **transitive verb** is an action verb that is followed by a word or words that answer the question *what?* or *whom?* An **intransitive verb** is an action verb that is not followed by a word that answers the question *what?* or *whom?*

Jason **telephoned** Andrea to invite her to the party. (transitive)
Jason's party **began** at eight o'clock. (intransitive)

▶ **Exercise 1** Draw two lines under each action verb. Write in the blank whether the verb is *T* (transitive) or *I* (intransitive).

___T___ Molly, our team captain, passed the ball to Deana.

_____ **1.** George and Ling brought chips and salsa to the meeting.

_____ **2.** Uncle Louis rides his horse three times each week.

_____ **3.** Marian sings beautifully in spite of her lack of practice.

_____ **4.** This city possesses more forms of entertainment than my hometown.

_____ **5.** After the thunderstorm a rainbow appeared in the sky.

_____ **6.** A flock of hummingbirds invaded the orchard.

_____ **7.** She respectfully declined the nomination for vice president.

_____ **8.** The Spanish Club travels to Spain next year.

_____ **9.** Both players work feverishly during the tennis match.

_____ **10.** The Riveras appreciate the space museum's newest exhibit.

_____ **11.** Tanya attends the symphony once a year.

_____ **12.** Roger's family took a ski trip last February.

_____ **13.** Dwight found his sneakers under the table.

_____ **14.** The explorers searched for treasure at the bottom of the sea.

_____ **15.** We watched the dolphin show at the amusement park.

_____ **16.** Jennifer's group displayed many crafts at the charity bazaar.

_____ **17.** The art gallery on Tenth Street holds a public showing once a week.

_____ **18.** A soft breeze playfully tugged at the last summer flowers.

Grammar

_____ **19.** The new lights on the pavement outline the road clearly.

_____ **20.** Tristan bought a road map from the convenience store.

_____ **21.** Renata's teammates waited impatiently.

_____ **22.** The toddler tripped on an uneven sidewalk.

_____ **23.** Our entire class contributed to the flood victims' relief fund.

_____ **24.** The space shuttle ascends through the clouds.

_____ **25.** Toby smells the tomato sauce hours before dinner.

_____ **26.** Many campers chose sites closer to civilization.

_____ **27.** The tourists complete their journey by train.

_____ **28.** Years ago, Simone wrote many letters.

_____ **29.** The celebration begins at two o'clock in the school gymnasium.

_____ **30.** William made a vase in pottery class.

▶ **Writing Link** Write a paragraph about a sporting event. Use transitive and intransitive verbs to describe the action.

_____

_____

_____

_____

_____

_____

_____

_____

_____

_____

_____

_____

_____

_____

_____

_____

Lesson 6
Linking Verbs

A **linking verb** links, or joins, the subject of a sentence with a word that identifies or describes the subject.

Sculpture **is** important.   The sculptor **seemed** dedicated.   Jo **will become** a sculptor.

LINKING VERBS
Forms of *be:* am, is, are, was, were, been, being

appear	feel	look	seem	sound
become	grow	remain	smell	taste

▶ **Exercise 1** Write *LV* in the blank if the verb is a linking verb and *AV* if the verb is an action verb.

LV   Frédéric Auguste Bartholdi was a sculptor.

AV   **1.** Scholars recognize Alsace as Barthldi's birthplace.

AV   **2.** His mother raised him in Paris.

AV   **3.** Alsace lies between Germany and France.

LV   **4.** Long ago it was an independent kingdom.

LV   **5.** However, today, as in 1834, it is part of France.

LV   **6.** Bartholdi was a poor student at first.

LV   **7.** Then he became interested in art.

LV   **8.** He seemed genuinely attracted to sculpture.

LV   **9.** However, sculpture is a difficult art to pursue.

AV   **10.** Sculpture requires much space.

LV   **11.** Its cost is often very great.

AV   **12.** The young Bartholdi dreamed of large sculptures.

AV   **13.** His options appeared limited.

LV   **14.** Bartholdi was nothing if not resourceful.

AV   **15.** His first success occurred in his hometown of Alsace.

AV   **16.** The town, Colmar, wanted a large statue to commemorate a local hero.

AV   **17.** Bartholdi's design appealed to the town leaders.

AV   **18.** He received the commission in 1856.

LV   **19.** The statue of the Napoleonic marshal Jean Rapp was a great success.

AV **20.** He made fountains, portrait busts, and a statue of the Celtic hero, Vercingetorix.

AV **21.** However, Bartholdi felt unsatisfied with these commissions.

AV **22.** He wanted his statues timeless.

AV **23.** He would express ideals with his works of art.

AV **24.** War, however, crushed his hopes.

AV **25.** In 1870 Prussia, a German state, invaded France.

LV **26.** The sculptor became an officer.

AV **27.** Bartholdi had command of fifteen soldiers in Colmar against some five thousand Germans.

AV **28.** The Germans forced his soldiers to retreat.

AV **29.** The Germans occupied his hometown.

LV **30.** His mood remained melancholy for some time.

AV **31.** In 1871 the unhappy Bartholdi sailed to America.

LV **32.** France and the United States had been strong friends since the American Revolution.

LV **33.** The French patriot Lafayette was also an American general in the Revolution.

AV **34.** Bartholdi liked America.

LV **35.** He was a guest at President Grant's summer cottage.

AV **36.** The French sculptor talked to Grant about an idea.

LV **37.** Edouard Laboulaye, a French journalist and politician, was the originator of the idea.

AV **38.** A Frenchman makes a monument to America's independence.

AV **39.** Bartholdi enlarges the notion into a fantastic idea.

AV **40.** He creates the Statue of Liberty.

▶ **Writing Link** Describe in two or three sentences a pet you or someone you know has had. Use a linking verb in at least two of the sentences.

_____

_____

_____

_____

_____

_____

Lesson 7
Verb Phrases

The verb in a sentence may consist of more than one word. The words that accompany the main verb are called **auxiliary**, or helping, **verbs** A **verb phrase** consists of a main verb and all its auxiliary verbs.

Miki and Steve **should finish** the posters before noon.

AUXILIARY VERBS
Forms of *be*: am, is, are, was, were, being, been
Forms of *have*: has, have, had, having
Other helping verbs: can, could, do, does, did, may, might, must, shall, should, will, would

▶ **Exercise 1** **Draw two lines under each verb phrase and circle each auxiliary verb.**

The performers may begin this concert early.

1. Jacques has played golf several times.

2. The majestic mountain will challenge any climber.

3. Three poodles have escaped from the Allingham estate.

4. An army captain could capture the attention of every private in the room.

5. Belinda might have seen the tornado from the basement window.

6. Mandy and Monica are visiting their aunt in Pittsburgh.

7. Walden Pond has become a popular destination for fans of Henry David Thoreau.

8. New rock bands will be featured on that radio station every Sunday evening.

9. This antique car did function well in its day.

10. The duchess may wear her diamond tiara to the embassy.

11. A new movie has sparked interest in Latin dancing.

12. Dorothy Parker was considered a great wit.

13. The history museum might acquire a collection of Civil War clothing.

14. The alarm will sound at precisely six o'clock.

15. Hernando must assist the band leader between songs.

16. Our plan could have succeeded at any other time of the year.

17. The Fadorsens shall hire a nanny for Angelina.

18. Dr. Carmichael is conducting a survey on sleep habits.

19. Though an amateur composer, Henri will create a memorable melody for the occasion.

20. Lisa will study phonetics next semester.

21. A detective would be gathering clues in this situation.

22. Champion divers are practicing for their Olympic event.

23. Eleanor Parker did play the baroness in *The Sound of Music.*

24. Irene and Ben will meet us along the parade route.

25. All of the horses were surging toward the finish line.

26. Alicia should recover in time for the next event.

27. Mr. Muldoon had conducted the orchestra since 1982.

28. I do worry about the effects of pollution on the environment.

29. Charlie is learning patience from his grandfather.

30. Jeanine might be chosen as a contestant on that game show.

31. Native American jewelry is sold at that store.

32. This discussion has been planned by the search committee.

33. The entire family shall fly to Paradise Island.

34. Don may give the precious music box to Teresa.

35. The incompetent sleuth had accused the wrong person.

36. Purple and yellow wildflowers were dotting the verdant meadow.

37. Katherine does enjoy each video game in her collection.

38. A number of potential buyers were being shown the Davises' house.

39. Mom could use some help with the neighborhood council meeting.

40. Nathan will be singing in the talent show.

▶ **Writing Link Write two or three sentences about an activity you enjoy. Use an auxiliary verb in at least two of the sentences.**

_____

_____

_____

_____

_____

_____

Lesson 8
Adjectives

(handwritten) which one, whatkind, How many, or ~~whose~~ who's.

An **adjective** is a word that modifies a noun or a pronoun by limiting its meaning.

dark clouds   **wet** snow   **clear** lake   **magnificent** lightning

Adjectives include the articles *a*, *an*, and *the*. *A* and *an* are **indefinite** articles; *the* is a **definite** article.

A dove glided over **the** orange trees.

Because they modify nouns, possessive nouns and pronouns are considered adjectives as well.

Place **your** jacket next to **Ryan's** jacket.

A **proper adjective** is formed from a proper noun and begins with a capital letter. Proper adjectives are often created by using the following suffixes: *-an*, *-ian*, *-n*, *-ese*, and *-ish*.

We ate **German** food and listened to **African** music at the international festival.

▶ **Exercise 1** Draw a line under each adjective in the following sentences.

A great number of adventurous people have immigrated to America.

1. European powers expanded their influence in the seventeenth century.

2. French explorers started North American colonies in Quebec.

3. English colonies started for religious freedom and business opportunities.

4. The Virginia colony was a business colony.

5. Large numbers of immigrants enabled the various colonies to prosper in the eighteenth century.

6. By the nineteenth century, Europe had a great number of unhappy people.

7. The common people's concerns were often ignored.

8. Therefore, many ordinary folk decided to emigrate.

9. They left their old homes and took a chance on America.

10. The first great immigration into the new nation came with the French Revolution.

11. The fierce Revolution caused many dramatic changes in France.

12. Every few years the weak government would be overthrown.

13. French immigrants to America included former royalists and radicals.

14. Very few people liked the constant twists and turns of the bitter struggle.

15. After the dictator Napoleon was defeated, however, emigration from France lessened.

16. Then aggressive Germany developed widespread troubles.

17. Many educated Germans fought for true, lasting political reform.

18. However, the strict Prussian government took over more and more of Germany.

19. Liberal Germans began immigrating to distant America.

20. Many Germans had immigrated to colonial America years before.

21. They found the rich farmland of Pennsylvania to be like the fertile regions they had left.

22. However, the new German immigrants often settled in wild frontier areas such as Wisconsin.

23. The American government gladly encouraged French and German immigration.

24. It saw this encouragement as a serious duty to European peoples.

25. One of the most numerous immigrant groups was the Irish.

26. Irish people had come to colonial America in the eighteenth century.

27. They fled the English government and its military occupation of Ireland.

28. In the 1840s, a terrible famine killed more than one million Irish people.

29. Many survivors considered America their only hope for lasting freedom.

30. Toward the end of the nineteenth century, the serious situation in eastern Europe became even worse.

31. Millions emigrated from their homelands in Russia, Austria-Hungary, Poland, and other areas.

32. Russia established a *Russification* policy for its people.

33. The Russian empire was a vast, gigantic empire stretching from the Pacific to Germany.

34. The Tsar's government sought to make everyone speak the Russian language.

35. His policy also persecuted the Jewish people within his lands.

36. The terrible attacks against Jews were known as *pogroms*.

37. Therefore, many Jewish people emigrated from Russia and came to America.

38. Large numbers of Chinese immigrants arrived in California after the Gold Rush.

39. They contributed to the economic successes of the West Coast.

40. Significant numbers of Japanese immigrants arrived in the late nineteenth century.

Lesson 9
Adverbs

An **adverb** is a word that modifies a verb, an adjective, or another adverb by making its meaning more specific. Adverbs answer the questions *how? when? where?* and *to what degree?*

When modifying a verb, an adverb may appear in various positions in a sentence. When modifying an adjective or another adverb, an adverb appears directly before the modified word.

The boy had run **quickly** home. (*Quickly* modifies the verb phrase *had run.*)
Kate is **very** nervous about her performance. (*Very* modifies the adjective *nervous.*)
Dr. Delacorte removed the bandages **quite carefully**. (*Quite* modifies the adverb *carefully; carefully* modifies the verb *removed.*)

The negatives *no, not,* and the contraction *-n't* are adverbs.

Other negative words, such as *nowhere, hardly,* and *never,* can function as adverbs of time, place, and degree.

I could**n't** remember where I left my science book.
The rain **never** begins until softball practice starts.

▶ **Exercise 1 Draw an arrow from each adverb to the word it modifies.**

The children were happily playing in the park for an hour.

1. We gleefully danced because of our victory.

2. My sister can type fast.

3. The maple tree in the yard is gradually losing its leaves.

4. The grandfather clock chimes merrily.

5. The big harvest moon shone brightly in the October sky.

6. Father loudly whistled for his dog.

7. The high school band marched proudly in the festival parade.

8. I thought the conductor was rather late in calling, "All aboard!"

9. The muddy creek flows very quickly.

10. The young artist watched the master closely.

11. The cooks in the cafeteria generously gave to the food drive.

12. The dairy cows grazed contentedly in the sweet clover.

13. It is nearly impossible to see butterflies this time of year.

14. Canadian geese gently settled down on the blue lake.

15. Boats that flew colorfully painted sails glided through the canal.

16. Karen and Brad seem very pleased with their score in ice dancing.

17. The cool air subtly reminds us that fall is approaching.

18. My family is planning this year's completely relaxing vacation.

19. The track team eagerly ate the soup and sandwiches.

20. The baby bird fluttered clumsily.

21. We noticed that the wildflowers had quickly withered.

22. The steam engine puffed loudly as it pulled slowly into the station.

23. The kids jumped happily on the sled and swiftly slid down the hill.

24. Caitlin searched everywhere for the missing locket.

25. My little brother's football team practiced hard for their first game.

26. The flame on the candle suddenly flickered.

27. Our lovely cactus bloomed beautifully in time for the holidays.

28. The antique bed was entirely covered by the homemade quilt.

29. The passenger was snoring loudly when the bus finally stopped at the station.

30. The aerobics class will meet again in two weeks.

31. Flowering shrubs totally surrounded the large porch.

32. The elephants in the circus were successfully trained for their job.

33. Wait here for the subway train.

34. The varsity team usually wore the school colors.

35. Jackets and sweaters were carelessly laid on the chairs and tables.

36. The art teacher artistically displayed the students' paintings.

37. Her older sister Gail will earnestly study anthropology in college.

38. The guides at the zoo skillfully led the group of tourists.

39. The new tractor deeply plowed the large field.

40. Uncle Dave certainly tells good stories.

▶ **Exercise 2** Draw a line under each adverb. Write in the blank the type of word it modifies: *V* (verb), *adj.* (adjective) or *adv.* (adverb).

_____V_____ The balloon floated <u>gently</u> toward the sky.

_____V_____ **1.** The wind whistled <u>sharply</u> through the trees.

_____V_____ **2.** The crowd <u>angrily</u> protested the court's decision.

_____V_____ **3.** He <u>hardly</u> had the ball, and then he dropped it.

___Adj___ **4.** I enrolled in a <u>slightly</u> unusual course.

__V, Adv__ **5.** Diane carried the carton of eggs <u>very</u> <u>carefully</u>.

__Adj V__ **6.** Teri and Samantha worked on their science project <u>yesterday</u>.

__V, Adv__ **7.** In spite of the setbacks, John succeeded <u>quite</u> <u>well</u>.

_____V_____ **8.** We <u>cheerfully</u> rode many miles in the restored train.

_____V_____ **9.** How will you maintain your grades?

__V, Adv__ **10.** She joined the club <u>extremely</u> <u>early</u> to qualify for the contest.

__Adv V__ **11.** The demonstration we witnessed was <u>truly</u> <u>extraordinary</u>.

__Adv V__ **12.** The announcer says the show will <u>begin</u> soon.

__Adv Adj__ **13.** The storm was <u>terribly</u> severe on the East Coast.

_____V_____ **14.** Jasmine <u>then</u> answered the question for the entire class.

___Adj___ **15.** The guest of honor was <u>very</u> knowledgeable.

_____V_____ **16.** Greg <u>barely</u> heard the news on the radio.

___Adv___ **17.** You will <u>never</u> guess whom I saw at the mall.

___Adj___ **18.** You will need one cup of <u>finely</u> chopped celery for this omelette.

_____V_____ **19.** They <u>recently</u> established their friendship.

Grammar

_____V_____ 20. I <u>nearly</u> grabbed the wrong suitcase from the luggage carousel.

____Adv, V____ 21. We <u>quite possibly</u> will launch the boat in the morning.

_____V_____ 22. Colleen waited <u>quietly</u> for me to demonstrate the program.

_____V_____ 23. Andre did <u>not</u> hear a shriek in the dark studio.

_____V_____ 24. She is <u>already</u> practicing for the school play.

_____Adj_____ 25. I have voiced my <u>well-researched</u> position on that issue.

_____V_____ 26. Joni <u>quickly</u> locked the front door.

_____V_____ 27. Cynthia says she <u>never</u> dreams about her job.

_____V_____ 28. The choir rehearsed <u>diligently</u> for the homecoming program.

_____V_____ 29. The evening sky <u>slowly</u> turned deep blue.

_____V_____ 30. The president <u>solemnly</u> opened the assembly.

_____Adj_____ 31. The bike was <u>totally</u> clean despite the rain.

_____V_____ 32. I <u>desperately</u> wanted to see the adventure movie at our local theater.

_____Adj_____ 33. This job seems <u>utterly</u> hopeless.

_____V_____ 34. Our team <u>firmly</u> defended the championship trophy.

____Adv, V____ 35. Sven <u>almost surely</u> will sell his computer to Alison.

_____V_____ 36. The yellow daffodils are <u>gently</u> swaying in the spring breeze.

_____Adj_____ 37. The tape in your videocassette recorder is <u>rather</u> tangled.

___Adv, V___ 38. Maria <u>certainly</u> seems devoted to the school newspaper.

_____Adj_____ 39. The soft drink can felt <u>extremely</u> cold in my hand.

_____V_____ 40. We saw the small sailboat drifting <u>aimlessly</u>.

▶ **Writing Link** Write a paragraph about a new activity you have tried recently. Use adverbs in your sentences.

_____

_____

_____

_____

_____

_____

_____

Lesson 10
Prepositions

A **preposition** is a word that shows the relationship of a noun or pronoun to some other word in the sentence.

The book **on** the table was written **by** Dr. Kotlinski.
The story **of** Hercules fascinates me.

COMMON PREPOSITIONS

aboard	as	but (=except)	in	out	toward
about	at	by	inside	outside	under
above	before	concerning	into	over	underneath
across	behind	despite	like	past	until
after	below	down	near	pending	unto
against	beneath	during	of	regarding	up
along	beside	except	off	since	upon
amid	besides	excepting	on	through	with
among	between	for	onto	throughout	within
around	beyond	from	opposite	to	without

A **compound preposition** is a preposition that is made up of more than one word.

according to	apart from	because of	in front of	next to	out of
ahead of	aside from	by means of	in spite of	on account of	owing to
along with	as to	in addition to	instead of	on top of	

Phrases that begin with a preposition usually end with a noun or pronoun called the **object of the preposition**.

The man arrived **with the pizza**. Everything went **according to plan**.

▶ **Exercise 1** Circle each preposition and underline each prepositional phrase.

The first American satellite was launched (from) Cape Canaveral.

1. Before this launch, the Soviet Union built a satellite named *Sputnik*.

2. It circled Earth (in) 1957.

3. *Sputnik* weighed only 184 pounds and fell (to) Earth (within) three months.

4. The Russians launched *Sputnik II* (on) November 3, 1957.

5. A dog was along (for) the ride.

6. The scientists wanted to see how long it would live (in) space.

7. It lived one hundred hours (after) takeoff.

8. The 1960 *Tiros I* demonstrated a satellite's value (in) weather forecasting.

Grammar

9. The year 1960 also saw the Soviet Discoverer capsules tested for passengers.

10. The Russians developed space capsules intended for human use, too.

11. The first man in space was Yuri A. Gagarin.

12. He made a single orbit around Earth.

13. According to records, the date was April 12, 1961.

14. Gagarin was two hundred miles above Earth.

15. The American project Mercury was initiated in 1958.

16. It was under the control of the National Aeronautics and Space Administration.

17. In May of 1961, Alan B. Shepard Jr. went into space.

18. Shepard, the first American in space, spent fifteen minutes there.

19. Two months after Shepard, Virgil I. Grissom became the second American to travel outside Earth's atmosphere.

20. Grissom's Mercury flight was like Shepard's suborbital flight.

21. A chimpanzee successfully orbited Earth in an American spacecraft during November 1961.

22. The first of the American astronauts in orbit around Earth was John H. Glenn.

23. The Atlas rocket lifted Glenn's Mercury capsule from the launch pad.

24. Millions watched on television as Glenn went into space.

25. He made three orbits around the planet.

26. On his way down, however, a signal indicated the capsule's heat shield had worked loose.

27. Everyone was terribly afraid; Glenn could die because of this problem.

28. Two minutes later, ground control discovered the problem was in the signal itself.

29. Without difficulty, Glenn and his capsule, which he called *Friendship 7*, were hauled out of the sea.

30. Besides these rocket efforts, Americans flew a rocket plane into outer space's lower reaches.

31. This was the famous rocket plane known as the X-15.

32. Today Russia and the United States, along with several other countries, are working together to move the boundaries of space ever further.

Lesson 11
Conjunctions: Coordinating, Correlative, and Subordinating

Grammar

A **conjunction** joins single words or groups of words. A **coordinating conjunction** joins words or groups of words that are equal in grammatical importance. Coordinating conjunctions include *and, but, or, nor, for,* and *yet.*

I wrote the letter **and** mailed it. It looked cloudy, **yet** we hoped for sunshine.

Correlative conjunctions work in pairs to join words and groups of words of equal importance. Correlative conjunctions include *both...and, just as...so, not only...but also, either...or, neither...nor,* and *whether...or.*

Either we leave now, **or** we don't leave at all.
Both Gina **and** Simone compete in gymnastics.

A **subordinating conjunction** joins a dependent idea or clause to a main clause.

COMMON SUBORDINATING CONJUNCTIONS

after	as long as	considering (that)	than	whenever
although	as soon as	if	though	where
as	as though	in order that	unless	whereas
as far as	because	since	until	wherever
as if	before	so that	when	while

The movie starts **after** the advertisements finish.
We finished early **so that** we could go home.

▶ **Exercise 1** Circle each conjunction. In the blank, write *coord.* if the conjunction is coordinating, *corr.* if the conjunction is correlative, or *sub.* if the conjunction is subordinating.

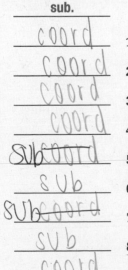

sub.   We are leaving (whenever) you are ready.

coord   1. The game began, (but) the rain stopped it.

coord   2. I have eaten, (yet) I am still hungry.

coord   3. The sun rose, (and) its light shone against the blue sky.

coord   4. (Do) you have enough money, (or) do you need more?

subcoord   5. Ogima walked home (because) he wanted to be alone.

sub   6. The branch fell (after) the storm had subsided.

subcoord   7. The television was muted (so that) Jeremy could hear the birds.

sub   8. He sought for more social importance (than) he really had earned.

coord   9. (Not only) does Mary volunteer at the hospital, (but also) she delivers meals to people who need them.

sub **10.** The crowds bustled all day, although the sale was over.

sub **11.** Darla waited by the escalator while Tina purchased a dress.

coord **12.** Whether lasagna or chicken is served at the banquet depends on us.

sub **13.** Drive down Front Street until you see the post office.

coord **14.** Either investigate the matter thoroughly, or ask someone else to do it.

coord **15.** They already inquired and were told the store was completely sold out.

sub **16.** Mercedes attended the ball last year, whereas I've gone the past two years.

coord **17.** Let's finish the project today, for tomorrow we will have other things to do.

coord **18.** The gift was neither requested nor expected.

sub **19.** Dr. Stevens spoke as though he had something on his mind.

sub **20.** Timothy will stay at the library as long as he can tonight.

sub **21.** If they do not arrive soon, we will start the movie without them.

sub **22.** Scott would rather see the movie before he reads the book.

sub coord **23.** We will arrive early so that we can find good seats.

coord **24.** Just as you helped me, so I try to help others.

sub **25.** The coach warned us we would lose unless we practiced harder.

sub **26.** After the assembly is over, Simon is going to leave.

coord **27.** I adore that actress, but I don't like her latest performance.

sub **28.** If the principal permits it, the chess club will host a tournament.

sub **29.** As soon as you finish packing, we will leave.

sub **30.** Courtney is in the habit of jogging every afternoon since she joined the track team.

coord **31.** Grandmother remembers not only Harry S Truman, but also Franklin D. Roosevelt.

sub. **32.** Everyone has a great time whenever Aunt Mae comes for a visit.

▶ **Writing Link** Write two or three sentences about a decision you have had to make. Use at least one **correlative conjunction** and one **subordinating conjunction**.

_____

_____

_____

_____

Lesson 12
Conjunctive Adverbs and Interjections

Grammar

A **conjunctive adverb** is used to clarify the relationship between clauses of equal weight in a sentence.

I won the archery contest; **nevertheless**, I still need to practice.

COMMON CONJUNCTIVE ADVERBS

again	further	indeed	nevertheless	still
also	furthermore	instead	nonetheless	then
besides	hence	likewise	otherwise	therefore
consequently	however	moreover	similarly	thus

An **interjection** is a word or phrase that expresses emotion or exclamation. An interjection has no grammatical connection to other words. Commas follow mild ones; exclamation points follow stronger ones.

Oh, is that so? **Hey**! Watch out or you'll get hurt!

▶ **Exercise 1** Draw a line under each conjunctive adverb and circle each interjection.

(Hey!) Casey won the contest; therefore, he became famous.

1. The *Hesperus* sank; moreover, there were no survivors of the wreck.

2. Dennis failed to follow the recipe; consequently, his pancakes did not turn out well.

3. We did not have enough money for the bus ride; besides, we enjoyed the walk.

4. General Douglas MacArthur was a great leader in World War II; similarly, George Patton won military glory in that conflict.

5. Those clouds are lovely; however, they signal coming bad weather.

6. (Oh!) You cleaned your room; therefore, you can have the last piece of pumpkin pie.

7. Dominique loves this ring; moreover, she actually has enough money to buy it.

8. You have to sit through a poor movie; however, a poor book you can put down.

9. Diego has to give a speech today; consequently, he is very nervous.

10. (Ouch!) I cut my finger on this stack of papers.

11. Sheila loves math class; similarly, she appreciates learning about chemistry.

12. I've always wanted to fly; indeed, I've even dreamed about it.

13. It is raining; otherwise, we would be outside.

14. Akira paints magnificently; moreover, he's even sold a few paintings.

15. Aha! I caught you raiding the refrigerator.

16. Larry passed his driving test; therefore, he wants to celebrate.

17. Denise is at swimming practice; likewise, Shawn is playing volleyball.

18. Well, how do you think the story ended?

19. Those new clothes in the store window look great; nevertheless, they're too expensive.

20. Let's enter the dance contest, Teri; furthermore, let's win it.

21. Bart slept until noon; then, he had to explain why he was late for his weekend job.

22. Wow! That is a blimp floating across the sky.

23. Guides led the visitors around the house; then, the party finally began.

24. Well, if you insist, I'll give him a call.

25. That blue one might be a reliable car; similarly, the red one could run well.

26. Cousin Martha has volunteered to help plan the party; moreover, she's willing to bring refreshments.

27. I love philosophy; indeed, it makes me see everything differently.

28. The old barn is beautiful; hence, I'll sketch it for art class.

29. Captain Ogden gave us a tour of his ship; moreover, he taught us how to steer it.

30. The Mongol hordes were powerful armies; otherwise, how could they have conquered so much territory?

31. The typhoon wrecked the shoreline; moreover, the wind damaged houses inland.

32. No! Don't put aluminum foil in the microwave oven.

▶ **Writing Link** Write a brief narration of a surprising event, real or imagined. Use at least one conjunctive adverb and two interjections.

_____

_____

_____

_____

_____

_____

_____

_____

✓ Unit 1 **Review**

▶ **Exercise 1** Write the part of speech above each italicized word: *N* (noun), *pro.* (pronoun), *V* (verb), *adj.* (adjective), *adv.* (adverb), *prep.* (preposition), or *conj.* (conjunction).

       adj.   **conj.**   **V**
  Lavender orchids *and* white roses *decorated* each table.

1. *The* [adj] aquarium was filled *with* [prep] *jellyfish* [n].

2. They were driving through town, so they *decided* [V] to pay *us* [pro] *a* [adj] visit.

3. Tony *and* [conj] Steve were *completely* [adv] finished painting the house by *six* [adj] o'clock.

4. The bullet train *sped* [V] through the countryside *at* [prep] an alarming *pace* [n].

5. *Dad* [n] ordered a *pizza* [n] with *pepperoni* [n], sausage, and *extra* [adj] *cheese* [n].

6. Learning to operate *theatrical* [adj] lights *is* [V] harder than *it* [pro] looks.

7. The *passengers* [n] will be boarding *the* [adj] airplane *soon* [adv].

8. *She* [pro] planned to vacation in Hawaii *but* [conj] had to settle *for* [prep] Hagerstown.

9. Who could imagine the *quaint* [adj] village would *have* [V] an entire store devoted to lamp *shades* [n]?

10. The children were *slightly* [adv] less *enthusiastic* [adv] about the move than *their* [pro] parents.

11. *This* [adj] *horse* [n] should run *freely*.

12. *Old* [adj] forty-five-speed records *have* [V] *become* [V] *collector's* [n] items.

13. How *did* [V] the broccoli *land* [V] *under* [prep] the kitchen *table* [n]?

14. The interviewer asked *several* [adj] difficult questions, *yet* [con] Stacy remained *calm* [adj].

15. *Corrine* [n] works as *an* [adj] intern *at* [prep] the Jefferson City Arts Council.

16. *We* [pro] hope to explore the new *bookstore* [n] after school *today* [adv].

17. Waiters *and* [con] waitresses *wear* [V] tuxedos at *that* [pro/adj] restaurant.

18. *Her* [pro] *perfume* [n] contains the scents *of* [prep] vanilla, lilies, and honeysuckle.

19. His *cheerful* [adj] smile *lit* [V] the room from the *moment* [n] he entered.

20. Ruth and Joc have lived *in* [prep] the same brick house *for* [pre] *thirty-five* [adj] years.

Cumulative Review: Unit 1

▶ **Exercise 1** Write the part of speech above each italicized word: *N* (noun), *pro.* (pronoun), *V* (verb), *adj.* (adjective), *adv.* (adverb), *prep.* (preposition), *conj.* (conjunction), or *int.* (interjection).

             adj.   **prep.**   **N**
       Virginia works as a *French* tutor *in* the *evening.*

1. The drama department *will* produce *a* musical *this* fall.

2. *We* stayed *late* to help clean up after the *banquet.*

3. *Glenna,* Tom, *and* Michael serve *on* *our* student council.

4. The glass *shelves* *were* full of unusual *objects.*

5. Though the piano *needs* tuning, *it* still sounds lovely when played by *Sydney.*

6. A folk art *exhibition* opens *at* the *museum* on Tuesday.

7. *Wow!* Imagine finding *oil* beneath *your* own backyard!

8. The wind *gradually* ceased, *and* the sun *peeked* through the clouds.

9. They *remembered* visiting *the* monument when *they* were children.

10. Roberto is interested in *Greek* history, *but* I prefer *geometry.*

11. Kyle brought *us* *brochures* describing several *beautiful* resorts.

12. Molly *was* waiting *for* the others on the steps *of* the statehouse.

13. *Everyone* looked *forward* to the *Silcrests'* dinner party.

14. *A* television news crew *videotaped* the entire *competition.*

15. *Well,* what *shall* we do *about* the broken pipe?

16. Neither steak *nor* rice sounds appetizing to *me* *tonight.*

17. In the spring, a *new* bridge will be *built* to replace *this* one.

18. Jerry *goes* skiing more *frequently* than *Sylvia* does.

19. Consumers *expect* to find *bargains* at *an* outlet store.

20. *Oh,* is the *concert* over *already?*

Unit 2: Parts of the Sentence

Lesson 13
Simple Subjects and Simple Predicates

Every sentence has a subject and a predicate. A **simple subject** is the main noun or pronoun that tells what the sentence is about. A **simple predicate** is the verb or verb phrase that tells something about the subject.

Clocks tick. (*Clocks* is the simple subject; *tick* is the simple predicate.)

▶ **Exercise 1** Draw one line under each simple subject and two lines under each simple predicate.

Andrea read from the book *Of Mice and Men*.

1. Bells were ringing in joyous celebration of the King's coronation.

2. According to poet John Keats, whales are "sea-shouldering" mammals.

3. Flowers were growing in every nook and cranny of the tiny backyard.

4. Paintings were displayed throughout the elaborate entryway.

5. The race at Cape White is on Saturday.

6. Those books are expensive.

7. I write poetry on rainy afternoons.

8. Julia has a rare coin from the seventeenth century.

9. We visited the Museum of Natural History in Cincinnati, Ohio.

10. The boxes of old clothes and toys are in a corner of the attic.

11. Our dog barks every morning at the mail carrier.

12. The exam was difficult.

13. I asked for a car for my birthday.

14. We stayed at the aquarium all day.

15. The sirens woke us in the dead of night.

16. The performance was impressive.

17. Time passed quickly.

18. Jake studies German.

19. Basketball is Ricardo's favorite sport.

Grammar

Grammar

20. The art of map production is called cartography.

21. Astronomy interests Derek and me.

22. Barb moved away a week or so ago.

23. Paul is the most responsible baby-sitter of all the teens on our block.

24. Luisa talks in her sleep.

25. I helped at my uncle's repair shop last week.

26. That intersection is dangerous due to a deep curve right before it.

27. My brother studied biology at Northwestern University.

28. Mrs. McCann completed the problem on the chalkboard.

29. Physics is my favorite subject.

30. The answer became clear as soon as I quit thinking about it.

31. Joel felt proud of his dog's blue ribbon.

32. The walk to town was more than a mile through soggy fields and low hills.

33. Amiua's archery team practices after school on Wednesdays and Thursdays.

34. The band will play in the gym.

35. Eduardo was absent for three days last week.

36. Her family includes three brothers and two sisters.

37. David put his shiny new baseball trophy on the top shelf.

38. Nicole will study in Paris this summer.

39. The spring concert is the biggest event for the choir.

40. Jill decided on a new stereo, speakers, and stand.

41. Ching-Li collects baseball cards of American ballplayers.

42. I worked on my term paper all day.

43. Pam borrowed my dictionary.

44. Mark laughed loudly at my lame joke.

45. Rashida works after school in the deli at Streber's Market.

Lesson 14
Complete Subjects and Complete Predicates

Grammar

A **complete subject** includes the simple subject and any words that modify it.

The driver of our bus waits patiently for the smallest children.

A **complete predicate** includes the simple predicate and any words that modify it.

The works of Monet **are on display at the museum**.

▶ **Exercise 1 Draw a vertical line between the complete subject and the complete predicate.**

The Vikings | were Scandinavian.

1. The seafaring Vikings traveled along the coasts of Europe during the period A.D. 800–1100.

2. This turbulent period is known as the Viking Age.

3. Vikings from Sweden, Norway, and Denmark raided many of Europe's coastal villages.

4. Viking traders exchanged goods with merchants in Byzantium, Russia, and France.

5. Rich iron deposits in Scandinavia allowed Vikings to develop advanced tools.

6. Ornamental spears, swords, and axes were used by Viking warriors.

7. Viking ships were superior to the rowboats of the time.

8. The Vikings often buried their wealthy deceased in ships under water.

9. Some Viking poetry and literature still exist.

10. Viking sea warriors could be vicious in their attacks.

11. Many people in coastal villages were killed or taken prisoner.

12. Swedish Vikings settled in areas around the Gulf of Finland.

13. The Orkney and Shetland islands were home to Norwegian Vikings.

14. Vikings known as Rus, or Varangians, established the first Russian state during the ninth century.

15. Some Vikings founded settlements in Ireland and northwestern England.

16. These daring explorers also settled in Iceland, Greenland, and North America.

17. Descendants of the Vikings in the city of Normandy, France, were called Normans.

18. Viking conquests slowed in the tenth century.

19. The political systems and armies of Europe grew stronger in the eleventh century.

20. This brought an end to the Viking Age.

▶ **Exercise 2** Draw one line under the complete subject and two lines under the complete predicate.

<u>The Vikings</u> <u><u>were probably the first Europeans in Nova Scotia.</u></u>

1. Nova Scotia was one of their first stopovers in the Northern Hemisphere.

2. The province of Nova Scotia lies on the eastern coast of Canada.

3. The Nova Scotia peninsula and Cape Breton Island make up Nova Scotia.

4. It is almost completely surrounded by water.

5. The Gulf of St. Lawrence separates Nova Scotia from Newfoundland.

6. John Cabot claimed Nova Scotia for the British in 1497.

7. He left no settlers in Nova Scotia.

8. French explorers Pierre du Gast and Samuel de Champlain later claimed part of Nova Scotia.

9. Nova Scotia was a battleground between the British and French during the seventeenth century.

10. An agreement called the Peace of Utrecht gave the mainland to the British.

11. The British gained control of Cape Breton Island in 1763.

12. The country joined the Dominion of Canada as one of its four primary provinces in 1867.

13. About eighty percent of Nova Scotia is covered by evergreen forests.

14. Nova Scotia and West Virginia are about the same size.

15. The city of Halifax is Nova Scotia's capital.

16. Fish, lumber, and ships were once important products of Nova Scotia.

17. Today coal, oil, and paper are the main products.

18. Nova Scotia's government is a parliamentary system.

19. It is headed by a lieutenant governor.

20. However, the provincial premier and an executive council make up the true executive branch.

▶ **Writing Link** Write one complete subject, and then write at least two complete predicates that will finish the sentence in an opposite manner.

_____

_____

_____

_____

_____

_____

Lesson 15
Compound Subjects and Compound Predicates

A **compound subject** has two or more simple subjects that are joined by a conjunction. The subjects share the same verb. A **compound predicate** has two or more verbs or verb phrases that are joined by a conjunction and share the same subject.

Pennies, nickels, and dimes filled the jar. (compound subject)
He **peeled and ate** a banana at lunch. (compound predicate)

▶ **Exercise 1** Draw a vertical line between the subject and predicate. Write *S* above each simple subject and *V* above each simple verb.

        S   V   V
The campers|slept outdoors and cooked over a campfire.

1. You and Tom have the best parts in the play.

2. I wrote the letter and mailed it the same day.

3. Grandmother sews our clothes and knits our sweaters.

4. The photographer took the photos and developed them himself.

5. The boy and the puppy ran toward the house.

6. A pencil case and a picture sat on the teacher's desk.

7. He makes crafts and sells them at the art fair.

8. For our club project, Jamal and I grilled and served hot dogs at the picnic.

9. Many friends and relatives came to my sister's graduation party.

10. Diane and Mitsu saw the movie and enjoyed it.

11. Clothes, jewelry, and baked goods were sold at the charity bazaar.

12. Richie and Peta walk or jog five miles each day.

13. Joy and my brother drove them to the party and dropped them off.

14. Both Tim and I take guitar lessons.

15. Jerry loaded the software and played his computer game.

16. They canceled and then rescheduled their ski weekend.

17. Leopards and tigers are members of the cat family.

18. Antonio and his family moved to Springfield and then settled in our city.

19. Hydrogen and oxygen combine to make water.

20. The little girl cried and reached up to her dad.

▶ **Exercise 2** Draw a vertical line between the subject and predicate. Write in the blank *CS* if the subject is compound, *CP* if the predicate is compound, or *B* if both are compound.

_CS_   Bala and Hannah|studied for the French test together.

_____ **1.** Mrs. Fabrizio announced the winner and called him to the front of the class.

_____ **2.** The coach, the team, and the fans stomped and cheered loudly after the touchdown.

_____ **3.** The librarian found us books and suggested some articles.

_____ **4.** Music and art were my favorite classes last year.

_____ **5.** Our government class chose two candidates and held a mock election.

_____ **6.** Four geese and one duck swim in the pond behind our house.

_____ **7.** The faculty and students held a car wash and started a food drive for the needy.

_____ **8.** Melon and cantaloupe are my favorite summer fruits.

_____ **9.** The car rattled and shook before stopping completely.

_____ **10.** Carl and Dimitri discovered the error and brought it to the teacher's attention.

_____ **11.** The newspaper carrier delivered the newspaper and collected his fee.

_____ **12.** Tornadoes and hurricanes are natural disasters.

_____ **13.** Quarters or dimes and nickels will work in that machine.

_____ **14.** Either you or I should call Phil and tell him the good news.

_____ **15.** We often remember the good times and forget the bad times.

_____ **16.** Tennis and baseball keep us busy in the summer.

_____ **17.** Kevin marched in the band and played the trumpet.

_____ **18.** The wind and rain pounded the windows and kept us awake all night.

_____ **19.** Either Nancy or Zack will mow the grass.

_____ **20.** Ricardo and Mitch bought new video games and played them all weekend.

80

Lesson 16
Order of Subject and Predicate

In most sentences, the subject comes before the predicate. In a sentence written in **inverted order**, the predicate comes before the subject.

Some sentences are written in **inverted order** for variety or special emphasis.

PREDICATE   SUBJECT
Around her neck **was**   a beautiful **necklace.**

The subject also follows the predicate in a sentence that begins with *there* or *here.*

PREDICATE   SUBJECT
There **are**   more **members** in the Chess Club than in the Pep Club.

When the subject *you* is understood, the predicate appears without a subject.

UNDERSTOOD SUBJECT   PREDICATE
    (You)   **Ask** her for help.

▶ **Exercise 1** Draw one line under each simple subject and two lines under each simple predicate.

Over the hill lies a valley rich with artifacts.

1. Here are the cookies for the bake sale.

2. Look at the photographs in the album.

3. There is no reason for the delay.

4. Behind Joey was the girl from my biology class.

5. In the pile on the left were the tests from our class.

6. Inside a box in the attic was a picture of her grandmother's wedding.

7. There goes my favorite kind of sports car!

8. Using a microscope, watch the movement of the bacteria.

9. Deep in the water was a swordfish partially hidden by a rock.

10. Finish the assignment for Friday.

11. There was no one left in the auditorium after the play.

12. Wear a heavy coat on your walk in the snow.

13. Here is the poem by e. e. cummings.

14. Inside the apartment building were the landlord and her dog.

15. Read the third paragraph aloud.

16. There exist many books about Martin Luther King Jr.

17. On the bird feeder was a tiny hummingbird.

18. Look in the mirror.

19. On the table were three gifts for Robert.

20. There is a trampoline in the gym.

▶ **Exercise 2** Write *C* beside each sentence that is a command (imperative). Write *I* beside each sentence that is in inverted order. If the sentence is in inverted order, draw one line under the subject and two lines under the verb.

____I____ Under the rock was a pile of earthworms.

_____ 1. Wait for the bus on the right side of the street.

_____ 2. There is nothing as colorful as a fireworks display.

_____ 3. Through the streets roared many fire engines and police cars.

_____ 4. Be quiet in the library.

_____ 5. Here lies the envelope with the letter inside.

_____ 6. Beyond the meadow was a forest of tall pines.

_____ 7. Send your entry to this address for the contest.

_____ 8. There are several students from China in our class.

_____ 9. There is no signature on her letter.

_____ 10. Out of the tunnel came a speeding train.

_____ 11. Come with me to the festival downtown.

_____ 12. Go to the store for some milk and butter.

_____ 13. Here is the best way to Shama's house.

_____ 14. Give Janine or Maria the camera.

_____ 15. Be ready to swing at the ball.

_____ 16. There was no one in the halls after the bell.

_____ 17. Over the net flew the volleyball.

_____ 18. Into the store walked a mother and five small children.

_____ 19. Sing us a song.

_____ 20. There was a party after our victory.

Lesson 17
Complements: Direct and Indirect Objects

A **complement** is a word or phrase that completes the meaning of a verb. A **direct object** is one type of complement. It answers the question *what?* or *whom?* after an action verb.

Marie Curie won two **Nobel Prizes**. (*Nobel Prizes* answers the question *what?*)

An **indirect object** is also a complement. It answers the question *to whom? for whom? to what?* or *for what?* after an action verb.

Harrison gave **Randy** a gift for his birthday. (*Randy* answers the question *to whom?*)

▶ **Exercise 1** Draw two lines under each verb. Circle each direct object.

The Bobcats won the (championship.)

1. We ate dinner earlier than usual.

2. My uncle in Singapore sent me flowers on my birthday.

3. Does Raoul like his new home?

4. Our family took a trip to Arizona last year.

5. Pam liked my new dress.

6. Keshia wrote a great speech for the assembly.

7. Henry Ford introduced the Model T Ford in 1908.

8. I carried Dana's backpack to the bus stop for her.

9. I left my algebra book in my locker.

10. Shari painted many pictures in art class.

11. I lost my favorite earrings at track practice.

12. Members of the class planted several trees to help the environment.

13. Melanie collects shells at the beach.

14. Teresa ate breakfast on the run.

15. Do you prefer golf or tennis?

16. Jamal chose Andy as his math tutor.

17. Maryam wrote the Arabic alphabet on the board.

18. Antonio hurt his knee in football practice.

19. We polished the surface of the car.

20. I needed a postage stamp for the letter.

▶ **Exercise 2 Circle each direct object. Draw one line under each indirect object.**

Mrs. Reynolds made <u>me</u> a (costume) for the masquerade.

1. She gave the museum a rare sculpture.

2. Did Tracy give you her tickets for the concert?

3. Reiko left Gretchen a message.

4. The candidate gave voters a chance for questions.

5. The librarian gave Isabel a book.

6. I gave the clerk a ten-dollar bill.

7. Has Jim told Marcos and Josh his plans?

8. The college awarded my sister a full scholarship.

9. Ben made Rachel and me a batch of cookies.

10. Jennie's mom brought her a warm-up suit for gymnastics practice.

11. David wouldn't tell me his secret recipe.

12. Tommy sold Ray his car.

13. The police officer gave him a ticket for reckless operation.

14. I gave Billy a copy of the periodic table.

15. Allyn told Kevin his ideas for the English project.

16. The referee awarded our team the ball.

17. Should Elliot bring Mother her robe?

18. My grandfather gave me his fishing pole.

19. We gave Tanya the award for most valuable player.

20. The teacher showed us a shortcut to the problem.

▶ **Writing Link Write four or more sentences about a special gift that someone has given you. Use a direct object and indirect object in at least two of your sentences.**

_____

_____

_____

_____

_____

Lesson 18
Object Complements and Subject Complements

An **object complement** is a noun, a pronoun, or an adjective that completes the meaning of a direct object by identifying or describing it.

Akira finds me a good **friend**. (noun)
Paul calls the car **his**. (pronoun)
He considered it **irrelevant**. (adjective)

▶ **Exercise 1** Above each object complement, write *N* for noun, *P* for pronoun, or *adj.* for adjective.

                            N
Frederick finds hockey a challenge.

1. Tara considers her education an investment in her future.

2. They call that land theirs.

3. We elected Tim class treasurer.

4. Errors make these baseball cards rare.

5. Yolanda found the German class a challenge.

6. Important landmarks make that city a tourist attraction.

7. My little sister named her hamster Rizzo.

8. A strong drive to excel makes my mother successful.

9. The club appointed Andrew leader of our group project.

10. Erica considers that technique hers.

11. Mr. Mottice found the chemicals potentially dangerous.

12. Dan considers TV a waste of time.

13. The museum considered the diamonds irreplaceable.

14. I consider Manuel a strong competitor.

15. The director will name Terri most improved singer at the choir banquet.

16. Julia considered the crafts in her display hers.

17. Todd finds vegetables essential for a healthy diet.

18. The Grangers now call Minnesota home.

19. We found the tragic climax of the play a shock.

20. The people of the village consider that way of life theirs.

A **subject complement** follows a subject and a linking verb. It identifies or describes a subject. The two kinds of subject complements are predicate nominatives and predicate adjectives.

A **predicate nominative** is a noun or pronoun that follows a linking verb and gives more information about the subject.

Montana is a **state**.

A **predicate adjective** is an adjective that follows a linking verb and gives more information about the subject.

He seemed **happy** with the results.

▶ **Exercise 2** Write *PN* above each predicate nominative and *PA* above each predicate adjective.

         PA
That coat seems expensive.

1. Suki Chen would be a good choice for cheerleader.

2. Uncle Paul is your father's brother.

3. Eric's notes are scraps of paper with unreadable writing.

4. The party was dull without a band.

5. The house looks ready for a fresh coat of paint.

6. Sunlight is one cause of skin cancer.

7. I felt lucky after the earthquake.

8. Neil Armstrong was the first person on the moon.

9. Doctors must be cautious about prescriptions.

10. Madelyn seems happy with her new brother.

11. Those boys are competitors.

12. Because of their unhappiness, I feel sad.

☑ Unit 2 Review

▶ **Exercise 1** Draw a vertical line between the subject and predicate. Write *DO* above each direct object and *IO* above each indirect object.

              DO
    Carol|wrote her paper about water pollution.

1. We recycle newspapers.

2. My friend Janet bought chips and soda for the party.

3. He gave us coins from his collection.

4. Rex served his parents breakfast on their anniversary.

5. Ken thanked me for my help.

6. I found a five-dollar bill on the ground.

7. Karen told her doctor the truth.

8. We saw the stars clearly with the new telescope.

9. Mrs. Fitzpatrick wrote her representative a letter about toxic waste.

10. We eat Mexican food once a week.

11. Vince bought his dad a new wallet.

12. Uncle Ellis often makes pudding for dessert.

13. My little brother brought a goldfish home from the fair.

14. Mike gives tennis all of his time.

15. The teacher assigned Kim a report for extra credit.

16. Beth gave Jim an extra folder for his book report.

17. The computer made a strange noise and then shut down completely.

18. The restaurant had burritos on the menu.

19. Nathaniel told Chris the best idea for a costume.

20. The newscaster reported an accident on Fifth Avenue.

Cumulative Review: Units 1–2

▶ **Exercise 1** Write *C* for concrete, *A* for abstract, or *col.* for collective above each noun in italics. Write *T* for transitive or *I* for intransitive above each verb.

      col.   I
The *team* waited patiently.

1. Abby took voice *lessons* with Dr. Vogelsang.

2. My grandfather began a story about his *childhood*.

3. David bought his favorite *magazine*.

4. He and his *sister* argue about everything.

5. Elliot's *camera* takes magnificent photographs.

6. Kenny leaves *clothes* everywhere.

7. The *band* visited Florida this year.

8. His *sadness* shows in all his actions.

9. The *geese* are flying south for the winter.

10. The *army* guarded the area night and day.

▶ **Exercise 2** Draw a line between the subject and predicate. Above each word in italics, write *OC* for object complement, *PN* for predicate nominative, or *PA* for predicate adjective.

                                OC
That teacher|considers final exams *unnecessary*.

1. Arachnids are *arthropods* with eight legs.

2. Susan found the race a *challenge*.

3. Some people are *realistic*, and others are *dreamers*.

4. Air pollution remains a *problem* in our state.

5. The family considers Uncle Jack a *character*.

6. Mr. Thomas may become our new basketball *coach*.

7. Ed became *anxious* about the noises downstairs.

8. His friendliness makes Li a popular *person*.

Grammar

Unit 3: Phrases

Lesson 19
Prepositional Phrases

A **prepositional phrase** begins with a preposition and ends with a noun or a pronoun called the **object of the preposition**. Some common prepositions are *against, at, for, in, to, on, by,* and *with*.

A prepositional phrase can function as an adjective, modifying a noun or a pronoun.

Darcy chose the bedroom **above the garage**. (*Above the garage* modifies the noun *bedroom*.)

It may also function as an adverb when it modifies a verb, an adverb, or an adjective.

That poem is meaningful **to me**. (*To me* modifies the adjective *meaningful*.)

▶ **Exercise 1** Underline the prepositional phrase or phrases in each sentence.

Architects design buildings and other structures for their clients.

1. Architecture is considered a form of art.

2. It is one of the oldest of the fine arts.

3. More is known about the structures of ancient times than about the builders.

4. Before the invention of construction equipment, architects relied on huge labor forces.

5. Examples of early architecture include the Egyptian pyramids and tombs of stone.

6. Mesopotamians used clay bricks in ziggurats at Uruk.

7. Ancient Greeks built magnificent palaces and the huge complex of Knossos.

8. Greeks used masonry and decorated the walls of their structures with frescoes.

9. Columns and beams were also among the Grecian trademarks.

10. Marble was widely used as a construction material during this classical period.

11. The Acropolis and the Parthenon are examples of the fine techniques of the Greeks.

12. The Romans later added their expertise to the Greek technology.

13. During the second century, Romans built structures made from concrete, terra cotta, and bricks.

14. Architectural refinements by the Romans included the arch, the vault, and the dome.

15. Aqueducts, the Colosseum, and the Pantheon are examples of Roman structures.

16. Gothic architecture originated in Northern Europe.

17. The use of buttresses, arches, and vaults characterizes this style.

18. Gothic architecture is seen in many cathedrals in Paris.

19. Examples of Gothic architecture are found throughout Europe.

20. Many of the traditions of the past are reflected in modern architecture.

▶ **Exercise 2** Draw one line under each prepositional phrase and two lines under the object of each preposition.

The name Frank Lloyd Wright is well known among architects.

1. American architect Frank Lloyd Wright was a key figure in modern architecture.

2. Wright produced designs for residences and commercial buildings.

3. His designs are known for their originality.

4. With a style based on natural forms, Wright's work is unique.

5. Though he studied civil engineering for a time, Wright worked in a design department.

6. On the side, Wright designed houses for clients of the firm.

7. The homes have low roofs and walls of windows.

8. Huge stone fireplaces are a central part of his home designs.

9. His commercial buildings have heavy walls with skylights for the primary light source.

10. At Robie House in Chicago, Wright blended the architecture with the surrounding landscape.

11. After 1893, Wright went out on his own.

12. He would become one of the most famous architects in the United States.

13. Taliesin West is a complex near Phoenix that became Wright's home, workshop, and school.

14. It is a series of structures with roofs of canvas and wood resting on walls of boulders.

15. The Guggenheim Museum in New York is another of Wright's creations.

16. It has a spiral design similar to the structure of seashells.

17. His designs are marked by the use of forms from nature.

18. One of his most famous buildings, Fallingwater, is located in a small town in Pennsylvania.

19. Cantilevers, or beams supported at one end, suspend the living room and terrace over a waterfall.

20. Fallingwater is now one of the most popular tourist attractions in Pennsylvania.

Lesson 20
Appositives and Appositive Phrases

An **appositive** is a noun or a pronoun that further identifies another noun or pronoun.

My music teacher, **Mr. Price**, studied with famous musicians.

An **appositive phrase** is the appositive along with any modifiers. If not essential to the meaning of the sentence, it is set off by commas.

We rented bicycles to ride through that area, **the most charming part of town.**

▶ **Exercise 1** Underline the appositive or appositive phrase in each sentence.

Mr. Thompson, <u>Dan's father</u>, works at a chemical plant.

1. Venus, the second planet from the sun, resembles Earth.

2. Some people prefer soft pretzels, large pretzels that are warmed, to ordinary pretzels.

3. My sister Pam marches in the band.

4. The rattlesnake, one of the most poisonous types of snake, is feared by many people.

5. My favorite comedians, Abbott and Costello, are in that movie.

6. The winner, the first runner to cross the finish line, will win a trophy.

7. My best friend Roberto is the treasurer of the Drama Club.

8. Asthma, a disease of the respiratory system, is sometimes controllable with medication.

9. The new boy in school, Derek Peterson, is from Montana.

10. My father, a former trumpet player, encouraged me to take lessons.

11. The chorus, a group made up of choir members, will perform tonight.

12. *Beowulf*, our assignment for English class, is about a hero of the middle ages.

13. That recliner, a lumpy old chair, is my uncle's favorite.

14. Our house, the two-story on the corner, is more than one hundred years old.

15. Her intelligence, a powerful asset, led her to a career in medicine.

16. Cindy and I always order the same dinner, a burrito and refried beans.

17. My neighbor Diane gives me a ride to school every morning.

18. In chemistry we worked on a chemical solution, a combination of two acids.

19. Only Mother, a very patient person, can tolerate Tommy's tantrums.

20. Davy Crockett, an American folk hero, was a pioneer who became a U.S. representative.

21. The teacher assigned a final project, a term paper.

22. Moussaka, a Greek dish, is my favorite food.

23. Every Friday after school we meet at the same place, the restaurant on the corner.

24. The test, a mixture of essay and multiple-choice questions, was easy.

25. Cairo, the capital of Egypt, has a hot, dry climate.

26. Janet's uncle Jake is a teacher at the middle school.

27. That book, a mystery novel, is suspenseful.

28. Edison's experiments led to an important discovery, the first central electric-light power station.

29. Samuel de Champlain, a French explorer, was the founder of Quebec.

30. The poet Robert Browning had an innovative style.

31. My cousin Tim came to watch me in the play.

32. Mr. Dixon, the new mayor, has been a politician for many years.

33. Daniel, our relief pitcher, finished the game.

34. Sarah is from Springfield, the capital of Illinois.

35. Mr. Ortega, our soccer coach, encourages us in our academic work.

36. Our favorite spot is Camp Lightfoot, a peaceful retreat.

37. Pegasus, a winged horse, is a mythical creature.

38. Lake Ontario, the smallest of the five Great Lakes, borders both Canada and New York.

39. The boy over there is Luis, the fullback of the football team.

40. Your breakfast, eggs and bacon, was easy to make.

41. Fans of baseball pitcher Orel Hershiser admire his longevity.

42. The artifact, an ornate bowl, was found in the desert.

43. Nathan became an Eagle Scout, the highest honor in scouting.

44. Our dog, a golden retriever, does many tricks.

45. The band concert, a series of songs by Gershwin, is scheduled for Tuesday.

46. Prince Edward Island, a popular vacation spot in Canada, is the setting for the TV series *Anne of Green Gables*.

47. Phoenix, the capital city of Arizona, lies in the Salt River Valley.

48. My friend Robert, the car expert, helped me choose new tires for my car.

Grammar

Lesson 21
Participles and Participial Phrases

A **participle** is one type of verbal. Remember that verbals are verb forms that function as nouns, adjectives, or adverbs. A participle functions as an adjective when it modifies a noun or a pronoun. A present participle always ends in *-ing*. Past participles usually end in *-ed*.

The child watched the **spinning** top.
We admired the freshly **planted** flowers.

A **participial phrase** contains a participle and any modifiers needed to complete its meaning.

Warmed by the fire, we took off our jackets.
Having misplaced my keys, I could not get into my house.

Copyright © by Glencoe/McGraw-Hill

▶ **Exercise 1** Draw a line under the participle or participial phrase in each sentence.

Looking around, we saw many friends.

1. The winding road led to a large house on a hill.

2. Knowing the answer, I raised my hand.

3. Alonzo's shaking hands gave away the fact that he was nervous.

4. Guided by a strong sense of direction, I found my way out of the forest.

5. The locked cage contained a Bengal tiger.

6. Playing major league hockey, Rafael fulfilled his dream.

7. We see Jenny racing to the curb for the mail every day.

8. Having discussed the matter at length, my father took the job out of state.

9. Paying attention, I heard a lovely ringing in the distant bell tower.

10. Disappointed by the loss, the fans quietly left the stadium.

11. We saw Junko courteously thanking everyone.

12. I listened to the willow's sad, creaking branches.

13. Finding the assignments difficult, Isra sought help from a tutor.

14. During the performance everyone could probably hear my pounding heart.

15. Having done my homework, I left for hockey practice.

16. Valerie finds her after-school job challenging.

17. The winning steer at the fair came from Springfield.

18. The sad film left many moviegoers sobbing gently.

19. Startled by the noise, we jumped from our chairs.

20. Protected by his seat belt, Sean walked away from the accident.

▶ **Exercise 2** Underline each participle or participial phrase and draw an arrow to the noun or pronoun it modifies.

The students, determined to make a difference, organized a clean-up effort.

1. Having concluded my speech, I stepped away from the podium.

2. Dressed as a pirate, my little brother had a cardboard sword.

3. The runners, tired from the race, rest on a nearby bench.

4. Having received her letter, I wrote back right away.

5. Searching the room for my jacket, I found my hat instead.

6. Tracked by the hunters, the deer ran swiftly.

7. Those arriving after the bell will be marked tardy.

8. The city's authorities felt a growing concern about the high crime rate.

9. Everyone came to the pep rally wearing the school colors.

10. That juice, derived from the leaves of the aloe plant, is used to treat burns.

11. Disturbed by the lack of cooperation, the coach dismissed us early.

12. Rescued by the firefighters, the kitten was shaking.

13. Promising he'd be home on time, Jeff left for the movies.

14. The insects, attracted by the food, ruined our picnic.

15. Yelling from across the field, Russ reminded us to bring our uniforms.

16. The tin can uncovered by my metal detector was worthless.

17. We chose the line by the field house as our starting point.

18. Covered with ice and snow, the car would not start.

19. Ty was confused by the note lying on the counter.

20. The dripping faucet got on everyone's nerves.

94 *Grammar and Language Workbook, Grade 10*

Lesson 22
Gerunds and Gerund Phrases

A **gerund** is another type of verbal that ends in *-ing*. It is a verb form that is used as a noun. A gerund may function as a subject, an object of a verb, or the object of a preposition.

Nina made us laugh by **packing** for the trip two weeks in advance.

A **gerund phrase** includes a gerund and any complements and modifiers needed to complete its meaning.

The rules prohibited **eating anywhere in the library.**

Grammar

▶ **Exercise 1** Underline the gerunds or gerund phrases in each sentence.

Rich is responsible for <u>bringing the equipment to practice</u>.

1. Logging is the process of harvesting trees and delivering them to manufacturing facilities.

2. Writing papers for English is something Jay enjoys.

3. Charlie complained of hearing noises outside.

4. My sister and I helped mom with her fall planting.

5. Doctors are constantly finding new cures for diseases.

6. Flying is our first choice of vacation transportation.

7. I told Laura that she should consider acting as a career.

8. Mrs. Baker's unique teaching made her class popular.

9. Being in enclosed places makes Tonya nervous.

10. My brother plans on returning home after a year in Spain.

11. Dividing the chores made life easier at our house.

12. After waiting for an hour, we gave up and went home.

13. Coloring is a popular activity with most children.

14. We enjoyed seeing videotapes of our childhood.

15. Carmen would like to try skydiving.

16. Practicing constantly helped Mike with his basketball layups.

17. Singing the fight song is a tradition before each football game.

18. Jessica's snoring keeps everyone awake.

19. Did Lena give a reason for refusing to go to class?

20. My sister studies toward a degree in accounting.

▶ **Exercise 2** Underline the gerund or gerund phrase in each sentence. Above each, write *S* if the gerund functions as a subject, *O* if it functions as an object of a verb, or *OP* if it functions as an object of a preposition.

0

Ray enjoys <u>listening to music from the 60's.</u>

1. Calling is the best choice.

2. David gives racing most of his time.

3. George lightened the mood by whistling.

4. Olivia devotes her time to helping others.

5. Omar and Brian are responsible for training their dogs.

6. Catching a big fish made the day at the lake worthwhile.

7. The ancients had no way of knowing the weather ahead of time.

8. Mother was against celebrating her birthday.

9. Living in the Middle East for a year was an adventure for the whole family.

10. Mining coal was my grandfather's job as a young man.

11. Brushing regularly protected me from cavities.

12. Kirsten devoted a week to preparing for the final exam.

13. Despite her injury, Diana still likes skating.

14. Listening is important in following directions.

15. His interest in wrestling began at an early age.

16. Zack is good at conveying his point to others.

17. The actors in the play were busy with learning their lines.

18. Gaining the trust of his friends is important to Len.

19. Meagan took pride in designing the homecoming float.

20. Watching television has never interested Mia.

Lesson 23
Infinitives and Infinitive Phrases

An **infinitive** is another type of verbal. It is a verb that is usually preceded by the word *to*. An infinitive functions as a noun, adjective, or adverb. The word *to* may also begin a prepositional phrase. However, when *to* precedes a verb, it is not a preposition but instead signals an infinitive.

We were content **to wait**.

An **infinitive phrase** includes the infinitive and any complements and modifiers.

To have lost the championship would have been devastating for the team.

▶ **Exercise 1** Circle the infinitive or infinitive phrase in each sentence.

In some areas of the country it is not easy (to find a job)

1. With her father in the military, Charlotte learned to adjust to new situations.

2. Rudy learned to ride a bike when he was very young.

3. Pedro refused to play by our rules.

4. Sharon's understudy was prepared to take her place in the play.

5. To save time in the mornings, Danny laid his clothes out each night.

6. Nicky hoped to learn French to study abroad.

7. Mother tried to limit the amount of fat in our meals.

8. Winter is the best time for some families to go on vacation.

9. Gabe's dream is to become a lawyer.

10. Joel was eager to save money for a new stereo.

11. Dan always tries to remain calm in emergencies.

12. We decided to order a pizza.

13. Several police officers were dispatched to control the traffic flow.

14. I was happy to help Dad wash the car.

15. To act on Broadway is Chip's wish.

16. We walked several blocks until we found something to eat.

17. Sheila always tries to be prepared for class.

18. It was difficult to identify the type of bacteria under the microscope.

19. Kim was anxious to leave for the concert.

20. It was fun to learn stained glass technique.

21. To delay the game would have angered the fans.

22. Gina helped me to solve my geometry problems.

23. The politician was ready to admit defeat.

24. The doctor gave me something to take for my stomachache.

25. Emilio was content to settle for the second-place award.

26. To build a new home will take a long time.

27. I am not ready to go to the park yet.

28. The teacher showed us how to diagram the sentence.

29. Jill wanted to march in the Thanksgiving Day parade.

30. Holly had a heavy backpack to carry.

31. Mr. Foltz encouraged us to try harder.

32. Some of the words on the test were hard to define.

33. To improve my tennis game, I began taking lessons.

34. Jamie began to develop symptoms of the flu.

35. Dad refined our diets to reduce the chance of heart disease.

36. Ben refused to watch the violent movie.

37. Allen was anxious to tell the story of the fire alarm at school.

38. The detective needed more evidence to prove his theory.

39. My aunt would like to run for office.

40. Rachel searched for a quarter to phone home.

▶ **Writing Link** **Write four or five sentences explaining how to prepare your favorite food. Use infinitives in each sentence.**

_____

_____

_____

_____

_____

✓ Unit 3 **Review**

▶ **Exercise 1** Write *P* above each word or phrase in italics if it is a participle and *G* if it is a gerund.

         P
Having finished the exam quickly, I felt I'd done well.

1. *Exercising* is a good stress reliever.

2. Erin's hobby is *ballet dancing*.

3. We will try to cover much of the material, *depending on our time limitations*.

4. The class split into groups, *forming two lines*.

5. The small boy, *working diligently to stack the blocks*, was disappointed when they tumbled down.

6. My uncle enjoys *walking through the mall*.

7. *Sue's screaming* woke everyone in the house.

8. Our cabin did not have *running* water.

9. *Fearing I would miss the rehearsal*, I hurried to get ready.

10. Anna's job was *finding volunteers for the project*.

11. The teacher pointed to a slide *showing the single-celled bacteria*.

12. *Doing the errand* took more time than usual.

13. *Studying* is necessary for good grades.

14. The hero of the play proposed to the girl on *bended* knee.

15. Everyone was excited about *going to the party*.

16. The dishes, *broken during the tremor*, were irreparably damaged.

17. *Having written the letter*, I mailed it promptly.

18. *Working under a tight deadline*, we delivered the school paper to the printer on time.

19. Paul's company makes money by *exporting goods*.

20. My father hates to do the *shopping*.

Cumulative Review: Units 1–3

▶ **Exercise 1** Draw a vertical line between the subject and the predicate in the sentences below. Draw a line under each adjective and circle each adverb.

Tamara | already has a new stereo.

1. We walked carefully away from the broken glass.

2. The delicious dinner was extremely high in calories.

3. The green sedan balanced precariously on the edge of the cliff.

4. Crystal left a mysterious message for me.

5. The baby slept soundly through the loud thunder.

6. Members of the cheerleading squad ran quickly for the bus.

7. The heavy rain made it extremely hard to see the road.

8. My old purse had more space than my new one does.

9. My biology teacher immediately reviewed the difficult items on the test.

10. Kevin finally agreed on a less expensive restaurant.

▶ **Exercise 2** Write *P* for participle, *I* for infinitive, or *G* for gerund above each phrase in italics.

Scott was asked *to present the award.*

1. Do you want me *to talk to Rhonda for you?*

2. *Placing her arms at her sides*, she took a deep breath.

3. *Weather forecasting* is very intricate.

4. I saw Antonio *standing by his locker.*

5. *To reach our goal*, we will need two hundred dollars more.

6. *To attend Harvard* was Lionel's dream.

7. My goal was *getting ahead of the other runners.*

8. *Having beaten me at rummy again*, Mother laughingly apologized.

9. I found Donna's *whining* tiresome.

10. Mitch was asked *to submit his story to the school paper.*

Unit 4: Clauses and Sentence Structure

Lesson 24
Main and Subordinate Clauses

A **main clause** is a group of words that contains a complete subject and a complete predicate. Also known as an **independent clause**, a main clause can stand alone as a complete sentence.

A light gray wall served as background for Lisel's paintings.

A **subordinate clause** also contains a subject and a predicate but cannot stand alone. Because it depends on a main clause to make sense, it is also known as a **dependent clause**. Usually, a **subordinating conjunction** introduces a subordinate clause, although it may begin with a relative pronoun (such as *who, whose, whom, which, that,* or *what*) or a relative adverb (such as *when, where,* or *why.*) In some subordinate clauses, the connecting word also serves as the subject of the clause.

Lisel's paintings stood out vividly **when they were displayed against a neutral background.**
The clown **who left his red nose in the dressing room** should report to Lost and Found. (The relative pronoun *who,* which connects the clauses, is the subject of the subordinate clause.)

SUBORDINATING CONJUNCTIONS

Time: after, as, as soon as, before, since, until, when, whenever, while
Place: where, wherever
Manner: as, as if, as though
Cause: as, because, inasmuch as, since, so that
Concession: although, even though, though
Condition: if, than, unless

▶ **Exercise 1** Check (✔) the blank before each sentence that contains a subordinate clause.

✔____ One of the men who had sailed with Christopher Columbus inspired a young swineherd to change his lot in life.

____ 1. Fifteen-year-old Francisco Pizarro listened intently to the old sailor's tales of adventure.

____ 2. He resolved that one day he, too, would explore the New World.

____ 3. Over the next few months, Pizarro plotted his escape from his employer.

____ 4. Finally, his chance arose.

____ 5. Young Pizarro and two of his friends set off to find their fortunes in Seville, 150 miles away.

Grammar

_____ **6.** The man who would one day mesmerize his Peruvian hosts with his powerful steed and gleaming armour made his most important journey on foot, clad in a coarse shirt and short breeches.

_____ **7.** Penniless, the young men lived on dry bread and whatever wild fruit they could scavenge.

_____ **8.** They slept wherever they could find hospice from nature—in peasants' hovels, under bridges, and in ancient Roman ruins.

_____ **9.** Finally, the long trek came to an end.

_____ **10.** The companions entered the great city and then went their separate ways.

_____ **11.** Because Spain was in the middle of a war, Pizarro's application to join the army was immediately accepted.

_____ **12.** It did not take the stalwart Spaniard long to earn the rank of lieutenant.

_____ **13.** In 1502, the swineherd-turned-soldier headed for the Americas.

_____ **14.** He lived for a while in Hispaniola (the main Spanish base in the New World).

_____ **15.** When Vasco de Balboa outfitted an expedition to South America and Central America in 1509, he chose young Pizarro as his chief lieutenant.

_____ **16.** Pizarro served under Balboa in several capacities over the next few years.

_____ **17.** Then in 1524, he set out with a small group to explore the west coast of South America.

_____ **18.** His goal was to find the Inca empire, legendary for its wealth.

_____ **19.** Perhaps through greed, or perhaps through a lust for power, Pizarro did not stop until he had conquered the Peruvian peoples.

_____ **20.** The Peruvians had built their empire by conquering their neighbors; their warriors were now the vanquished.

_____ **21.** Although Spain ruled the colony for nearly 300 years, Peru won independence in 1826.

_____ **22.** The campaign for Peru's independence was led by José de San Martin of Argentina and Simón Bolívar of Venezuela.

_____ **23.** The goal of both men was to end foreign rule throughout South America.

_____ **24.** The last of the Spanish troops surrendered in 1826; the following year, Peru's first constitution went into effect.

▶ **Writing Link** **Write a sentence that contains at least two subordinate clauses.**

_____

_____

_____

_____

Lesson 25
Simple and Compound Sentences

A **simple sentence** has one complete subject and one complete predicate. The subject, the predicate, or both may be compound.

SUBJECT	PREDICATE
Long strands of ivy	curled around the window ledge.
Ivy and juniper	filled the flower boxes.
Plants	breathe air and absorb sunlight.

Two or more simple sentences, each considered a main clause, comprise a **compound sentence**. Main clauses can be joined to build a compound sentence by using a comma followed by a conjunction such as *or, and,* or *but.* However, a conjunction is not necessary to form a compound sentence. A semicolon may be used to join two main clauses without a conjunction. A semicolon is also used before a conjunctive adverb, such as *moreover.*

Spring arrived late this year, **but** Mona's garden was as beautiful as ever.
Spring arrived late this year; Mona's garden was as beautiful as ever.
Spring arrived late this year; however, Mona's garden was as beautiful as ever.

▶ **Exercise 1 Write in the blank whether the sentence is *simple* or *compound*.**

__compound__   Terri bought the ingredients, but Jason baked the cookies.

_____ **1.** Valery ran her fingers through her long, straight hair.

_____ **2.** I may seem calm to you, but inside I'm really quite nervous.

_____ **3.** That song always melts my heart!

_____ **4.** Get used to hearing a racket; Glenna's moving next door!

_____ **5.** I was nervous about asking Marcia to dance; therefore, I stumbled on my way across the room.

_____ **6.** The grandfather clock chimed the hour.

_____ **7.** Darkness descended on the countryside, and many stars became visible.

_____ **8.** Jan and Steve walked to the grocery store.

_____ **9.** Last year our family enjoyed our trip to Iowa; however, this year we are going to visit Vermont.

_____ **10.** The old car's engine sputtered and died.

_____ **11.** Suzanne practices acrobatics every night after school.

_____ **12.** Bring me the videotape, or put it in the VCR.

_____ **13.** The marching band won a top rating at the state band contest.

_____ **14.** The ski club members are raising money for a trip to Aspen, but they will probably pay most of the expenses themselves.

_____ **15.** Wildflowers grew in the back corner of the abandoned lot.

_____ **16.** Either Jacques will meet us here, or he will meet us at the mall.

_____ **17.** Tiffany is bringing decorations, and the Wilsons are supplying the food.

_____ **18.** Magenta is Claire's favorite color, but Nora prefers turquoise.

_____ **19.** Place the painting on the wall above the couch.

_____ **20.** Dr. Calavaris may speak on atom smashing, or Dr. Yee may give a presentation on forces.

▶ **Exercise 2** Underline each main clause. If there is more than one main clause in a sentence, add a comma or a semicolon as needed.

<u>Roses grow near the fence</u>, and <u>pansies grow beside the walk</u>.

1. Books lined the shelves but no one noticed them.

2. Our school colors are purple and white.

3. Wait for the bus or you will have to walk several miles.

4. Jason cleaned the garage and cut the grass.

5. Tina is redecorating her half of the room but Tammy is keeping her half the same.

6. The trees swayed with the breeze the birds twittered and fluttered as they tried to hang on.

7. Crimson silk was Joanna's choice for her prom dress.

8. The school newspaper printed my story but they omitted the picture.

9. Quentin's journal has never been read by anyone.

10. Lisa bought three CDs and one poster at the music store.

11. Dad is cooking pasta for dinner and I can't wait to eat it!

12. George and Martha were the main characters in the play.

13. Three players hit home runs during the baseball game.

14. Muriel will hand out the yearbooks or you can pick up one in the student government office.

15. I am eager to learn the solution to this mystery.

Lesson 26
Complex and Compound-Complex Sentences

Grammar

A **complex sentence** contains a main clause and one or more subordinate clauses.

MAIN CLAUSE   SUBORDINATE CLAUSE
We played charades by candlelight   when the electricity went out.

Do not be confused by *the electricity went out*, which is a complete sentence (or main clause). The complete subordinate clause is *when the electricity went out*, which cannot stand alone as a sentence.

A **compound-complex** sentence has more than one main clause and one or more subordinate clauses.

      SUBORDINATE CLAUSE   MAIN CLAUSE   MAIN CLAUSE
Whenever we have an ice storm, the twins go skating, and I enjoy the peace.

▶ **Exercise 1** Draw one line under each main clause and two lines under each subordinate clause. Write *C* in the blank if the sentence is complex and *CC* if it is compound-complex.

____C____   Emily breaks out in hives whenever she eats strawberries.

_____   **1.** When ice is on the road, drive more cautiously.

_____   **2.** After I heard Sylvia McNair, I bought one of her CDs, and I sent her a fan letter.

_____   **3.** Jim is going with us Wednesday if he can take time off from work.

_____   **4.** As long as Rick is going to the store, could he buy some nachos for me?

_____   **5.** After I have written a story, I often feel amazed that the words are mine, but I'm still hesitant to show it to anyone else.

_____   **6.** After Bruce spilled paint on the couch, he decided he should have hired a professional painter.

_____   **7.** Although February is a short month, it seems longer because its day are gray.

_____   **8.** Unless I've misunderstood the store clerk, the package should arrive next Thursday; however, it may have to be back-ordered.

_____   **9.** We'll have pizza for supper tonight if we get home before the store closes.

_____ **10.** After I saw a Kenneth Branagh movie (*Henry V*), I was hooked!

_____ **11.** When the apartment manager asked if we needed anything, we requested new window shades because the old ones had holes in them.

_____ **12.** Jason wrote out a schedule of his time so that he could practice the guitar more often.

_____ **13.** If you have never heard a National Opera Ebony performance, you should make a point to check it out.

_____ **14.** We cannot start the concert until the weather clears.

_____ **15.** Elise wants to sell her stereo system so that she can buy a newer one.

_____ **16.** Some of the teachers really enjoyed themselves at the Homecoming Dance; Mr. Osborne, for example, strutted across the floor as if he were a peacock.

_____ **17.** While the mechanic changed the tire, the driver received last minute instructions from the racing team's manager.

_____ **18.** I'll do the dishes tonight so that you can go to the movies with Jan.

_____ **19.** After the dance was over, Lila and Alan decided to stop for hamburgers.

_____ **20.** We'd better tell Mr. Nash the truth before he finds out for himself.

_____ **21.** Here is the house where President Roosevelt grew up.

_____ **22.** When Carol and I went shopping, I thought I would buy school clothes; I bought three pairs of shoes instead.

_____ **23.** Although she is only five, Carrie Sue solved a Rubrick's cube!

_____ **24.** After the rain ceased, the stuffy air cleared.

_____ **25.** Cin writes poetry while she rides the bus to and from school.

_____ **26.** Because Todd stays up so late, he keeps the rest of us from sleeping, and we are getting tired of it.

_____ **27.** Lucy will come after she babysits if we haven't already concluded the meeting.

_____ **28.** When he called, Zack explained the mix-up, and he apologized for it.

▶ **Writing Link** Describe a familiar setting. Use at least two complex sentences and one compound-complex sentence.

_____

_____

_____

_____

_____

_____

Lesson 27
Adjective Clauses

When a subordinate clause modifies a noun or a pronoun it is called an **adjective clause.** Often, an adjective clause is introduced by a relative pronoun. An adjective clause can also begin with *where* or *when*.

The present **that I bought for Ron's birthday** was lost when I moved. (modifies the noun *present*)

Do you know anyone **who will lend me a computer?** (modifies the pronoun *anyone*)

RELATIVE PRONOUNS

that	whom	whomever
which	whose	what
who	whoever	whatever

▶ **Exercise 1** Draw one line under each adjective clause and two lines under each word that introduces an adjective clause.

The song <u>that I heard on the radio</u> brought back many memories.

1. The horse that Danny owns is a well-trained Tennessee walking horse.

2. Tell everyone whom you see about Tara's surprise party.

3. There is no one whose cooking tastes better than Mom's.

4. For his science project, Geoffry collected every specimen that he could find.

5. I don't like driving in traffic where the vehicles are bumper to bumper.

6. Lana often goes to the mall, where she shops with her friends.

7. At the fashion show, Paula saw many outfits that she liked.

8. The boy whose face is red fell down the stairs in the music building.

9. The house, which was made of brick, stayed cool in the summer.

10. I finally saw the TV series that you recommended.

11. The television program, which was quite long, contained some valuable insights.

12. Luigi chose the tie that had musical notes on it.

13. The place where we will have the picnic is five miles outside of town.

14. Shelly sold tickets to the people who live down the street.

15. The person whose guess is closest to the correct answer will win the prize.

16. The bike race will begin on Columbus Day, which is Saturday.

17. The couple who spoke to us in the lobby are professional ice dancers.

18. The computer that Jack wants to buy has many impressive features.

19. This is the area where the demonstration will take place.

20. Is Ms. Ferguson the chairperson who will be in charge this year?

▶ **Exercise 2** **Underline each adjective clause and draw an arrow to the word it modifies.**

The student <u>who finishes first</u> may collect the tests.

1. My mom put the trophy, which was engraved with my name, on our mantel.

2. Isaac is a boy whom you will like.

3. This is the beach where I saw the sand crab.

4. Students who are well organized seem to get good grades.

5. The medicine that the doctor prescribed made me very sleepy.

6. The lion whose cub was in danger scared the hyena away.

7. The Mississippi River, where Mark Twain spent most of his childhood, is the setting for many of his novels.

8. Do you remember the time when our choir entertained at the senior citizens center?

9. I am planning a surprise party for my best friend, whose birthday is Saturday.

10. The ballet that we saw last night was breathtaking.

11. This is a remake of a song that was originally sung by Frank Sinatra.

12. My mom will take anyone who wants to go.

13. Is this the restaurant where Yesmin met her boyfriend?

14. At our school bake sale, the cookies that were homemade sold the best.

15. Lakes where people can swim and fish are very popular in the summer.

16. Cole gave the coach who was retiring a picture of the team.

17. Everyone whom I nominated for student council got elected.

18. The loggerhead turtle is the endangered species that my uncle is trying to save.

19. The time when I should exercise is before dinner in the evening.

20. Luisa's electric guitar, which she bought at a flea market, takes up all her spare time.

Adjective clauses may be either essential or nonessential. **Essential clauses** are necessary to make the meaning of a sentence clear. A clause beginning with *that* is essential. **Nonessential clauses** add interesting information but are not necessary for the meaning of a sentence. A clause beginning with *which* is usually nonessential.

Use commas to set off nonessential clauses from the rest of the sentence.

Georgia has a talent **that is hard to match.** (essential clause)
My uncle, **who was born in New York,** moved to California when he was twelve. (nonessential clause)

▶ **Exercise 3** Underline each adjective clause in the sentences below. Write *E* (essential) or *non.* (nonessential) in the space provided to identify the type of clause.

__non.__ Aunt Betty, <u>who lives in New England</u>, finds treasure on the beach.

_____ **1.** Those players who can stuff the basket make basketball fun to watch.

_____ **2.** The tour guide told us to take the staircase that curves around the left side of the foyer.

_____ **3.** My pen pal, who lives in Hong Kong, writes to me at least once a month.

_____ **4.** Our state flag, which is red, white, and blue, stands in the corner of the room.

_____ **5.** The moment when the first debator begins speaking will be Jordan's cue to start the timer.

_____ **6.** The lady whose car is parked in the driveway is visiting Mom.

_____ **7.** The statue that Kurt sculpted will be displayed at the art show.

_____ **8.** Pour the hot chocolate into the blue mugs, which are sitting on the kitchen counter.

_____ **9.** The coffee table book that Aunt Rhoda received for her birthday has many beautiful
pictures in it.

_____ **10.** The hour when the performance begins is swiftly approaching.

_____ **11.** Maria is attending the Irish step dancing class, which meets on Friday nights.

_____ **12.** The school festival that we are planning should be fun.

_____ **13.** Tom interviewed Mrs. Lewis, who developed the international studies program.

_____ **14.** The bagels that the bakery sells are onion and poppyseed.

_____ **15.** The fish that occupy Gwen's aquarium are a rare tropical breed.

_____ **16.** Everyone asked Tomaika for the recipe to make the salad that she brought to the carry-in dinner.

_____ **17.** Mr. Greenwood, whose farm we stayed at last summer, plans to invite us back this year.

_____ **18.** The second when the clock strikes midnight will signal the beginning of a new year.

_____ **19.** When we drive through Missouri, I will show you the city where I grew up.

_____ **20.** A little girl pointed to the spot where her kitten disappeared.

_____ **21.** Naylor Road, which curves to the left, leads to an old stone quarry.

_____ **22.** The bill that Representative Joyce introduced could help many needy persons.

_____ **23.** Monique is the student who designed these shirts.

_____ **24.** The desk that Philip bought appears to be an antique.

_____ **25.** George and Janet hosted a party that I will never forget.

▶ **Writing Link** Write a brief paragraph describing a character in a TV series or movie. Use at least four adjective clauses in your description.

_____

_____

_____

_____

_____

_____

_____

_____

_____

_____

_____

_____

_____

_____

_____

_____

Grammar

Lesson 28
Adverb Clauses

An adverb clause is a subordinate clause that modifies a verb, an adjective, or an adverb. It is used to tell *when, where, why, to what extent,* or *under what conditions.* An adverb clause is usually introduced by a subordinating conjunction.

The deliciously cold breeze blows **after the thunderstorm has passed.**

An adverb clause that seems to have missing words is called an **elliptical adverb clause** The words that are left out are understood in the clause.

Marcie can sing higher than Jill (can sing).

▶ **Exercise 1** Place a check (✔) beside each sentence that contains an adverb clause.

_____ Polynesian peoples explored throughout the Pacific Ocean.

_____ 1. The Pacific Ocean is more than empty sea.

_____ 2. It contains as many as ten thousand islands.

_____ 3. Early explorers settled these islands hundreds of years ago.

_____ 4. Because many of the islands offered poor farming opportunities, islanders moved often.

_____ 5. After many centuries, people had settled all the inhabitable islands.

_____ 6. These islands exist because of different geological events.

_____ 7. Some of the large islands in the western Pacific came into being when ocean levels rose after the last Ice Age.

_____ 8. As the ice melted into the seas, the rising water drowned vast mountain chains.

_____ 9. Many other islands started from volcanic activity.

_____ 10. If deep-sea volcanoes keep growing, they eventually break through to the surface.

_____ 11. Whole volcanic-island chains eventually develop because the Pacific Ocean plate keeps shifting over hot spots deep in the earth's mantle.

_____ 12. The Hawaiian Islands extend 1,523 miles long as a result of this phenomenon.

_____ 13. Although the Pacific has many volcanic islands, coral formed most of them.

_____ 14. The soil of coral islands is poor.

_____ 15. This is true because the volcanic soil is rich in iron and magnesium oxides.

_____ **16.** Although the volcanic soil has a greater variety of minerals, the coral islands are merely consolidated limestone platforms.

_____ **17.** Coral islands develop slowly wherever coral-producing polyps and algae build up to the water surface.

_____ **18.** Without the variety of minerals found in volcanic soil, plants that take root on coral islands cannot create very fertile soils.

_____ **19.** This is why island settlers kept moving as often as they did.

_____ **20.** Because they were so successful as navigators and sailors, the Polynesians colonized islands over a vast area.

_____ **21.** As time went by, they planted settlements from Samoa to Easter Island, from New Zealand to Hawaii.

_____ **22.** Although they were great sailors, they were also accomplished farmers.

_____ **23.** After they reached a new island, they quickly established a new community.

_____ **24.** Before the Europeans came, Polynesians lived in hamlets and villages.

_____ **25.** Houses were built on raised platforms of varying height so that social distinctions could be observed.

_____ **26.** While a chief might live in a house on a platform seven to eight feet high, a commoner possessed a house with a platform only a few inches high.

_____ **27.** Wherever a village existed, the Polynesians laid it out around a central plaza, known as a *tohua*.

_____ **28.** The tohua served as village center and ceremonial focal point.

_____ **29.** Made up of three or four generations, the Polynesian family centered around a descent group.

_____ **30.** The Polynesians kept extensive genealogies so they could maintain information on their descent groups.

_____ **31.** Their genealogists counted descent through both the female line and the male line.

_____ **32.** Village genealogies often indicated that everyone was related to a mythical ancestor so that everyone felt kinship with each other.

_____ **33.** Polynesian society was very much class oriented.

_____ **34.** The Polynesian chief, of course, ranked highest.

_____ **35.** In the midst of this stratified society, craftsmen were held in great honor.

_____ **36.** They were able to use wood very skillfully so that great canoes could be built for sea voyages.

_____ **37.** Before any European ships appeared, the Polynesians were constructing huge double canoes up to 150 feet long.

_____ **38.** The great ocean-going vessels were built of small wood pieces held together by careful fitting and tight lashing because the Polynesians had no metal.

_____ **39.** Although everyone in Polynesian society was important, navigators were especially honored.

_____ **40.** That is not surprising, since the successful ocean crossings depended upon their skills.

▶ **Exercise 2** Underline the adverb clause in each sentence. Circle the verb, adverb, or adjective it modifies.

<u>While the sailboat bobbed at anchor</u>, we (slept)

1. The first Hawaiian settlers may have come from the Marquesas Islands, although the Marquesas are thousands of miles to the south.

2. Wherever they landed, powerful Polynesian princes and priests established kingdoms.

3. These great lords fought over territory after they started their kingdoms.

4. Although we have searched for the origin of the name *Hawaii*, we have not found it.

5. One idea is widely believed because it is very old.

6. As this story goes, the island was named for an early chieftan.

7. Wherever they came from, the Hawaiian people prospered in their islands.

8. Before the English arrived, Spanish, Dutch, or Japanese explorers may have visited Hawaii.

9. Although others may have landed first, the English naval officer Captain James Cook is credited with "discovering" Hawaii.

10. After he landed there on January 18, 1778, he brought the news of the islands' existence to the outside world.

11. The Hawaiians were quite impressed with Cook because they attributed divine powers to him.

12. As the eighteenth century drew to a close, King Kamehameha grew politically powerful.

13. After he obtained guns from European traders, the king waged a war of conquest.

14. King Kamehameha consolidated Hawaii into a single kingdom as soon as he was victorious.

15. His son's coming to the throne in 1819 was more important than anyone realized.

16. Reading and writing first appeared in 1820 when the young king welcomed Christian missionaries to his kingdom.

17. King Kamehameha III and his chiefs earned the people's respect because they provided a constitution, a legislature, and a public school system.

18. Americans settled in Hawaii in the early 1800's because it was in such a strategic location.

▶ **Exercise 3** Underline each adverb clause and adjective clause. Write *adv.* if the underlined clause is an adverb clause, and *adj.* if it is an adjective clause.

___adj.___ It is my sailboat that is the larger of the two.

_____ 1. It is the island of Oahu that is the most populated Hawaiian island today.

_____ 2. Although Oahu is well known, the island named *Hawaii* is bigger.

_____ 3. There are seven other main islands that make up the Hawaiian archipelago.

_____ 4. Kahoolawe is smaller than the other main islands are.

_____ 5. Kahoolawe is the only main island that is unpopulated.

_____ 6. The island of Maui has the largest volcano crater that is known on Earth.

_____ 7. Scientists know the crater's circumference (twenty miles around the rim) and depth (three thousand feet) because they have made careful measurements.

_____ 8. When you visit Hawaii, you may want to include an excursion to Molokai.

_____ 9. Everyone knows it is the people of Molokai that make the island such a nice place to visit.

_____ 10. A mountain on the island of Kauai is wetter than any other spot on Earth.

_____ 11. This mountain where you find the most rainfall is Mount Waialeale.

_____ 12. Vacationers have many happy memories after they leave the islands.

Lesson 29
Noun Clauses

A **noun clause** is a subordinate clause that acts as a noun.

That barren part of town is **Carson Village.** (noun)
That barren part of town is **where the tornado hit.** (noun clause)

The clause in the second sentence above replaces the noun (predicate nominative) in the first sentence.

Noun clauses can be used in the same way as nouns—as subject, direct object, object of a preposition, and predicate nominative.

Whoever sat in that chair broke it! (subject)
I have learned the hard way **that some people are just plain lazy.** (direct object)
I pay attention to **what the teacher says.** (object of preposition)
Prom Eve is **when the king and queen will be announced.** (predicate noun)

WORDS THAT INTRODUCE NOUN CLAUSES

how	what	where	who	whomever
however	whatever	which	whoever	whose
that	when	whichever	whom	why

▶ **Exercise 1** Underline each noun clause.

Sylvia, a student nurse, knew <u>when she would be on duty</u>.

1. Our choice will have to be whatever is the least expensive.

2. That we heard the weather report was lucky for us!

3. Joan discovered where I hid her keys.

4. Whatever the lady at the next table is eating is what I'll have, too.

5. I don't know what she expects of me.

6. Why he does that is a mystery to me.

7. I wonder when news of Marcus will arrive.

8. I'll do whatever you say.

9. However much you plan in advance makes the overall job that much easier.

10. Whoever wrote that essay should be very proud.

11. What this story lacks is a strong ending.

12. The report explains how Gem Lake became polluted.

13. What makes a great hamburger is the right seasoning and lots of onions.

14. The principal announced that Friday would be a teacher in-service day.

15. Can you tell me where the new restaurant is?

16. When the whistle blows is the signal to begin.

17. How you can eat that is beyond me!

18. Mary realized that she would never have solved the mystery without Jack's help.

19. This is where we came in.

20. Kim shouted that we were headed in the wrong direction.

Grammar

▶ **Exercise 2** Underline each noun clause. In the blank, indicate its use in the sentence: *S* (subject), *DO* (direct object), *OP* (object of a preposition), or *PN* (predicate nominative).

_____S_____ <u>What we had hoped for</u> was delayed.

_____ 1. This frayed cord is where the fire began.

_____ 2. Your question about how we came to be here requires a long explanation.

_____ 3. The one who gets the last piece of cake will be whoever eats the fastest.

_____ 4. This room is where President Lincoln slept.

_____ 5. Do you understand how to write a theme?

_____ 6. I'm not sure about which of these is mine.

_____ 7. Where the gymnasium now stands was once the baseball diamond.

_____ 8. Krista wondered why the classroom door was locked.

_____ 9. Do you understand how I feel?

_____ 10. Give these paper fans to whomever you want.

_____ 11. This chemical goes in whichever bottle is airtight.

_____ 12. Why we have to do this today is what I want to know.

_____ 13. How to find the sine and cosine perplexed Joseph.

_____ 14. Whichever key you pick will determine which prize you will win.

_____ 15. Wherever the dog buried that bone is a secret.

_____ 16. How the clown was able to pull a rabbit from under the chair puzzled her young audience.

_____ 17. The flight attendant told me which seat was mine.

_____ 18. Whichever you choose is fine with me.

_____ 19. First, let's learn why the cabbage juice turned this blue mixture to pink.

_____ 20. A raft is what I am showing at the county fair in August.

▶ **Exercise 3** Place a check (✔) in the blank next to each sentence that contains a noun clause.

_____✔_____ What I don't understand is why the culprit confessed so early in the movie.

_____ **1.** The note she left tells me why Kate drove to Kentucky.

_____ **2.** Please choose whichever seat you find most comfortable.

_____ **3.** Mrs. Matthews, who taught history for thirty years, will be honored at the banquet.

_____ **4.** Who the winner is remains a mystery until the envelope is opened.

_____ **5.** Miki made a cake that had a race car made of icing on top.

_____ **6.** Where do you keep the extra plates?

_____ **7.** I screamed when everyone jumped up and yelled, "Surprise!"

_____ **8.** The horse is kept where Billy can see him.

_____ **9.** How a bill becomes a law was the topic of Mr. Rodriguez's lecture.

_____ **10.** Several valuable jewels were missing from the safe where they had been stored.

_____ **11.** A newscaster explained that the president would be arriving momentarily.

_____ **12.** The perfume that Celeste bought smelled enchanting to me.

_____ **13.** Whatever the jury decides will satisfy the judge.

_____ **14.** Kylee wrote an interesting article for *YP Magazine*.

_____ **15.** Dr. Courter knew when the test results would be ready.

_____ **16.** Giorgio paints what others can only look at.

_____ **17.** The puppy who frolicked in the window wagged his tail at me.

_____ **18.** Whichever hole I play the best is my favorite hole at the miniature golf course.

_____ **19.** Charlie will vote however everyone else votes.

_____ **20.** You will find the treasure where the road meets the sea.

_____ **21.** What Joey said really made sense to me.

_____ **22.** The trophy goes to whoever crosses the finish line first.

_____ **23.** Where our dog Mitzi went remains a question.

_____ **24.** That the book might be wrong never occurred to anyone.

_____ **25.** Tracy, who had not practiced long, sang beautifully in the musical production.

▶ **Exercise 4** Fill in the blank with a word to introduce each noun clause.

_____That_____ the Corderos were coming was a complete surprise to Grandma.

1. _____ Lois didn't discover the truth puzzles me.

2. Give the tickets to _____ is at the door to collect them.

3. The rest of the group will support _____ decision you make.

4. Choose _____ you want to go for your birthday dinner.

5. _____ the cat ended up in a tree does not matter.

6. The role of Elizabeth I will be given to _____ presents the best audition.

7. Everyone asked _____ fur coat that was.

8. Cindy was amazed at _____ the magic trick was performed.

9. Address your complaints to _____ is responsible for the problem.

10. _____ one can see the sun setting on the lake is my favorite place to be.

11. _____ Bob said certainly had a tremendous effect on Maria.

12. Jennifer's favorite part is _____ the prince searches for the special rose.

13. Jaun and Marta believe _____ anything is possible.

14. The sun filtered through _____ must have been a window.

15. Send me a postcard from _____ you vacation.

16. _____ the master of ceremonies enters will be the cue to begin the music.

17. _____ this issue is important has yet to be discussed.

18. Rich and Chris debated _____ television program was better.

19. Davina deduced _____ the letter opener landed in the shrub.

20. _____ collected these shells must have done a lot of traveling.

21. _____ the temperature is warm seems the most popular destination.

22. Pick _____ type of fabric will look best.

23. When will we discover _____ happens next?

24. Janice inquired _____ the committee members wished to meet.

25. Tell me _____ wrote this incredible novel.

Lesson 30
Kinds of Sentences

A **declarative sentence** makes a statement. It usually ends with a period.

I love swimming.   Carey said, "I want some cookies."

An **imperative sentence** gives a command or makes a request. The subject *you* is understood. Imperative sentences end with a period or an exclamation point.

Get moving.   Please hurry up!

An **interrogative sentence** asks a question. It ends with a question mark.

You did what?   The man asked, "Would you like one?"

An **exclamatory sentence** expresses strong emotions. It ends with an exclamation point.

What a sight you are!   The sign read, "Hurry, or you'll miss the sale!"

▶ **Exercise 1** Label each sentence *dec.* if it is declarative and *imp.* if it is imperative.

__dec.__   The air feels as if rain is on the way.

_____ **1.** The herd of cattle grazed daily in the pasture.

_____ **2.** Put your dishes in the dishwasher when you have finished lunch.

_____ **3.** Howard doesn't feel well today.

_____ **4.** School starts on the Monday following band camp.

_____ **5.** Turn the music down.

_____ **6.** Every afternoon my dog Boulder sits at the bus stop and waits for me.

_____ **7.** Louie XIV was known as the "Sun King."

_____ **8.** I need change for a dollar.

_____ **9.** If I'm not home by seven, start the movie without me.

_____ **10.** Some readers think that Li Po was China's greatest poet.

_____ **11.** Set the alarm clock carefully this time.

_____ **12.** The fresh breeze filled the billowing sails.

_____ **13.** Shawna is our fastest runner.

_____ **14.** Oil the bike chain, Will.

_____ **15.** The legendary hero Hercules had many great adventures.

_____ **16.** Sook won the door prize at Karen's party.

Grammar

_____ **17.** Take out the garbage before you forget about it.

_____ **18.** We're sailing from Cleveland to Erie Beach, Ontario.

_____ **19.** James Watt, for whom the electric unit of power is named, was a Scottish inventor.

_____ **20.** Smith, do twenty push ups and twenty sit-ups.

▶ **Exercise 2 Insert a question mark if the sentence is interrogative or an exclamation point if the sentence is exclamatory.**

Who's there?

1. Watch out

2. Heads up

3. Are you ready

4. When does school start

5. Don't do it, Ashford

6. Did you sign up for drivers' education yet

7. Isn't Sri Lanka south of India

8. I don't want sugar on my cereal

9. You're going to be late for school

10. Are you in a big hurry

11. Didn't you say I could use it

12. Billy Collins got to go with them, and I didn't

13. Samantha, didn't you say you studied violin

14. Hold the mayonnaise, and definitely, no tomatoes

15. Who told you I said that to him

16. I thought you ordered a cheeseburger

17. That last candy bar is mine

18. No one could tell those twins apart

19. Well, didn't you have the whole weekend to study

20. What time do you want to get up to go fishing

21. Of course, the Queen of England is the Queen of Canada, too

22. I thought everybody in town knew her parents' car

Lesson 31
Sentence Fragments

A **sentence fragment** is an incomplete sentence. It may lack a subject, a verb, or both. It might also be a subordinate clause that cannot stand alone. Correct sentence fragments by adding the missing words or phrases.

▶ **Exercise 1** Write *F* next to each sentence fragment. Write *S* next to each complete sentence.

_____ F _____   When you are ready.

_____ **1.** If you said I was going to go.

_____ **2.** The lake is beautiful.

_____ **3.** I don't like.

_____ **4.** Whom he told to take the letter to.

_____ **5.** Travel to the store on Tuesday?

_____ **6.** Run of the mill place with the usual scenery.

_____ **7.** The bird in the air.

_____ **8.** Cammila told me the tale.

_____ **9.** The books on the table that my friend found at the antique mall.

_____ **10.** The french fries are too hot.

_____ **11.** Hamal wants to be a scientist.

_____ **12.** Said to tell you about it.

_____ **13.** I prefer orange juice to apple juice.

_____ **14.** Which book is best to start with?

_____ **15.** Stories of children, some of my favorite.

_____ **16.** Tina laughed loudly.

_____ **17.** A kind of milky white?

_____ **18.** The moose by the river that runs through our town.

_____ **19.** The speckled trout are difficult to catch.

_____ **20.** The VCR still on?

_____ **21.** The old bicycle tire is flat.

_____ **22.** The swans float slowly and majestically.

_____ **23.** The rain comes down like a blue curtain.

_____ **24.** Runs from the park northward to the bench and then south.

_____ **25.** Michigan on map like a giant mitten.

▶ **Exercise 2** Write whether you should add a subject (*S*), verb (*V*), or a main clause (*M*), to form a complete sentence.

___M___   Under the rose bush.

_____ **1.** In from the cold weather.

_____ **2.** The children the blue bird in the tree.

_____ **3.** The trolley car.

_____ **4.** Rolled along the sidewalk.

_____ **5.** Napoleon at Waterloo.

_____ **6.** Fell out of the sack.

_____ **7.** Beyond the trees.

_____ **8.** Next to the mossy boulders.

_____ **9.** Sat by the statue.

_____ **10.** Until tomorrow.

_____ **11.** Lovely California chaparral country.

_____ **12.** Located near Lake Huron.

_____ **13.** Chief Pontiac the great leader.

_____ **14.** Over the third base line.

_____ **15.** Sank in 1912.

_____ **16.** The rhino magnificently.

_____ **17.** Swam the English Channel.

_____ **18.** Because I said so.

_____ **19.** I think the T'ang dynasty greatest in Chinese history.

_____ **20.** Opened Tutankhamen's tomb in 1922.

Lesson 32
Run-On Sentences

A **run-on sentence** is two or more complete sentences written as though they were one sentence. A comma splice is perhaps the most common kind of run-on sentence. It occurs when two main clauses are separated by a comma rather than a semicolon or a period. Another kind of run-on sentence is formed when there is no punctuation between the two main clauses. A third kind of run-on sentence is formed when there is no comma before a coordinating conjunction that joins two main clauses.

Jake is planning a trip to Orlando, he will leave Tuesday.
(Correct by adding a coordinating conjunction, such as *and,* by replacing the comma with a semicolon, or by making each main clause a separate sentence.)

The sun shone brightly the birds sang with glee. (Correct by adding a comma and a coordinating conjunction, by adding a semicolon, or by making each main clause a separate sentence.)

Carla hoped to finish her project this afternoon but she ran out of time. (Correct by adding a comma before *but.*)

▶ **Exercise 1** Write *R* in the blank before each run-on sentence.

_____R_____ Scott asked us to help set up the festival, we were glad to help.

_____ **1.** Every year, the local dance community holds a festival it celebrates the many different kinds of dance.

_____ **2.** Ballet is a classical form of dance; it has been performed for hundreds of years.

_____ **3.** Modern dance uses similar steps, but the dancers perform them differently.

_____ **4.** Many folk dances exist and nearly every culture has its own dances.

_____ **5.** Some of these folk dances represent ancient rituals and they retain the symbolic steps even though they are no longer performed as rituals.

_____ **6.** For example, in Ukrainian dances that were once rituals, the dancers' movements represent the movement of the moon.

_____ **7.** Armenians have dances in which the intricate steps mirror the process of carpet weaving.

_____ **8.** Some groups, such as the Hopi, still use dance as a form of worship.

_____ **9.** Other dances, such as the flamenco, began as improvised movements, the flamenco was created by the Andalusian Romany peoples.

_____ **10.** Many European folk dances evolved into modern social dances and these include the waltz and the polka.

_____ **11.** Today, we think of the waltz and polka as ballroom dances.

_____ **12.** The tango and fox-trot are also ballroom dances.

_____ **13.** In addition to social and folk dances, there are theater dances, these are dances performed chiefly for entertainment.

_____ **14.** Anyone who has seen a Broadway musical such as *Guys and Dolls* or *West Side Story* is familiar with theater dance.

_____ **15.** All of these forms of dance will be represented at the festival it should be both educational and fun.

▶ **Exercise 2 Correct each run-on sentence.**

Dance is composed of rhythmic movements of the body; persons may always have danced in one form or another.

1. Ballet is perhaps the best known classical dance it is based on steps developed in the sixteenth and seventeenth centuries.

2. The nineteenth century saw the development of the Romantic style of ballet this style is characterized by soft, fluid movements.

3. The Romantic style was gradually replaced by a more vigorous technique, it included more jumps and complicated turns.

4. Vaslav Nijinsky became one of the first choreographers to incorporate modern movements into classical ballet his dancers wore modern clothes and performed movements resembling those of sports players.

5. As the twentieth century progressed, modern dance techniques were included as well, classical ballet retained its traditional positions.

6. Modern dance actually formed as a reaction against ballet dancers had grown tired of ballet's rigid stances and limited ranges of movement.

7. Isadora Duncan, an innovator in modern dance, believed balletic movements were unnatural she wanted to dance in a more natural fashion.

8. Duncan drew inspiration from nature her dances used wild leaps and flowing rhythms.

9. In the 1960s and 1970s, yet another school of thought arose and it was called postmodernism.

10. Instead of traditional dance steps, postmodernists advocated simplistic movements these movements, such as walking, rolling, and running, were meant to convey natural impulses.

✓ Unit 4 Review

▶ **Exercise 1** Underline the clauses and note whether they are adjective (*adj.*) clauses, adverb (*adv.*) clauses, or noun (*N*) clauses.

_____adj._____   The car that my brother bought is really neat.

_____ **1.** The sailboat that glided into the harbor was beautiful.

_____ **2.** The model airplane soared as if it were a real fighter aircraft.

_____ **3.** I become very sleepy whenever it rains hard.

_____ **4.** We forgot that you said it would rain today.

_____ **5.** The detective asked whose coffee mug this is.

_____ **6.** The last Russian tsar, who was murdered in 1918, was Nicholas II.

_____ **7.** Tio Sancho was very happy when he saw us.

_____ **8.** Mr. Dyer and Ms. Peabodie, who judged the science fair, spoke highly of

your project.

_____ **9.** Chen said he would buy whichever one you suggested.

_____ **10.** Terri thinks Jules Verne was a much better writer than H.G. Wells was.

_____ **11.** This little Virginia town is where Robert E. Lee surrendered.

_____ **12.** The children cried because the storm knocked out the lights.

_____ **13.** When the submarine surfaced, the water hardly rippled.

_____ **14.** Why they believe that is a question I don't think about.

_____ **15.** The scientist who won the award is my father's cousin.

_____ **16.** *The Tale of Genji* is a famous Japanese novel that my brother read for a class.

_____ **17.** I know whose bike this is.

_____ **18.** Your story about how the detective solved the mystery is very interesting, Patti.

_____ **19.** I was really sorry after I nonchalantly told her secret to our friends.

Cumulative Review: Units 1–4

▶ **Exercise 1** Label each italicized word with its part of speech: *N* (noun), *V* (verb), *adj.* (adjective), *adv.* (adverb), *pro.* (pronoun), *prep.* (preposition), or *con.* (conjunction).

prep.   **N**
With a loud crash, the vase fell to the *floor*.

1. His *leaving caused* a lot of comment.

2. *After* the shower, the *entire* world seemed refreshed.

3. Is *Ethan Frome* fiction *or* biography?

4. Brunhilda, a character in *Wagnerian* operas, *was* the beautiful leader *of* the Valkyries.

5. I found Ms. Lopez *extremely* well *prepared* for the debate.

6. Running and weight *lifting* are Alpesh's *favorite* activities.

7. *Both* the advisors spoke with a *Brooklyn* accent.

8. Do you understand that there will be more *responsibility* placed *on those* who can handle it?

9. The pigeons *outside* his window awakened Geraldo with *their soft* cooing.

10. The Walkers' new van *runs* on diesel *fuel*.

11. The *entire* surprise party came off *without* a hitch.

12. *Because of* a disease called *blight*, chestnut trees have become *very* rare.

13. *Your* gear *should include* the following: *extra* socks, a first-aid kit, *and* a rain poncho.

14. After *thirty* years of marriage, Renaldo *still* enjoyed being with *his* wife.

15. The MVP award went to *her*, the girl *with* the red *hair*.

16. Durrell *is being scouted* by three major *colleges* because of his outstanding passing ability.

17. Can a person from *our* tiny community understand the *pressures* of life in the city?

18. *Interestingly* enough, Jo *wrote* the story that appeared in the newspaper, *but* she hasn't seen a printed copy yet.

19. Kahlil ate *two* eggs *besides* the pancakes.

20. Please hand me the jars, *those* with the green *labels*.

Name _____ Class _____ Date _____

Unit 5: Diagraming Sentences

Lesson 33

Diagraming Simple Sentences

To diagram a simple sentence, write the simple subject and verb on a horizontal line and then draw a vertical line between them. Add adjectives and adverbs on a slanted line under the words they modify.

The new computer arrived yesterday.

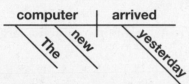

Place a direct object on the same line as the simple subject and the verb. Separate it from the verb with a vertical line. An indirect object is placed under the verb.

Did you lend them money?

you | Did lend | money
      them

To diagram a simple sentence with a compound part, follow the model diagrams below.

I love my dog and my cat.   A dog or a rabbit dug up our garden.

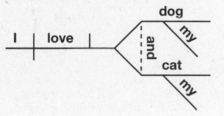   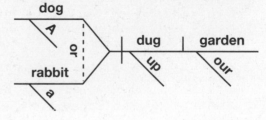

We roasted and ate marshmallows.

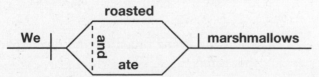

To diagram a simple sentence with a subject complement (a predicate nominative or a predicate adjective), follow the model diagrams below.

This CD sounds great!   She is the team captain.

CD | sounds \ great   She | is \ captain
  This   the team

▶ **Exercise 1 Diagram each sentence.**

1. Dad ordered pizza.

5. Mom gave me the grocery list.

2. Ships and boats roam the blue sea.

6. The Inca created and maintained a large empire.

3. The team appears eager.

7. Mammoths and mastodons roamed North America.

4. Beth has registered three cats and two dogs.

8. Trent and Franz invented and developed that game.

Grammar

Lesson 34
Diagraming Simple Sentences with Phrases

To diagram a prepositional phrase, place the preposition on a diagonal line under the word it modifies. Place the object of the preposition on a horizontal line that joins the diagonal. An infinitive phrase is diagramed like a prepositional phrase, except that its diagonal line extends a little below the horizontal line.

Who is afraid of the big, bad wolf? (prepositional phrase)

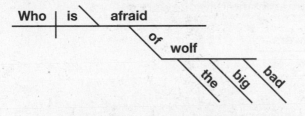

At the restaurant, Shirushi ordered the food to go. (infinitive phrase)

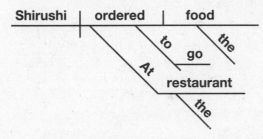

An infinitive phrase used as a noun is diagramed like a prepositional phrase and then placed on a "stilt" in the subject or complement position.

To stand up to a bully is a very brave action.

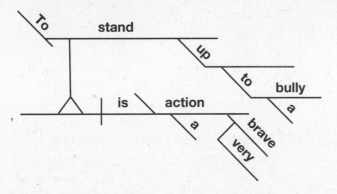

Place an appositive in parentheses after the noun or pronoun it identifies. Beneath it add any new words that modify the appositive. Any words that modify the noun or pronoun itself, and not the appositive, should be placed directly beneath the noun or pronoun.

Grammar

New York City, the "big apple," has a very large population.

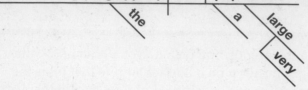

Place a participle or participial phrase under the word it modifies. The participle should curve along the line.

Working efficiently, the three energetic women planted the flowers.

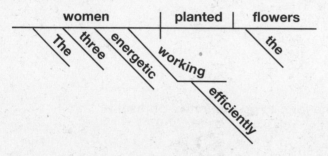

Place a gerund on a "step," and add complements and modifiers in the usual way. Position the gerund according to its role in the sentence. Remember that a gerund can be a subject, a complement, an object of a preposition, or an appositive.

Elmer enjoys swimming in the pond.

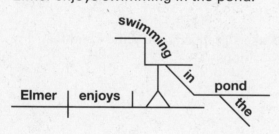

Diagram each sentence.

1. Gary, the store manager, hired me yesterday afternoon.

2. Angry citizens gathered outside the courthouse.

3. The sound of that new group is particularly vibrant.

7. Beautiful clipper ships once sailed across the seas.

4. Coach asked us to run five laps.

8. The removing of the Berlin Wall in Germany signaled the fall of communism.

5. The man in the moon is just a series of craters on the surface of the moon.

9. The old dilapidated car was difficult to steer.

6. Sue tried to win Sally's friendship.

10. I would like to pass by Grandma's house.

Grammar

11. Alicia, a veterinarian, loves training puppies.

12. The continent of Antarctica is a frigid environment.

13. Fala wants to write a story for the school paper.

14. The flowers in the garden by the side of the house are beautiful.

15. The wall needed scraping and washing.

16. This recipe is easy to make.

17. Tailoring garments requires special skill.

18. Kristen, my oldest sister, is now a freshman in college.

Lesson 35
Diagraming Sentences with Clauses

Copyright © by Glencoe/McGraw-Hill

Diagram separately each main clause in a compound sentence. Clauses joined by a semicolon have a vertical dotted line between their verbs. Clauses joined by a conjunction have the conjunction on a solid horizontal line connected to the verbs of each main clause by vertical dotted lines.

Bruno arrived late, and the teacher sent him to the office.

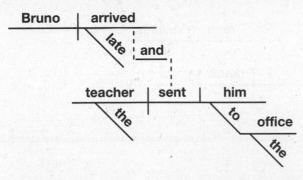

To diagram a complex sentence with an adjective clause, place the adjective clause beneath the main clause. Draw a dotted line between the relative pronoun that introduces the clause and the noun or pronoun it modifies. Diagram the relative pronoun according to its function in its own clause.

Tyler, who is captain of the swim team, plans to swim tomorrow.

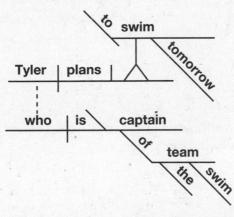

The diagram of an adverb clause is also placed beneath the diagram of the main clause. Place the subordinating conjunction on a diagonal dotted line connecting the verb in the adverb clause to the modified verb, adjective, or adverb in the main clause.

Angie plans to show her paintings before she graduates.

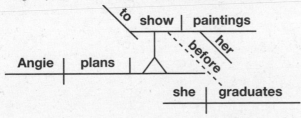

When diagraming a noun clause, first determine its function in the sentence: subject, direct object, predicate nominative, or object of a preposition. Then diagram the main clause, placing the noun clause on a "stilt" in the appropriate position. Place the introductory word of the clause in the position of the subject, object, or predicate nominative within the noun clause itself. If the introductory word merely begins the noun clause, place it on a line of its own above the verb in the subordinate clause, connecting it to the verb with a dotted vertical line.

You are what you eat.   I know that Ariel swims well.

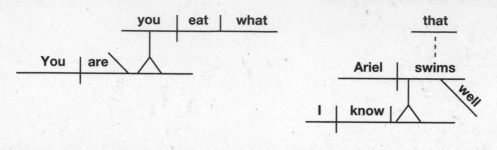

▶ **Exercise 1 Diagram each sentence.**

1. I was told that the neighbors had moved.

3. I wish that I had worked harder.

2. Our coach hates to lose Katie, but she has to quit.

4. Controlling the water supply was their responsibility.

5. Whoever brought the first gift wrapped it in red foil.

9. The new student inquired where he could find the classroom.

6. The African elephant is the largest land mammal; the blue whale, which lives in the ocean, is the largest of all mammals.

10. Some people believe that Elvis Presley, the King, is still alive.

7. The sundae that I bought is yours to eat.

11. Collecting two hundred signatures, they expressed their views.

8. Lightning and thunder scare me when I am home alone.

12. What this bike needs is a day in the shop.

13. Mongolian paleontologists find reptilian fossils when they dig in the Gobi.

16. The smell of roast beef woke Ben, for he had not eaten anything.

14. The pies that have Evelyn's special crust will be delicious.

17. Shooting with bow and arrow is a great skill.

15. The storyteller knew what tales his audience would like.

18. Francis, who always leaves behind something, will not want to forget his suitcase.

✓ Unit 5 **Review**

▶ **Exercise 1 Diagram each sentence.**

1. Kenji makes kites.

5. The apple proved tasty.

2. Venus and Mars are Earth's neighbors in the solar system.

6. People inhabiting the seashore collected great amounts of shellfish.

3. To write a good composition takes discipline.

7. Sheila's friend lost her radio near the church.

4. *Caveat emptor,* a Latin phrase, means that all purchases have risk.

8. The twister dropped Dorothy's house on the witch, and the ruby slippers appeared on Dorothy's feet.

Cumulative Review: Units 1–5

Grammar

▶ **Exercise 1** Read the two italicized sentences. Using these sentences, write at least one example of the word, phrase, or clause described.

Our general policy is to give the customer whatever she wants.

Thinking of something special that I can do for each of my friends has been fun, but it has

taken a lot of my time.

1. possessive pronoun _____

2. adjective _____

3. noun _____

4. linking verb _____

5. infinitive phrase _____

6. gerund phrase _____

7. indirect object _____

8. preposition _____

9. complete subject _____

10. complete predicate _____

    _____

11. prepositional phrase _____

12. simple subject _____

13. simple predicate _____

14. infinitive _____

15. adjective clause _____

16. indefinite pronoun _____

17. noun clause _____

18. conjunction _____

19. direct object _____

20. definite article _____

21. gerund _____

Copyright © by Glencoe/McGraw-Hill

22. indefinite article _____

23. personal pronoun _____

24. action verb _____

25. object of preposition _____

▶ **Exercise 2** Identify the part of speech (*POS*) and the use in the sentence (*USE*) of the italicized word or words. Be very specific.

The *uncertain* silence was almost tangible.

POS: **adjective** _____ USE: **modifies the noun *silence***_____

That the decision was tentative was obvious to everyone in the room.

POS: **noun** _____ USE: **subject of the sentence**_____

1. Classes were cancelled due to a *ruptured* water main.

POS: _____ USE: _____

2. Lisa eagerly dived into the frigid water and immediately climbed *back* into the boat.

POS: _____ USE: _____

3. Though it had been raining for an hour, we could still see dry circles under the shelter *of the*

large maple trees.

POS: _____ USE: _____

4. Shyly *looking* at Ramon for encouragement, Sarena gathered her thoughts and began her

presentation.

POS: _____ USE: _____

5. *Caring* for other people is a noble virtue.

POS: _____ USE: _____

6. *Intensely* engrossed in the novel, Kim hardly noticed the commotion.

POS: _____ USE: _____

7. Her answer certainly seemed *definite* to me.

POS: _____ USE: _____

8. Suddenly *realizing* the importance of his message, Simon stopped talking and began to think.

POS: _____ USE: _____

9. Mark Twain is one author *whom I have read extensively.*

POS: _____ USE: _____

10. Try *to do your best.*

POS: _____ USE: _____

11. Cold *and* shivering, LaToya wondered why she hadn't listened to the weather forecast.

POS: _____ USE: _____

12. Send *Mr. Yurkovich* the bill.

POS: _____ USE: _____

13. Golding's novel, *Lord of the Flies,* was copyrighted in 1954.

POS: _____ USE: _____

14. Sasha *paused and cleared* her throat.

POS: _____ USE: _____

15. *Neither sleet nor snow* closed schools last year, but icy roads did.

POS: _____ USE: _____

16. *To improve my typing skills* is one of my goals for this vacation.

POS: _____ USE: _____

17. Mrs. Essman is the *principal* of East High.

POS: _____ USE: _____

18. Hand me your *papers,* and return to your seats.

POS: _____ USE: _____

19. My parents think it *important* that I start looking at colleges this year.

POS: _____ USE: _____

20. Sharon was disappointed *when she saw her work schedule.*

POS: _____ USE: _____

_____

21. *Concentrating,* Mr. Yedon followed the printed directions.

POS: _____ USE: _____

22. *Hoping for success* just isn't enough; we have to develop a plan.

POS: _____ USE: _____

Unit 6: Verb Tenses and Voice

Lesson 36
Regular Verbs

Grammar

All verbs have four **principal parts**—a base, or present, form, a present participle, a past form, and a past participle. All the verb tenses are formed from these principal parts.

Different types of verbs form their past participles differently. A **regular verb** forms its past and past participle by adding the suffix -*ed* to the base form.

PRINCIPAL PARTS OF REGULAR VERBS

BASE	PRESENT PARTICIPLE	PAST	PAST PARTICIPLE
call	calling	called	called
roar	roaring	roared	roared

Used alone, the base form (except the base form of *be*) and the past form are main verbs. However, one or more auxiliary verbs are required for the present participle and the past participle to function as the simple predicate.

Doctors **confer.** (base form)
Doctors **conferred.** (past form)
Doctors **are conferring.** (present participle with the auxiliary verb *are*)
Doctors **have conferred.** (past participle with the auxiliary verb *have*)

▶ **Exercise 1** Complete each sentence by writing the form of the verb indicated in parentheses.

Archaeologists have _____discovered_____ that music existed in ancient civilizations. (past participle of *discover*)

1. Dictionaries have _____ music as the organization of sounds. (past participle of *define*)

2. Some experts believe that people _____ music by rhythmically repeating a sound. (past form of *create*)

3. A voice or an instrument _____ a series of sounds called a melody. (past form of *produce*)

4. Harmony is _____ when a number of sounds are made at the same time. (present participle of *occur*)

5. Throughout history, rhythm, melody, and harmony have _____ into complex arrangements. (past participle of *evolve*)

6. Remnants of musical instruments are _____ at excavations. (past participle of *uncover*)

7. In ancient China, musicians often _____ together in groups. (past form of *play*)

8. The *king* _____ of stone slabs on a frame, which were struck with mallets. (past form of *consist*)

9. Other Chinese instruments _____ flutes, lutes, and bells. (past form of *include*)

10. The Chinese _____ a gourd to make a wind instrument. (past form of *use*)

11. The Chinese still are _____ instruments from many different materials. (present participle of *construct*)

12. Other countries also have been _____ music since ancient times. (present participle of *develop*)

13. Music has _____ the festivities of Egyptian pharaohs, or rulers. (past participle of *accompany*)

14. Egyptian musicians _____ music mainly for the harp, lyre, and flute. (past form of *compose*)

15. Archaeologists _____ many of these artifacts in the tombs of pharaohs. (past form of *discover*)

16. The tomb of King Tutankhamen _____ trumpets that can still be played today. (past form of *contain*)

17. Middle Eastern peoples have _____ to music since prehistoric times. (past participle of *listen*)

18. The Assyrians _____ music to help their soldiers gain confidence. (past form of *utilize*)

19. David, a Hebrew king, was _____ for his talent with a harp. (past participle of *know*)

20. Ancient Greeks _____ music in their children's education. (past form of *include*)

21. Greek bards _____ from city to city, singing heroic tales. (past form of *travel*)

22. Greek flutists _____ at feasts. (past form of *entertain*)

23. The Romans _____ the horn from the Germanic peoples. (past form of *adapt*)

24. We are _____ more and more about the beginnings of music. (present participle of *learn*)

Lesson 37
Irregular Verbs

An **irregular verb** forms its past and past participle in some way other than by adding *-ed* to the base form. Following are some common irregular verbs.

PRINCIPAL PARTS OF IRREGULAR VERBS

Base Form	Past Form	Past Participle	Base Form	Past Form	Past Participle
be	was, were	been	lose	lost	lost
become	became	become	make	made	made
begin	began	begun	pay	paid	paid
build	built	built	rise	rose	risen
buy	bought	bought	see	saw	seen
choose	chose	chosen	seek	sought	sought
drink	drank	drunk	sell	sold	sold
drive	drove	driven	sing	sang	sung
feel	felt	felt	sink	sank	sunk
fly	flew	flown		*or* sunk	
give	gave	given	sleep	slept	slept
keep	kept	kept	steal	stole	stolen
know	knew	known	swing	swung	swung
lay	laid	laid	take	took	taken
lead	led	led	tear	tore	torn
leave	left	left	think	thought	thought
lie	lay	lain	throw	threw	thrown

▶ **Exercise 1** Complete each sentence by writing the form of the verb indicated in parentheses.

The pitcher _____**threw**_____ the ball more than ninety miles per hour. (past form of *throw*)

1. Yana _____ two picture frames for her grandmother. (past form of *choose*)

2. The talented photographer has _____ stunning pictures. (past participle of *take*)

3. The Saint Bernard _____ two big bowls of dog food. (past form of *eat*)

4. We have _____ to our favorite campsite dozens of times. (past participle of *drive*)

5. The crowd _____ ecstatic as the home team won at the buzzer. (past form of *become*)

6. The Marzetti family _____ to Florida to see their relatives. (past form of *fly*)

7. Why haven't you _____ to me more often? (past participle of *write*)

8. The police officer _____ her new uniform with pride. (past form of *wear*)

9. The thieves have _____ money from five banks. (past participle of *steal*)

10. The toddler _____ his tricycle up and down the sidewalk. (past form of *ride*)

11. Olivia has _____ her best friend for seven years. (past participle of *know*)

12. In 1497, Vasco da Gama _____ an expedition around Africa's Cape of Good Hope. (past form of *lead*)

13. The corn has _____ very quickly this summer. (past participle of *grow*)

14. Mrs. Schmidt has _____ the same bus every day for nine years. (past participle of *ride*)

15. I _____ the bell four times before anyone came to the door. (past form of *ring*)

16. The cat _____ on the windowsill in the afternoon sun. (past form of *lie*)

17. The rain has _____ into a slick sheet of ice. (past participle of *freeze*)

18. Shoppers have _____ crowding into stores all day. (past participle of *be*)

19. The choir _____ its last song. (past form of *sing*)

20. The hungry baby has _____ all of the milk. (past participle of *drink*)

21. I _____ only two people in line for the new movie. (past form of *see*)

22. The pilot _____ that we might experience turbulence. (past form of *say*)

23. Missy _____ nervous about opening night. (past form of *feel*)

24. The paramedic _____ calmly to the accident victim. (past form of *speak*)

25. They _____ and listened attentively. (past form of *sit*)

26. A giggling little boy _____ the limelight from the older and more experienced performers. (past form of *steal*)

27. Many students _____ the scavenger hunt was a huge success. (past form of *think*)

28. The flight attendant _____ some passengers blankets. (past form of *give*)

29. The kite slowly _____ below the horizon. (past form of *sink*)

30. The sun _____ in a burst of oranges and reds. (past form of *rise*)

31. Gina has _____ in many swim meets. (past participle of *swim*)

32. My grandmother _____ us exciting tales about her childhood. (past form of *tell*)

33. Janet _____ out of bed when the alarm rang. (past form of *spring*)

34. I have _____ a very relaxing summer. (past participle of *have*)

35. The teacher _____ the papers down on the desk. (past form of *lay*)

36. The school's football team _____ all of their games. (past form of *lose*)

Lesson 38
Verb Tenses: Present, Past, and Future

Verb tenses help to show when events take place—in the present, the past, or the future.

The **present tense** expresses a constant, repeated, habitual, or customary action or condition. It can also express a general truth or an action or condition that is happening right now.

The Volga River **flows** southward to the Caspian Sea. (a constant action)
Mercury **is** the planet nearest the sun. (a condition that is generally true)
Samantha **feels** happy. (not always but just now)

The present tense of all verbs except *be* is the same as the base form of the verb. To form the third-person singular of these verbs, add *-s* or *-es* to the base form.

SINGULAR			PLURAL		
I lift.	You lift.	She, he, or it lifts.	We lift.	You lift.	They lift.
I am.	You are.	She, he, or it is.	We are.	You are.	They are.

The **past tense** expresses an action or condition that was started and completed in the past.

The dogs **chased** the car until it turned the corner.

Except for *be*, all regular and irregular verbs have one past-tense form. The past-tense form of *be* may be either *was* or *were*.

SINGULAR			PLURAL		
I drifted.	You drifted.	She, he, or it drifted.	We drifted.	You drifted.	They drifted.
I was.	You were.	He, she, or it was.	We were.	You were.	They were.

▶ **Exercise 1 Complete each sentence by writing the tense of the verb indicated in parentheses.**

Scientists _____ study _____ weather patterns carefully. (study, present)

1. Temperature records _____ back as far as the mid-1800s. (*go*, present)

2. Studying the records, climatologists _____ a worldwide increase in temperature. (*find*, past)

3. They _____ the increase is about 1°F since 1860. (*think*, present)

4. Several years in the 1980s _____ among the warmest ever recorded. (*be*, past)

5. However, scientists _____ no overall warming trend in the United States. (*discover*, past)

6. Still, the continental United States _____ only about 1.5 percent of Earth. (*cover*, present)

7. Climate on Earth _____ dramatically from region to region. (*vary*, present)

8. Scientists _____ mathematical models and powerful computers to predict changes in the earth's climate. (*use*, present)

9. Weather _____ from day to day and sometimes from year to year. (*change*, present)

10. Global warming _____ to much debate among scientists. (*lead*, present)

Use the **future tense** to express an action or condition that will occur in the future. To form the future tense of any verb, use *will* or *shall* before the base form of the verb.

I shall try.   **You will come.**

Future time also can be expressed without using *shall* or *will*. Use *going to* or *about to* with the present tense of *be* and the base form of the verb. Or, use the present tense with an adverb or adverb phrase that states a future time.

I am about to leave the house.   **Luan arrives next week.**

▶ **Exercise 2** Change the verb or verbs in each sentence to future tense. Write the new verb in the blank. For those sentences indicated, use other words besides *will* or *shall* to express future time.

One major effect of global warming was changes in weather. _will be_____

1. Temperatures rose more quickly in the Northern Hemisphere. _____

2. There was greater warming in winters than in summers. (Do not use *will* or *shall*.)

    _____

3. Winter temperatures increase by an even greater amount in the Arctic and Antarctic.

    _____

4. Snow and ice melted. _____

5. An increase in evaporation put more water vapor into the atmosphere. _____

6. Water flooded low-lying areas. _____

7. Sea levels are as much as 25 feet above normal. _____

8. Ocean currents slowed down or shifted direction. _____

9. Hurricanes became more powerful and frequent. _____

10. Global warming brought many unexpected changes. _____

11. Perhaps some areas benefited from global warming. (Do not use *will* or *shall*.)

    _____

12. Small organisms were more adaptable to a rapid change in climate. _____

Lesson 39
Perfect Tenses: Present, Past, and Future

There are three perfect tenses in the English language: the present perfect, past perfect, and future perfect.

The **present perfect tense** expresses an action or condition that occurred at some indefinite time in the past. This tense also shows an action or condition that began in the past and continues into the present. To form the present perfect tense, use *has* or *have* with the past participle of a verb.

She **has heard** this song. (past indefinite action)
They **have remained** at the hospital for three days. (action began in past, continues into present)

Use the **past perfect tense** to indicate that one past action or condition began and ended before another past action started. To form the past perfect tense, use *had* with the past participle of a verb.

By the time I **left** (past), our team **had scored** (past perfect) twenty points.

Use the **future perfect tense** to express one future action that will begin and end before another future event begins. To form the future perfect tense, use *will have* or *shall have* with the past participle of a verb.

By tomorrow, Jean **will have finished** her project.

▶ **Exercise 1** Identify each perfect tense verb by underlining it and writing either *present perf.*, *past perf.*, or *future perf.* in the blank.

___present perf.___   The children have played the same game all day long.

_____   **1.** Frederick had worn glasses for five years before he got contact lenses.

_____   **2.** The puppy has grown two inches in five weeks.

_____   **3.** By next year the doctor will have treated two thousand patients.

_____   **4.** The diligent carpenter has built ten cabinets in one month.

_____   **5.** By the end of the year the sun will have risen 365 times.

_____   **6.** Cleo had written the story that everyone liked so much.

_____   **7.** In May the Cruzes will have lived in Tucson for five years.

_____   **8.** I have ridden every roller coaster in the park.

_____   **9.** Massachusetts had joined the Union before Vermont became a state.

_____   **10.** California has been a favorite vacation spot for years.

_____ **11.** By the time my mother leaves work, I will have put dinner in the oven.

_____ **12.** Miguel has written in his journal every day this week.

_____ **13.** We have taken a trip to the river every summer since we moved here.

_____ **14.** Frances has shown animals in the fair for five years.

▶ **Exercise 2** **Complete each sentence by writing the tense of the verb indicated in parentheses.**

No one ____has found____ the watch I lost last week. (present perfect of *find*)

1. The wildflowers in the field _____ every year. (present perfect of *bloom*)

2. I _____ of visiting the Ukraine. (present perfect of *dream*)

3. Texas _____ a state for two hundred years in the year 2045. (future perfect of *be*)

4. We _____ everything to keep the cold air from coming under the door. (present perfect of *try*)

5. Next week, the basketball player _____ the record for most games played. (future perfect of *break*)

6. Linda _____ two hundred miles before she stopped for gas. (past perfect of *drive*)

7. By the time I shoveled the walk, an inch of new snow _____ to the ground. (past perfect of *fall*)

8. Zina _____ each of her many visits to the art museum. (present perfect of *enjoy*)

9. The museum of natural history _____ countless artifacts for more than a century. (present perfect of *display*)

10. In February, the corner grocery _____ in the same location for thirty years. (future perfect of *be*)

11. Mr. Landis _____ a gift for his daughter's fifteenth birthday when she mentioned the new radio. (past perfect of *buy*)

12. My family _____ aluminum cans for as long as I can remember. (present perfect of *recycle*)

13. Rabbits _____ vegetables from our garden every summer. (present perfect of *eat*)

14. By the time Mary finished her paper route, the sun _____. (past perfect of *rise*)

15. Next week, the astronauts _____ their tenth journey into space. (future perfect of *make*)

Lesson 40
Distinguishing Tenses

At times it is difficult to determine which tense to use when writing. Use this summary of the six tenses to help you understand when and where each should be used.

TENSE	EXPRESSES	FORMS
present	current or habitual action	same as base form; add -s or -es to form third-person singular
past	action completed at some time in the past	one past-tense form, such as *won* or *lived*
future	action or condition that will occur in the future	*shall* or *will* before the base form
present perfect	action or condition that occurred in the indefinite past	past participle form with present-tense auxiliary verb *has* or *have*
past perfect	one past action that began and ended before another past action	past participle form with auxiliary verb *had*
future perfect	one future action that will begin and end before another future action begins	past participle form with auxiliary verbs *will have* or *shall have*

▶ **Exercise 1** **Underline each verb. Identify the tense of each verb by writing either *present, past, future, present perfect, past perfect,* or *future perfect* in the blank.**

_____present perfect_____ The Aztecs <u>have captured</u> the interest of many archaeologists.

_____ 1. Archaeologists have discovered Aztec stone temples, as well as metal and pottery artifacts.

_____ 2. Years before the Spaniards arrived in what is now Mexico, the Aztecs had established a vast empire.

_____ 3. The Aztecs had a different name for themselves—the *Mexica.*

_____ 4. The Valley of Mexico, now the location of Mexico City, was once the center of activity for the Mexica and their neighbors.

_____ 5. The Aztecs wrote books in pictograms about such things as their histories, beliefs, and censuses.

_____ 6. Archaeologists call these books *codices.*

_____ 7. At one time, hundreds of these books existed.

Grammar

_____ 8. Unfortunately, most of these books have disappeared.

_____ 9. If archaeologists ever discover more books, it will help to piece

together the Aztec past.

_____ 10. Historical documents fill in some of the gaps about Aztec culture.

_____ 11. Some fragments of perishable items such as clothing and feathers

also have survived.

_____ 12. The Spaniards and the native peoples of Mexico recorded

information about the Aztec culture.

_____ 13. By the year 2019, it will have been 500 years since the Spanish

arrived in Mexico.

_____ 14. Many of the Spanish conquerors built their own churches and

houses over those of the Aztecs.

_____ 15. As a result, many Aztec artifacts remain lost forever.

▶ **Exercise 2 Complete each sentence by writing the tense indicated in parentheses.**

The northernmost country in Latin America _____**is**_____ Mexico. (present tense of *be*)

1. Mexico's population today _____ third in the Western Hemisphere. (present tense of *rank*)

2. Mexico City _____ the largest city in the world. (present tense of *remain*)

3. The city _____ more than 7,500 feet above sea level in a high valley. (present tense of *lie*)

4. The Spanish _____ Mexico City on the ruins of Tenochtitlán. (past tense of *build*)

5. Tenochtitlán _____ the Aztec capital well before the Spanish arrived. (past perfect of *become*)

6. By the time the Spanish arrived, Tenochtitlán's population _____ almost 200,000. (past perfect of *reach*)

7. Today, Mexico City's population _____ to about twenty-two million people. (present perfect of *grow*)

8. Mexico _____ independence from Spain in 1821. (past tense of *gain*)

9. Before Mexico won independence, its inhabitants _____ against the Spanish rulers. (past perfect of *revolt*)

10. Mexico _____ a flag in 1821. (past tense of *adopt*)

11. The Mexican flag _____ green, white, and red. (present tense of *be*)

Lesson 41

Verbs: Progressive and Emphatic Forms

Each of the six verb tenses has a **progressive** form that expresses a continuing action. To make the progressive form, use the appropriate tense of the verb *be* with the present participle of the main verb.

They **are trying.** (present progressive)
They **were trying.** (past progressive)
They **will be trying.** (future progressive)
They **have been trying.** (present perfect progressive)
They **had been trying.** (past perfect progressive)
They **will have been trying.** (future perfect progressive)

The present and past tenses have additional forms, called **emphatic**, that add force, or emphasis, to the verb. To make the emphatic forms, use *do, does,* or *did* with the base form of the verb.

I **do try.** (present emphatic)   I **did try.** (past emphatic)

▶ **Exercise 1** Underline the progressive or emphatic verb form in each sentence and write in the blank which form it is.

_____ past progressive _____   The cows were chewing their cud.

_____   1. The corn had been growing at a record pace until the dry spell.

_____   2. The farmers were hoping for a bountiful harvest.

_____   3. They did work hard this year.

_____   4. Have you been watching the progress of the soybeans?

_____   5. The cold weather in Florida will be affecting the growth of citrus fruits.

_____   6. I do hope the weather improves.

_____   7. My cousin had been eating cantaloupe all summer until it became

too expensive.

_____   8. The neighbors have been tending to their own vegetable garden.

_____   9. Will they be giving the neighbors any fresh vegetables?

_____   10. George was weeding his garden when a rabbit came along.

_____   11. The birds are eating the seeds we have planted.

_____   12. My parents are making a scarecrow.

_____ **13.** By tomorrow, they will have been canning tomatoes for two solid weeks.

_____ **14.** We will be enjoying garden tomatoes in the winter!

_____ **15.** I do love fresh tomatoes!

▶ **Exercise 2 Complete each sentence by writing the form of the verb indicated in parentheses.**

They _____ are listening _____ closely to the band. (present progressive of *listen*)

1. By tomorrow morning, the telethon _____ for 48 hours. (future perfect progressive of *broadcast*)

2. The dog _____ nonstop for an hour. (present perfect progressive of *bark*)

3. My aunt and uncle _____ for a baby girl. (present progressive of *hope*)

4. The bus driver _____ this route as long as she could remember. (past perfect progressive of *take*)

5. I _____ you before I left! (past emphatic of *call*)

6. The old cow _____ peacefully in the field. (past progressive of *graze*)

7. The rancher _____ the horses in the stable at nightfall. (future progressive of *put*)

8. Ten of us _____ cars for two hours. (present perfect progressive of *wash*)

9. We _____ in our team! (present emphatic of *believe*)

10. In ten minutes, we _____ in line for a full five hours for these tickets. (future perfect progressive of *wait*)

11. We _____ about moving practice to Friday. (present progressive of *think*)

12. My friends and I _____ all of this group's music recently. (present perfect progressive of *buy*)

13. Just before the speaker came out, the audience _____ his name. (past perfect progressive of *chant*)

14. The judge _____ carefully to both sides. (past emphatic of *listen*)

15. Reporters _____ the mayor now. (present progressive of *interview*)

16. The principal _____ us about the incident in the parking lot. (past progressive of *tell*)

17. The spectators _____ the arena soon. (future progressive of *leave*)

18. Paul _____ the house all afternoon in anticipation of the party. (present perfect progressive of *clean*)

Lesson 42
Compatibility of Tenses

When writing about two or more events that occur at the same time, do not shift, or change, tenses.

INCORRECT: During the night the barn owl hunted, and it catches a fieldmouse. (Tense shifts from past to present.)

CORRECT: During the night the barn owl hunted, and it caught a fieldmouse. (Clearly the two events happened at nearly the same time in the past.)

Shift tenses only to show that one event precedes or follows another in time.

INCORRECT: By the time the movie ended, everyone left the theater. (The two past-tense verbs give the mistaken impression that both events happened at the same time.)

CORRECT: By the time the movie ended, everyone had left the theater. (The shift from the past tense verb *ended* to the past perfect verb *had left* clearly shows that the departure from the theater had happened before the movie ended.)

▶ **Exercise 1** Underline the second verb in each sentence and change it so that its tense is compatible with the first. Write the new verb in the blank.

_____fought_____ Abolitionists began their struggle against slavery, which they <u>fight</u> during the 1700s and 1800s.

_____ 1. Many abolitionists were African Americans who are determined to put an end to slavery.

_____ 2. They wrote pamphlets and edit newspapers.

_____ 3. Others worked on the Underground Railroad, work that is very dangerous.

_____ 4. By the time the Civil War began, the Railroad helped thousands of slaves to freedom.

_____ 5. The abolition movement produced many leaders, among whom are both African Americans and white.

_____ 6. African American abolitionists such as Harriet Tubman, David Walker, and Sojourner Truth were selfless individuals who are risking their lives for others.

_____ 7. By the time he was nine years old, Henry Highland Garnet escapes with his family from Maryland to the free state of Pennsylvania.

_____ 8. By the time he reached twenty-two years of age, Garnet became an eloquent speaker.

Grammar

_____ **9.** He later became a minister and serves as pastor of a Presbyterian church in
Washington, D.C.

_____ **10.** Robert Purvis attended Amherst College in Massachusetts and then settles in
Pennsylvania.

_____ **11.** He devoted most of his time and money to the Underground Railroad, which
he had believed in.

_____ **12.** When the war began in 1861, Purvis helps some 9,000 slaves to freedom.

_____ **13.** Samuel Cornish went to Philadelphia, where he organizes the first African
American newspaper with another abolitionist, John Russworm.

_____ **14.** They named the newspaper *Freedom's Journal*, and print articles from other
writers as well.

_____ **15.** James W.C. Pennington ran away from a cruel slaveholder in Maryland to New
York, where he goes to school.

_____ **16.** Before he left Maryland, he has learned the blacksmith trade.

_____ **17.** In 1849 Pennington wrote *The Fugitive Blacksmith*, which had been about his
own experiences.

_____ **18.** He became a great speaker, and he will speak before dignitaries in Europe.

_____ **19.** James Forten was fourteen years old when he joins the navy.

_____ **20.** While he was in the navy, he invents a device to handle ship sails.

_____ **21.** One famous African American female abolitionist was Harriet Tubman, who is
the "conductor" of the Underground Railroad.

_____ **22.** She grew up a slave in Maryland, where she was interfering with a supervisor
to save a fellow slave from punishment.

_____ **23.** The supervisor hit Harriet in the head and fractures her skull.

_____ **24.** In 1844 she married John Tubman, who has gained his freedom earlier.

_____ **25.** She escaped from slavery five years later and has gone to Philadelphia through
the Underground Railroad.

_____ **26.** By the time Harriet returned to Maryland, Congress has been passing the
Fugitive Slave Act of 1850.

Lesson 43
Voice of Verbs: Active and Passive

An action verb is in the **active voice** when the subject of the sentence performs the action.

The dog **chased** the cat.

An action verb is in the **passive voice** when the action is performed on the subject.

The cat **was chased** by the dog.

The active voice is generally stronger. However, sometimes the passive voice is preferred or even necessary. Use the passive voice if you do not want to call attention to the performer, or if you do not know the performer.

The cookies **were eaten.** (You may not want to identify who ate them.)
The dishes **were washed.** (You may not know who did the washing.)

To form the passive voice, use a form of the auxiliary verb *be* with the past participle of the verb. The tense of the auxiliary verb determines the tense of the passive verb.

The cat **is chased** by the dog. (present tense, passive voice)
The cat **was being chased** by the dog. (past progressive tense, passive voice)
The cat **will have been chased** by the dog. (future perfect tense, passive voice)

▶ **Exercise 1** Write *A* if the action verb in each sentence is in the active voice and *P* if it is in the passive voice.

___P___ Thomas Edison was regarded as a great inventor by the world.

_____ **1.** Our furniture was carried inside by the movers.

_____ **2.** The door was held open by me.

_____ **3.** A standing ovation was received by the speaker.

_____ **4.** The reporter interviewed the movie star.

_____ **5.** Betina has played softball every Tuesday for a month.

_____ **6.** The landscape was carefully painted by the artist.

_____ **7.** His grandfather told the boy many stories.

_____ **8.** Mrs. Miles donates time to the women's shelter.

_____ **9.** A crayon was pulled from the box by the little girl.

_____ **10.** She displays her drawing with pride.

_____ **11.** All ten pins were knocked down by the skilled bowler.

_____ **12.** The last score was missed by the scorekeeper.

_____ 13. Five hundred students were graduated by the university.

_____ 14. My aunt telephones our apartment every week.

_____ 15. Hot dogs are being eaten by the students.

_____ 16. Two authors wrote the book.

_____ 17. Twenty dollars had been earned by Ernest.

_____ 18. A patient called the doctor.

_____ 19. The park was covered by tall pines.

_____ 20. A truck is being driven by the forest ranger.

_____ 21. The test was taken by the class.

_____ 22. Our team has won the game.

_____ 23. The blaze was fought tirelessly by the firefighters.

_____ 24. The spelling bee has been won by Hiro.

_____ 25. An amusing story was written by the six-year-old.

_____ 26. The tennis player hit the ball hard.

_____ 27. The plane is being flown by the new pilot.

_____ 28. By tomorrow, a relative will have taken the Jeffersons to the airport.

_____ 29. The building is jealously protected by the watchdog.

_____ 30. The toy has been hidden by William.

_____ 31. Four books had been read by Rhetta in one week.

_____ 32. The school board closed the school.

_____ 33. The class was passing around the sign-up sheet.

_____ 34. We will take two burgers.

_____ 35. I have already eaten lunch.

_____ 36. The salad dressing was tasted by Anna.

_____ 37. My sister was singing the same song for an hour.

_____ 38. The spark plug had been removed by the mechanic.

_____ 39. The mechanic replaced the headlight and tail light.

_____ 40. The Smiths will take in the stray dog.

✓ Unit 6 **Review**

▶ **Exercise 1** Complete each sentence by writing the form of the verb indicated in the parentheses.

The eagle was _____**soaring**_____ higher and higher. (present participle of *soar*)

1. Am I _____ too picky? (present participle of *be*)

2. The beachcombers have _____ beautiful shells at low tide. (past participle of *find*)

3. After the crowd went home, trash _____ everywhere. (past tense of *lie*)

4. The cyclists have _____ fifty miles on the first leg of their trip. (past participle of *ride*)

5. Boats will be _____ late into the afternoon. (present participle of *sail*)

6. James _____ applying for a part-time job. (present tense of *be*)

7. I _____ some litter at the edge of the beach. (past tense of *see*)

8. Leah has _____ too far to give up now. (past participle of *come*)

9. Louis _____ his waterproof watch in the locker room. (past tense of *lose*)

10. At the end of the day we will have _____ here for six hours. (past participle of *be*)

11. The wind has been _____ dust in our faces. (present participle of *blow*)

12. He had _____ a mistake in not putting new batteries in his calculator. (past participle of *make*)

13. The temperature dropped when the sun _____ behind the clouds. (past tense of *go*)

14. Our family _____ a picnic lunch. (past tense of *bring*)

15. We had _____ all the pizza before Jake arrived. (past participle of *eat*)

16. I was _____ my time so I wouldn't get lost. (present participle of *take*)

17. I haven't _____ that much since last summer! (past participle of *swim*)

18. We _____ our announcements on the cafeteria wall. (past tense of *hang*)

19. I _____ happy we spent the day together. (present form of *be*)

20. I _____ we would be late if we didn't run. (past tense of *know*)

Unit 6 Cumulative Review: Units 1–6

▶ **Exercise 1** Draw one line under each transitive verb and two lines under each intransitive verb. Draw three lines under each direct object and circle each indirect object.

Archaeologists have discovered many Etruscan tombs.

1. These richly decorated tombs give archaeologists valuable information.

2. The Etruscans lived in Etruria, an area north of Rome, Italy.

3. In this area, hills cover the countryside.

4. According to most historians, the Etruscans migrated to Etruria by sea around 800 B.C.

5. By the seventh century B.C., twelve Etruscan states existed.

6. Each state had its own capital city.

7. Together they conquered lands beyond Etruria.

8. They spread across the Apennine Mountains in the north, and across the Po Valley.

9. In the south, they crossed the Tiber River.

10. The Etruscans grew grain, olives, grapes, and other foods.

11. They also made money by trade.

12. The Etruscans also worked as skilled metalworkers and pottery makers.

13. They believed in life after death.

14. Rich Etruscans built underground tombs.

15. They buried their relatives with objects such as vases, statues, and jewelry.

16. Artists gave the tombs additional atmosphere.

17. They painted scenes of daily Etruscan life on the walls.

18. Greeks influenced Etruscan art.

19. The Etruscans gave early Romans some important customs.

20. The Romans would eventually rule Etruria.

▶ **Exercise 2** Draw one line under each participle, two lines under each gerund, and three lines under each infinitive. Write *SF* after each sentence fragment.

We are learning more and more about ancient civilizations every day. _____

1. To study ancient civilizations in school. _____

   2. The Latins, living around the city of Rome before Roman kings came to power, arrived in this

   area most likely from across the Alps. _____

   3. Romans enjoyed the telling of the story of Romulus and Remus. _____

   4. To listen to the legend of Romulus and Remus is entertaining. _____

   5. The twins Romulus and Remus, left to die as babies in a basket on the Tiber River. _____

   6. To survive in the wilderness, the twins drank the milk of a wolf. _____

   7. Romulus, angered by his brother, killed Remus. _____

   8. Romulus, believed to be Rome's founder by the early Romans. _____

   9. Consisting of seven separate villages on seven hills, early Rome was not a unified

   region. _____

10. The early Etruscan rulers oversaw the combining of the seven cities into the first proper town

   of Roma. _____

11. The seven villages, overlooking the Tiber River, grew. _____

12. To build houses and shops in the valleys. _____

13. Connecting the city to the sea, the Tiber River allowed for easy trade abroad. _____

14. Disappointed with rule by kings, the Roman people began a new form of government. _____

15. Under this new government, called *res publica,* the people elected their governing

   officials. _____

16. Two officials, or consuls, together having the power of a king. _____

17. A parliament, known as a *senate,* helped the consuls with decisions. _____

18. Voting was not a right all Romans enjoyed. _____

19. To cope with an emergency, the consuls appointed a dictator for six months. _____

20. The Roman people, eventually composed of four classes. _____

▶ **Exercise 3 Write the form of the verb indicated in parentheses to correctly complete each
sentence.**

   The Latin people in Rome _____needed_____ a powerful army. (past tense of *need*)

   1. Historians _____ the Roman army for hundreds of years. (present perfect

   progressive of *study*)

   2. Rome _____ many enemies. (past tense of *have*)

3. Three groups of peoples close to Rome _____ the Latins for centuries. (past perfect of *threaten*)

4. The groups _____ as the Sabines, the Aequi, and the Volsci. (past tense of *know*, passive voice)

5. By 304 B.C., the Romans _____ all three groups. (past perfect of *conquer*)

6. The Etruscans still _____ power in Italy. (past tense of *hold*)

7. They, too, _____ by the Romans. (past tense of *defeat*, passive voice)

8. We _____ Rome twice by next spring. (future perfect of *visit*)

9. This time I _____ to Roman ruins. (future tense of *go*)

10. The Gauls _____ a Celtic people who came across the Alps looking for new lands. (past tense of *be*)

11. The Gauls _____ a reputation as fierce warriors. (past perfect of *earn*)

12. In 390 B.C. the Gauls _____ a threat to Rome itself. (past tense of *become*)

13. The Romans _____ to pay them a large amount of gold to leave. (past tense of *force*, passive voice)

14. The Romans also _____ problems with the Samnites. (past progressive of *experience*)

15. Originally, the Romans _____ an agreement with the Samnites to conquer the Volsci people. (past perfect of *sign*)

16. The Romans and the Samnites _____ historians. (present perfect of *fascinate*)

17. War _____ out between the two in 343 B.C. (past tense of *break*)

18. They _____ each other for fifty years. (past progressive of *fight*)

19. The Samnites _____ heavy armor. (past tense of *wear*)

20. The Romans _____ the Samnites before they agreed to be Rome's allies. (past perfect of *defeat*)

Unit 7: Subject-Verb Agreement

Lesson 44

Subject-Verb Agreement

Every verb must agree with its subject in person and in number. Most verbs have a different form only in the present tense; when the subject is third-person singular, an -*s* or -*es* is added to the base verb. The linking verb *be* is an exception. It changes form in both the present and past tenses.

SINGULAR   PLURAL
He **takes**.   They **take**.
She **is** friendly.   They **are** friendly.
It **was** ripe.   They **were** ripe.

The auxiliary verbs *be*, *have*, and *do* change form in verb phrases to show agreement with third-person subjects.

He **is running** home   They **are running** home.
She **has arrived.**   They **have arrived.**
Does she **have** a ride?   **Do** they **have** a ride?

▶ **Exercise 1** Draw one line under the simple subject and two lines under the correct verb form in parentheses.

Agriculture (remains, remain) vital to the interest of every person.

1. The United States still (produces, produce) a majority of the world's food supply.

2. Modern farms (has, have) become more efficient than ever.

3. A new science called agribusiness (has, have) been responsible for much of the improvement.

4. Farmers (takes, take) a keen interest in market conditions and efficiency techniques.

5. One day's work for a farmer today (equals, equal) about a week's effort for our grandparents.

6. Scientifically balanced fertilizers (keeps, keep) the nutrients in the soil high.

7. Better seeds (yields, yield) larger crops.

8. The seeds (is, are) developed to withstand extremes in climate and disease.

9. The only product of many large companies (is, are) hybrid seeds.

10. Newly developed weed-killers (increases, increase) crop yield.

11. Efficient pest control (has, have) reduced crop loss.

12. Almost every year the yield per acre (rises, rise).

13. Computers (performs, perform) many tasks on modern farms.

14. They (records, record) statistics on crop production and even (tracks, track) the weather.

15. Despite all of these advances, the number of farms (grows, grow) smaller every year.

16. Many young people (leaves, leave) the family farm in search of another profession.

17. Large corporations (has, have) purchased many of the successful farms.

18. These huge companies (involves, involve) themselves in every facet of agriculture.

19. To some people, that practice (is, are) beneficial.

20. Others (thinks, think) it (hurts, hurt) the small farmer.

▶ **Exercise 2** **Place a check (✔) next to each sentence in which the subject and verb agree.**

___✔___ Many advances have been made in livestock production.

_____ 1. Fewer animals die from disease because of advances in veterinary science.

_____ 2. New antibiotics decreases the number of deaths in young animals.

_____ 3. Scientists continues to search for ways to increase the meat supply.

_____ 4. One new product are beefalo.

_____ 5. It is a cross between a cow and the American bison.

_____ 6. Some people is experimenting with ostrich farms.

_____ 7. Supermarket shelves of the future might hold packages of ostrich meat.

_____ 8. In southern states, some farmers raise alligators.

_____ 9. Many people enjoys eating the meat from alligator tails.

_____ 10. Factory farming is a popular way to raise livestock today.

_____ 11. On factory farms, buildings holds large numbers of animals in a small space.

_____ 12. This type of farming produce more meat, milk, or eggs in less time and more cheaply than on traditional farms.

_____ 13. On some factory farms, a chicken house holds as many as 100,000 chickens.

_____ 14. It takes about 1.4 hours of labor to raise 100 chickens today, compared to 16 hours in 1945.

_____ 15. Some people criticizes the use of factory farms.

_____ 16. They says it is cruel to raise animals in such confined conditions.

_____ 17. To create better breeds of livestock, some scientists experiment with animal genes.

_____ 18. This type of science is called genetic engineering.

Lesson 45
Agreement: Intervening Prepositional Phrases

When a prepositional phrase comes between the subject and the verb, do not mistake its object for the subject. The verb must agree with the subject, not with the object of a preposition.

The **letters** from Paul **were** lost in the mail. (*Letters* is the plural subject. *Paul* is the object of the preposition *from* and is singular. The verb, *were,* is plural to agree with the subject *letters.*)

The **color** of the uniforms **is** red and gold. (The subject, *color,* is singular. *Uniforms* is the object of the preposition and is plural. The verb, *is,* is singular to agree with the subject, *color.*)

▶ **Exercise 1** Write *C* in the blank if the verb agrees with its subject. Write the correct verb form if the verb does not agree with its subject.

____specialize____   Two pet shops in town specializes in birds only.

_____   **1.** My favorite of the two shops is Winged Delights.

_____   **2.** Its knowledge of birds seems to be superior to the other store.

_____   **3.** "My selection of feathered tropicals are the largest in town," said Mrs. Cho, the

                owner.

_____   **4.** My interest in pets are limited to the parrot family.

_____   **5.** Brilliantly colored macaws from South America make attractive pets.

_____   **6.** However, the price tag on a macaw is beyond my means.

_____   **7.** The gray birds beside the cockatoo looks interesting.

_____   **8.** Those in the corner are African gray parrots.

_____   **9.** Their lack of color is offset by the parrots' intelligence.

_____   **10.** African grays, without question, is the best talkers in the entire parrot family.

_____   **11.** What type of foods are necessary for a healthy African gray?

_____   **12.** This bird, like other tropical birds, thrives on seeds, nuts, and fruit.

_____   **13.** Several food mixtures of good quality are available commercially.

_____   **14.** Fruits of almost any kind provides extra variety to the diet.

_____   **15.** The African gray, along with its cage, were priced well within my budget.

_____   **16.** My parents' reservations about having a bird in the house is unfounded.

_____ **17.** The chores of caring for the bird are readily shared by the entire family.

_____ **18.** The best of all the names we considered was Nestor.

_____ **19.** A parrot in our lives has proven to be a good decision.

_____ **20.** Nestor, with his heart-winning antics, are becoming a member of the family.

▶ **Exercise 2 Draw one line under the simple subject and two lines under the correct verb form in parentheses.**

Bird <u>fanciers</u> around the world (enjoys, <u><u>enjoy</u></u>) the beauty of tropical species.

1. Every variety of parrot, macaw, and cockatoo (is, are) a member of the family Psittacidae.

2. The birds of this family (varies, vary) in length from three to forty inches.

3. Other relatives in this family (includes, include) lories, cockatiels, and conures.

4. A relatively large head in proportion to the body (distinguishes, distinguish) these birds.

5. Most members of the family (has, have) short, round tails.

6. The toughest of nuts (represents, represent) little challenge for their large, hooked bills.

7. Birds in this family, without exception, (uses, use) their beaks like a third foot when climbing.

8. One of their unique features (is, are) their special feet.

9. This foot, with two toes pointing forward and two pointing backward, (gives, give) them greater dexterity than any other group of birds.

10. Most tropical regions of the world (provides, provide) suitable habitat for parrots.

11. Many temperate regions of the Southern Hemisphere (houses, house) parrot families, too.

12. The lifespan of Psittacidae (averages, average) thirty to fifty years.

13. Some parrots with the ability to mimic human speech (has, have) developed extensive vocabularies.

14. The talent of talking African gray parrots (is, are) unsurpassed.

15. The owl parrots from New Zealand (is, are) nocturnal birds.

16. Of all parrots, only the kakapos (is, are) entirely flightless.

17. Measuring only three inches long, the pygmy parrots of New Guinea (represents, represent) the smallest parrots in the world.

18. Macaws with their brilliant plumage (is, are) distinguished by their pointed wings and exceptionally long tails.

Lesson 46
Agreement: Linking Verbs

A predicate nominative that is different in number from the subject can be confusing. Only the subject affects the linking verb.

The first **act was** jugglers. (The singular verb, *was,* agrees with the singular subject, *act.* The verb is not affected by the predicate nominative, *jugglers.*)

Cookies were Mike's favorite dessert. (The plural verb, *were,* agrees with the plural subject, *cookies.* The verb is not affected by the predicate nominative, *dessert.*)

▶ **Exercise 1** Underline the verb in parentheses that best completes the sentence.

Notes (is, <u>are</u>) an excellent way to remember lesson material.

1. The biggest attraction in town (remains, remain) the antique shops.

2. The team members (is, are) a pleasure to coach.

3. The mint in the Lascombe Gardens (smells, smell) good, even from two blocks away.

4. The Ramirez family (is, are) a sponsor for the event.

5. Encyclopedias (stands, stand) a ready resource for writing term papers.

6. Gold pens (was, were) the women's prize.

7. When I am trying to concentrate, a dripping faucet (becomes, become) a nuisance.

8. A truce (means, mean) no aggression for a specific time period.

9. The twins (turns, turn) sixteen in three weeks.

10. Comic strip characters (was, were) the theme at the banquet.

11. Rawhide bones (is, are) candy to my dog, Beethoven.

12. The first topic (was, were) accidents in the home.

13. Berries (is, are) a mainstay in the diets of many birds.

14. The book (was, were) a collection of short stories.

15. The captains (is, are) the leaders of the volleyball team.

16. Her entire investment (was, were) fifty dollars.

17. The clouds (appears, appear) a threat to our baseball game.

18. Parties (is, are) a good opportunity to get to know people.

19. Sophomores (has, have) twice been student council secretary.

20. The girls (shows, show) great effort even though they are far behind.

21. The consequences (is, are) worth the risk.

22. Dances (remains, remain) our favorite social activity.

23. The juniors (feels, feel) their choice for class president was a good one.

24. Pets (becomes, become) a member of the family.

25. Compliments (is, are) a gift that anyone can give.

26. Oak trees (has, have) become a symbol for strength.

27. Concrete lions (stands, stand) guardian over the library entrance.

28. Mr. Jefferson (thinks, think) these assignments are simple.

29. Apologies (seems, seem) like bitter medicine, but the results are gratifying.

30. It (appears, appear) pot-bellied pigs are gaining popularity as pets.

31. The rhythms of the percussion section (was, were) the highlight of the concert.

32. Holidays (means, mean) exciting sights and sounds.

33. Lien's favorite Sunday breakfast (is, are) scrambled eggs.

34. Her songs (remains, remain) a hit week after week.

35. The majority of people (feels, feel) a rain shower ruins their day.

36. Hikers (is, are) the largest category of park visitors.

37. Rainbows (was, were) a spectacular sight after the thunderstorm.

38. In Japan, railroads (has, have) become the standard for mass transit.

39. Precautions (is, are) an indispensable part of safe operation.

40. Sonya (seems, seem) miles above the rest of the class.

▶ **Writing Link Write three or four sentences describing the person you most admire. Use examples of subject-verb agreement with linking verbs and predicate nominatives in at least two of your sentences.**

_____

_____

_____

_____

_____

_____

Grammar

Lesson 47
Agreement: Inverted Sentences

An **inverted sentence** is one in which the subject follows the verb. Take care to locate the subject accurately, making sure that the verb agrees with it. Because an inverted sentence often begins with a prepositional phrase, the object of the preposition can be easily mistaken for the subject. Remember that the subject follows the verb in an inverted sentence.

Singular: Under the bush **sits** a **rabbit.** (The verb, *sits,* must agree with the subject, *rabbit.*)

Plural: Under the bush **sit** three **rabbits.** (The verb, *sit,* must agree with the subject, *rabbits.*)

Inverted sentences often begin with the word *there* or *here.* These words are almost never the subject of a sentence.

Singular: There **is** a **shadow** across the page.   Here **comes** my **brother.**
Plural: There **are cracks** in the foundation.   Here **are** five **examples.**

The subject in an interrogative sentence may follow an auxiliary verb. In this event, the subject will appear between the auxiliary verb and the main verb.

Singular: **Does** the **price include** tax?
Plural: **Do** our **privileges include** free admission?

▶ **Exercise 1** Draw one line under each simple subject and two lines under the correct verb or helping verb in parentheses.

Beneath the water (was, <u>were</u>) two very hungry <u>sharks</u>.

1. (Is, Are) the doctor attending the sessions?

2. Under the tree (lurks, lurk) the hungry cats.

3. (Is, Are) electric vehicles becoming more popular?

4. There (goes, go) Oko's sisters.

5. (Does, Do) he live in the mountains?

6. Inside that house (was, were) the object of my affections.

7. (Was, Were) Jamal helping with the pamphlets?

8. Beside the fence (grows, grow) black raspberries.

9. Except for Tamiko, (has, have) all the others paid the fee?

10. Here (comes, come) one of the prettiest floats in the parade.

11. (Was, Were) the basket full of apples?

12. There (is, are) only fifty tickets left.

13. (Does, Do) that dish contain peanuts?

14. On top of the car (was, were) perched three pigeons.

15. (Was, Were) the three of them excused for the day?

16. In these humble surroundings (was, were) born our sixteenth president.

17. For the boat's deck (has, have) Benny used treated boards?

18. There (sits, sit) his forgotten papers.

19. Here (comes, come) your favorite part.

20. (Does, Do) the Joneses like golf?

▶ **Exercise 2** Place a check (✔) next to each sentence in which the subject and verb agree.

___✔___   Are there any leftovers from yesterday?

_____   **1.** Around the corner speeds the little terrier.

_____   **2.** There walks a proud woman.

_____   **3.** Is the teachers glad for the holiday break?

_____   **4.** Into the yard flies the hungry birds in search of a meal.

_____   **5.** Here is three copies of today's *Times*.

_____   **6.** Does Enrico have enough money for lunch?

_____   **7.** Above the staircase was the secret passageway.

_____   **8.** There is the misplaced textbook.

_____   **9.** Has any other activities generated this much enthusiasm?

_____   **10.** Were all of them in the car?

_____   **11.** Near the pond grows a weeping willow.

_____   **12.** There goes the dog in search of her missing puppy.

_____   **13.** Was the views spectacular from the bridge?

_____   **14.** On the fence post hangs several pieces of twine.

_____   **15.** Here comes the best musicians in the world.

_____   **16.** Do the players provide their own shoes?

_____   **17.** Around the city speeds the delivery trucks.

_____   **18.** There are many sources for the information you need.

Lesson 48
Agreement: Special Subjects

A **collective noun** names a group. It is considered singular when it refers to a group as a whole. It is plural when it refers to each member individually.

SINGULAR
The **flock is** ready to be sheared.
Our **team is** the best.

PLURAL
The **flock are** sheared one at a time.
Our **team are** all seniors.

Some nouns that end in *-s* are singular and take singular verbs.

Mumps is a painful childhood disease.

Other singular nouns ending in *-s* take plural verbs.

The scissors are on the shelf.

Many nouns ending in *-ics* may be singular or plural depending on their meaning.

Singular: **Politics is** a challenging field. (one type of field)
Plural: Her **politics are** confusing to many people. (more than one political standpoint)

Nouns of amount are singular when they refer to a total that is considered one unit. They are plural when they refer to a number of individual units.

Singular: Nine **dollars is** the price. (one unit)
Plural: Nine **dollars were found** under the bleachers. (nine individual units)

A title is always singular, even if it contains plural words.

Travels with Charley is an engrossing book.   "Cycles" is my latest poem.

▶ **Exercise 1 Underline the verb in parentheses that best completes each sentence.**

The faculty (is, <u>are</u>) required to return their keys on the last day of school.

1. The herd (passes, pass) through the orchard on the way to the pasture.

2. Mumps sometimes (requires, require) quarantine.

3. Eight dollars (is, are) too much to pay for that hat.

4. Statistics (is, are) a branch of mathematics.

5. The flock (is, are) preening their feathers.

6. Mark's favorite pants (is, are) faded blue denim.

7. Several hours (was, were) wasted while we waited for Tasha.

8. The economics of South Africa (is, are) closely tied to the diamond industry.

9. The team (wins, win) frequently.

10. The scissors (needs, need) sharpening.

11. Three months (is, are) the waiting period for a license.

12. Women's gymnastics (has, have) been dominated by adolescents for several years.

13. The class (is, are) finishing their assignments.

14. Measles (is, are) still a dangerous disease in many parts of the world.

15. Ten yards (is, are) the minimum distance for a first down.

16. Optics (deals, deal) with the changes and properties of light.

17. To keep communication lines open, the faculty (meets, meet) every week.

18. Checkers (is, are) her favorite board game.

19. Three weeks of concerts (has, have) been booked.

20. The acoustics (makes, make) this theater superior to the others.

21. Because of boredom, the audience (is, are) leaving a few at a time.

22. These binoculars (magnifies, magnify) by fifty times.

23. Six inches (makes, make) a big difference in a hemline.

24. Of all his educational pursuits, genetics (was, were) his favorite.

25. The readership of the *Times* (leans, lean) toward conservatism.

26. The United States (has, have) two major political parties.

27. Thirty days at hard labor (was, were) his sentence.

28. His tactics (proves, prove) he is an honorable man.

29. *Canterbury Tales* (describes, describe) life during the time of the Black Death.

30. Maria's glasses (contains, contain) bifocal lenses.

31. The Toronto Maple Leaf (is, are) the name of a National Hockey League.

32. Several species (was, were) on the endangered list.

33. Most of the national news (is, are) on the front page.

34. The remains of the collapsed buildings (was, were) buried.

35. Twenty-eight days (is, are) the average gestation period for a rabbit.

36. Mathematics (requires, require) an understanding of formulas.

37. Our squadron (practices, practice) flight patterns daily.

38. The committee (has, have) signed their names on the contract.

39. The Chicago Bulls (reworks, rework) their strategy daily.

40. The Corps of Engineers (builds, build) dams and bridges.

Grammar

Lesson 49
Agreement: Compound Subjects

A compound subject that is joined by *and* or *both ... and* is plural except when the joined words make a single unit or when they both refer to the same person or thing.

Singular: Cheese **and** crackers **is** a favorite snack. (compound subject as a single unit)
Her friend **and** mentor **believes** she will win the election. (*friend* and *mentor* are the same person)

Plural: The man **and** the woman **are** co-chairpersons.
Both Ali **and** Eduardo **enjoy** soccer.

When a compound subject is joined by *or* (or by *either...or*) or *nor* (or by *neither... nor*), the verb always agrees with the subject nearer the verb.

Singular: **Either** the coach **or** a player **is** commenting.
Singular: **Neither** the players **nor** the coach **is** commenting.
Plural: **Neither** the coach **nor** the players **are** commenting.

When *many a, each,* or *every* precedes a compound subject, the subject is singular.

Singular: **Many a** dog and cat **has** passed through the shelter.
Each boy and girl **has** a locker.
Every worker and supervisor **is** united on this issue.

▶ **Exercise 1 Complete each sentence by writing the correct present-tense form of the verb indicated.**

Both Anya and Kareem _____**like**_____ the new teacher. (like)

1. Horses, cattle, and sheep _____ on the lush pastures. (thrive)

2. My brother or my sister _____ the menus tonight. (choose)

3. Every plate and cup _____ a chip in it. (have)

4. Either the Hopkins family or the Ferreras _____ our house when we

are away. (watch)

5. Many a friend and traveler _____ passed this way. (have)

6. Neither Kathy nor her sisters _____ about the schedule change. (know)

7. Both Dad and Mom _____ peace and quiet on the weekends. (want)

8. Neither Mr. Watkins nor my neighbor _____ squash. (plant)

9. After the meeting, Antonio and Jalisa _____ riding home with me. (be)

10. Alberto or the twins _____ using the encyclopedia. (be)

11. Every gesture and movement _____ something specific. (mean)

12. Either flowers or candy _____ a nice gift. (make)

13. Many a man, woman, and child _____ hunger every day. (feel)

14. Neither the steers nor the cow _____ wandered far. (have)

15. Both robins and blue jays _____ my backyard. (frequent)

16. Neither my sister nor my brothers _____ willing to lend me five dollars. (be)

17. My friend and teacher _____ me on the piano. (accompany)

18. A Nintendo or a CD player _____ his Christmas list. (top)

19. Though I get very nervous on stage, every smile and nod _____ me confidence. (give)

20. Either a broken string or a faulty tuning peg _____ a violinist. (unnerve)

21. Many a teacher and student _____ through these halls every day. (pass)

22. Neither Blake nor I _____ to lose her as a friend. (want)

23. Both the newspaper and the radio station _____ plugging our spring concert. (be)

24. Neither Cooper nor Longfellow _____ the author of *The Scarlet Letter*. (be)

25. Before the commencement, the chorus and the orchestra _____ the national anthem. (perform)

26. Spaghetti or lasagna _____ first on my list of favorites. (rank)

27. Regardless of the cost, every letter and postcard _____ being answered. (be)

28. Either rain or snow _____ a slowdown on the freeway. (cause)

29. After the performance, each boy and girl _____ an autographed picture. (receive)

30. Neither Charlene nor Mia _____ well today. (feel)

31. Both pork and beef _____ high levels of fat. (have)

32. Neither the store nor the restaurant _____ until nine o'clock. (open)

33. Ham and eggs _____ a regular breakfast at our house. (be)

34. Mr. Caron or the boys _____ cleaning the garage. (be)

35. Every man and woman _____ your concerns. (share)

36. Either my sister or my parents _____ picking us up after the ballgame. (be)

37. Each player and cheerleader _____ for a victory tonight. (hope)

38. Before each performance, both the actors and the stagehands _____ the props carefully. (check)

Lesson 50
Agreement: Intervening Expressions

Expressions such as *accompanied by, as well as, in addition to, plus,* and *together with* have a meaning similar to *and* but do not form a compound subject. They are a part of a phrase that modifies the subject but does not change its number.

Max, accompanied by An-Li, **is** on his way to the fair.
The **governor,** as well as his press secretary, **is flying** to Washington.

▶ **Exercise 1** Underline the verb in parentheses that best completes each sentence.

Stamp collecting, enjoyed by teenagers as well as adults, (is, are) a popular hobby.

1. Oko, together with Toby and Cara, (enjoys, enjoy) the hobby of stamp collecting.

2. They, plus other members of their families, (spends, spend) a lot of time on their hobby.

3. Oko, along with her parents, (collects, collect) only Japanese stamps.

4. The beauty of stamps, plus the large variety, (is, are) the reason that Toby prefers a general collection.

5. Cara, as a horse-lover, (likes, like) to collect stamps depicting horses.

6. Cara, together with her two friends, (wants, want) to join a local philatelic society.

7. *Philately,* as most collectors know, (is, are) another name for stamp collecting.

8. Dabblers, along with serious collectors, (meets, meet) monthly to share their hobby with others who have similar interests.

9. The president, plus nine other members, (collects, collect) only stamps with unusual cancellations.

10. One member, along with his son, (has, have) a collection of nearly 50,000 stamps.

11. Locating sources for new stamps, along with trading or selling duplicates, (ranks, rank) as a practical benefit of membership.

12. Annually the society, together with local stamp clubs, (sponsors, sponsor) an exhibition of the members' collections.

13. Cara, along with Oko and Toby, (hopes, hope) to attend the show this year.

14. Every Saturday, Oko, accompanied by Toby, (visits, visit) the local stamp store.

15. The shop, besides stocking supplies and accessories, (carries, carry) a large selection of stamps.

Grammar

16. A set of six stamps from Zimbabwe, along with a single issue from Brazil, (has, have) captured

Toby's attention.

17. The set, plus some new display mounts, (costs, cost) about fifteen dollars.

18. A 1967 Japanese stamp, as well as a 1988 air mail stamp, (catches, catch) Oko's eye.

19. Many of Toby's friends, including Consuelo, (is, are) now asking for help in starting a

collection.

20. The great variety of subjects, together with the hobby's adaptability to individual interests,

(provides, provide) a lifelong pastime.

▶ **Exercise 2** **Complete each sentence by writing the correct present-tense form of the verb**
indicated.

Many other things, in addition to stamps, _____ are _____ fun to collect. (be)

1. Young children, as well as older children, often _____ collecting leaves or rocks. (like)

2. Having fun, plus putting things into categories, _____ children to learn. (help)

3. Many serious collectors, together with not-so-serious collectors, _____ things they

have a special interest in. (collect)

4. An interest in sports, accompanied by a love of baseball, _____ baseball card

collectors. (drive)

5. Ball caps, in addition to T-shirts, _____ the interest of other sports enthusiasts. (draw)

6. Animal figures, as well as stuffed animals, _____ the interest of some collectors.

(draw)

7. Many a stuffed rabbit, together with stuffed bears and pigs, _____ become part of a

collection. (have)

8. Something a person likes to do, such as riding horses or listening to music, often _____

interest in collecting. (spark)

9. Many people who like music, in addition to going to concerts, _____ autographs. (collect)

10. A special poster, together with old photos, _____ interesting to someone who likes

old movies. (be)

11. Much of the excitement, as well as the fun, _____ from the discovery of a new item.

(come)

12. Something rare, plus something unusual, _____ most collectors. (excite)

Lesson 51
Agreement: Indefinite Pronouns as Subjects

When an indefinite pronoun is used as a subject, its verb must agree with it in number. Indefinite pronouns can be grouped into three categories.

INDEFINITE PRONOUNS

ALWAYS SINGULAR: *each, anything, nothing, everything, one, something, everyone, either, someone, anyone, no one, nobody, everybody, neither, somebody, anybody*

Examples: After the inspection, **everything was** in its place.
   No one wants to go first.

ALWAYS PLURAL: *several, many, few, both*

Examples: **Few are** ready for the examination.
   Several of the townspeople **are planning** to attend.

SINGULAR OR PLURAL: *some, most, all, none, any*

Examples: **Most** of the team **is** healthy. (*Most* refers to *team,* which is singular.)
   Most of the sophomores **attend** the class meeting. (*Most* refers to *sophomores,* which is plural.)

▶ **Exercise 1** Complete each sentence by writing the correct present-tense form of the verb indicated.

A few of my friends _____ like _____ anchovies. (like)

1. Some of the puppies _____ constantly. (whine)

2. Everybody in the two towns _____ about the rivalry. (know)

3. Somebody in the bleachers _____ constantly. (scream)

4. Neither of the boys _____ the key to the house. (have)

5. Most of the band _____ regularly. (practice)

6. Everybody in the auditorium _____ patiently for the opening curtain. (wait)

7. Several of my friends _____ a computer with ease. (operate)

8. During a test, nobody _____ the room. (leave)

9. All of the blackberries _____ picked. (be)

10. No one _____ choosing him as captain. (regret)

11. _____ anyone show signs of fatigue? (do)

12. Someone with very large feet _____ through the flower bed. (walk)

13. Because information is lacking, none of the committee _____ to vote on the issue today. (want)

14. No matter what Chandra thinks, either of the candidates _____ qualified. (be)

15. Everyone for miles around _____ in the Oktoberfest. (participate)

16. Something about that person _____ Tia to be suspicious. (cause)

17. If you need more information, any of the clerks _____ the expertise to help you. (have)

18. One of the cockatiels _____ twice every year. (molt)

19. We should be there on time, if everything _____ well. (go)

20. Since the tornado, many people _____ thunderstorms. (fear)

21. After lunch, all of the class _____ sleepy. (feel)

22. Nothing about the situation _____ a sense of security. (foster)

23. Anything that is broken _____ our immediate attention. (need)

24. During the concert, each of the four Garcias _____ a solo. (sing)

25. Most of the neighbors _____ spending time together. (enjoy)

26. Any of the leftover food _____ stored in the refrigerator. (be)

27. Because we are so busy, no one _____ a break. (take)

28. Nobody _____ that kind of treatment. (expect)

29. After the siren sounds, all of the force _____ on alert. (be)

30. Due to all the changes, few of the girls _____ confident about the contest. (feel)

31. None of the class _____ a perfect attendance record. (maintain)

32. Either of those necklaces _____ this outfit. (match)

33. None of the disks _____ formatting. (require)

34. Of the two chapters, neither _____ difficult material. (contain)

35. Once the schedule is set, both of the part-timers _____ to be on time. (try)

36. Few of the players _____ a beard. (wear)

37. Any of the squad _____ fully certified in first aid. (be)

38. Some of the drivers _____ the yellow flashing light. (ignore)

39. Within our class, everyone _____ the new teacher. (like)

40. Several of the musicians _____ in a local band. (play)

☑ Unit 7 **Review**

▶ **Exercise 1** Underline the verb in parentheses that best completes each sentence.

This brick sidewalk (<u>needs</u>, need) repair.

1. Our principal (sings, sing) in a barbershop quartet.

2. April showers (rains, rain) steadily but softly.

3. The waves (crashes, crash) rhythmically against the giant rock close to the beach.

4. (Does, Do) we need to pack that much for a weekend trip?

5. Aunt Carla (writes, write) that she is coming to visit this summer.

6. Jamal and Frank (races, race) every day to the bus stop.

7. The limbs of the old oak tree (sways, sway) in the breeze.

8. Somebody (needs, need) to fix this step before an accident occurs.

9. I hope that our school (wins, win) the big game this year!

10. Smells of hot coals and cooking beef (fills, fill) the backyard.

11. Chocolate candies with fruit fillings (was, were) the dessert of choice for visitors at the chocolate festival.

12. Martin's binoculars (is, are) what we need.

13. There (is, are) many reasons we need today off.

14. Charles (tells, tell) funny stories.

15. Can members of the flag corps (rides, ride) on the bus with the football team?

16. The first item on Julie's shopping list (was, were) socks.

17. These scissors (cuts, cut) through every kind of material.

18. Many of this year's participants (was, were) in last year's tournament, too.

19. Bill and Sancho (thinks, think) their classmates overemphasize weight lifting.

20. Few (argues, argue) as well as Fred, the president of the Debate Club.

21. In the trunk there (is, are) a spare tire.

22. The street car (is, are) late this morning.

23. Our yard (becomes, become) bigger every time I mow it!

24. The moon (seems, seem) exceptionally bright tonight.

Cumulative Review: Units 1–7

▶ **Exercise 1** Draw one line under each compound subject and two lines under each compound predicate. Write *C* in the blank if the conjunction in parentheses is a coordinating conjunction. Write *S* if it is a subordinating conjunction.

___C___   Jennifer (or) Pedro will bring the refreshments.

_____ **1.** The dog (and) the cat belong to Mr. Spinoza.

_____ **2.** Cara will remain happy (as long as) she is treated with respect.

_____ **3.** Dad and Mom were stranded (because) my brother brought the car home late.

_____ **4.** The stag shook his antlers (and) pawed the ground.

_____ **5.** The car looks beautiful (since) it has been waxed.

_____ **6.** The red shoes were available, (but) the black ones were out of stock.

_____ **7.** Mr. Jefferson, (though) he wanted to be present, had to decline the invitation.

_____ **8.** Alice practiced her clarinet (and) watched television.

_____ **9.** I don't know if Ken went home (or) if he went to practice.

_____ **10.** Getting up early (so that) I would be prepared gave me a head start on the others.

_____ **11.** Angie bought a new notebook (before) she went to class.

_____ **12.** Sitting on the front porch (and) reading the newspaper took up the whole morning.

_____ **13.** I usually collapse on the couch (when) I get home from practice.

_____ **14.** The pup looked at me (as if) it were guilty of something.

_____ **15.** The neighbors own a Ford (and) a Cadillac.

_____ **16.** Brown trout will study the bait (before) they eat it.

_____ **17.** Felipe, (if) he gets the job, will work twelve hours a week and earn five dollars an hour.

_____ **18.** The sparrows were feeding in the backyard, (but) the blue jay drove them off.

_____ **19.** I must watch my baby brother (until) my mother returns.

_____ **20.** The players don't want sympathy (or) pity.

▶ **Exercise 2** Write *N* in the blank if the clause in italics is used as a noun, *adj.* if it is used as an adjective, or *adv.* if it is used as an adverb.

___adj.___   The shed *where I keep my motorbike* belongs to my uncle.

_____ **1.** Alonzo, *who is making funny faces,* is my little brother.

_____ **2.** Arriving home, I saw the tree *that you told me about.*

Grammar

_____ 3. The cat looked *as if it had fallen into water.*

_____ 4. Did the reporter say *why the road has been closed?*

_____ 5. Who was the player *that fumbled the ball?*

_____ 6. Ms. Conrad whispered *so that no one else could hear.*

_____ 7. Jamal can win the race *if he concentrates on pacing himself.*

_____ 8. Ben Franklin first said *that a penny saved is a penny earned.*

_____ 9. Cassandra rested *while she was recuperating from a cold.*

_____ 10. Do you have the manual *that came with the television set?*

_____ 11. Carol gasped *when the race car crashed.*

_____ 12. The medal will be awarded to the runner *who finishes first.*

_____ 13. This is the bracelet *that Connie gave me for Christmas.*

_____ 14. Is this the horse *that shies at passing cars?*

_____ 15. *That the water is undrinkable* is an established fact.

_____ 16. *So that I would be surprised,* Melinda kept the party a secret.

_____ 17. The brook *that runs near the woods* is on our property.

_____ 18. Aunt Rita told us *that José got home last night.*

_____ 19. The snowbank, *which was four feet high,* stopped all traffic.

_____ 20. Orville shouted at me *as loud as he could.*

▶ **Exercise 3 Underline the verb in parentheses that best completes each sentence.**

The squadron (is, <u>are</u>) taking their vacations at the same time.

1. The caretaker of the palace grounds (do, does) a splendid job.

2. The pile of leaves (was, were) an eyesore.

3. In the train station (sit, sits) three weary travelers.

4. Phonics (is, are) a method of teaching reading.

5. Seven dollars (is, are) too much to pay for that shirt.

6. Mike's politics (is, are) rather conservative.

7. Neither the twins nor Alberto (has, have) enough money for lunch.

8. Somebody (get, gets) all the lucky breaks.

9. The mechanics from the garage (charge, charges) reasonable rates.

10. (Do, Does) the Tofts know the score?

11. Most of the team (respects, respect) the opponents' skills.

12. The stereo, as well as both radios, (needs, need) repair.

13. The Templetons of Barkersville (visits, visit) us every spring.

14. Spruce trees or oak trees (grow, grows) best in this type of climate.

15. Nina and An-Li (miss, misses) the point completely.

16. The first signs of morning (is, are) a whistling tea kettle and the smell of bacon frying.

17. Snow or heavy rains (is, are) expected tonight.

18. No one in the group (keeps, keep) track of their expenses.

19. First aid, plus CPR training, (top, tops) the agenda for Wednesday.

20. *Antlers by the Thousands* (describe, describes) the life cycle of reindeer.

21. Measles (is, are) a common childhood disease.

22. This tape and CD (belongs, belong) to Sook.

23. The orchestra (was, were) ready for the overture.

24. Neither books nor a magazine (is, are) left on the shelf.

25. Some of the clouds (has, have) scattered.

26. Both of them (is, are) late.

27. Either bike (is, are) a good buy.

28. Everybody in the chorus (is, are) on time for practice.

29. Most of my cousins (lives, live) in Boston.

30. Several of the videos (is, are) on sale.

31. Many of his jokes (is, are) old.

32. Everybody (was, were) tired after the run.

33. Few of the flowers (looks, look) ready to bloom.

34. None of it (is, are) useful.

35. There (goes, go) my two best friends.

36. Both of them (arrives, arrive) late all the time.

37. Either bike (pedals, pedal) equally well.

38. Everybody in the chorus (sings, sing) well.

Unit 8: Using Pronouns Correctly

Lesson 52

Personal Pronouns: Case

Pronouns that refer to persons or things are called **personal pronouns**. Personal pronouns have three cases, or forms, called nominative, objective, and possessive. The case of a personal pronoun depends on the pronoun's function in the sentence.

CASE	SINGULAR	PLURAL	FUNCTION IN SENTENCE
Nominative	I, you, she, he, it	we, you, they	subject or predicate nominative
Objective	me, you, her, him, it	us, you, them	direct object, indirect object, or object of preposition
Possessive	my, mine, your, yours, her, hers, his, its	our, ours, your, yours, their, theirs	replacement for possessive noun(s)

Use the **nominative case** for a personal pronoun in a compound subject.

Ricardo and **she** are taking the advanced placement test.

Use the **objective case** for a personal pronoun in a compound object.

The guide handed the questionnaire to Mom and **me**.

In formal writing, after a form of the linking verb *be,* use the nominative case. People often use the objective case, however, in informal writing and speaking.

The person at the door was **he**.   The best player is **I**.

Use **possessive pronouns** to indicate ownership and before gerunds (-*ing* forms used as nouns). Do not spell possessive pronouns with apostrophes.

His playing is getting better.   That canoe is **theirs**.

▶ **Exercise 1** Underline the pronoun in parentheses that best completes each sentence.

If your tent is leaking, you can sleep in (our's, <u>ours</u>).

1. Lina and (she, her) expect to hear from the representative very soon.

2. Dell's parents are quite pleased about (him, his) attending summer school.

3. Address your complaints to Mr. Bowles and (they, them).

4. Lupe believes that pile of trash is (theirs, their's).

5. The person on the phone is (he, him).

6. Thomas, Tran, and (I, me) are going to represent the school at the conference.

7. In spite of (it's, its) injured beak, the seagull was able to feed itself.

8. The heaviest responsibility for the project fell on Sarah and (she, her).

9. Anyone interested in working on the scrap paper drive should contact Gina or (I, me).

10. (Me, My) singing finally put the baby to sleep.

11. The Red Raiders, the Yellow Jackets, and (they, them) are tied for second place in the league.

12. It looks as though the leaders after the first round will be Forrest and (she, her).

13. Frederick Douglass and (him, he) are two well-known African American leaders of the last century.

14. I imagine your parents are happy about (you, your) practicing for the recital.

15. The man standing between my sister and (I, me) is Uncle Drake.

16. Peter and (she, her) will perform a scene from *Our Town* for the class.

17. Ask Josh about (his, him) joining the Spanish Club.

18. David and Jacob turned the mountain bike on (it's, its) side to replace the chain.

19. Moira and (he, him) have been researching the Underground Railroad for their presentation.

20. Are you certain that book is (your's, yours)?

21. The others in the group were getting a little tired of (him, his) joking and teasing.

22. There's no doubt the championship is (their's, theirs).

23. Tonya ran to pick up the phone, certain it would be for (she, her).

24. The teachers in charge of the video yearbook are Ms. Ramey and (he, him).

25. Is that prize-winning steer (your's, yours)?

26. I hope you don't mind (us, our) laughing so hard at the movie, but it's awfully funny.

27. What really concerns John and (I, me) is the distance to the cabin.

28. Danielle is convinced the bracelet in the school Lost and Found is (her's, hers).

29. Michael, Brian, and (we, us) are planning an Open House after the game.

30. The coach tried to encourage (them, their) running to and from school every day.

31. The gloves on the radiator by the art room are (her's, hers).

32. Do you and (her, she) want to meet us after school by the chemistry lab?

33. The plot of the movie revolved around the wolves and (he, him).

34. That blue truck with the white cap is (ours, our's).

Lesson 53
Pronouns with and as Appositives; After *Than* and *As*

Use the nominative case for a pronoun that is in apposition to a subject or a predicate nominative.

The representatives, **Sherlyn** and **he,** attended the meeting. (*Representatives* is the subject.)

The only other people there were teachers, **Mr. Blaine** and **she.** (*Teachers* is the predicate nominative.)

Use the objective case for a pronoun that is in apposition to a direct object, an indirect object, or an object of a preposition.

The audience applauded the stars of the show, **Armando** and **her.** (*Stars* is a direct object.)

Aunt Rachel sent her nieces, **Sonia** and **me,** the book. (*Nieces* is an indirect object.)

The warning must have been meant for both groups, **them** and **us.** (*Groups* is an object of the preposition *for.*)

When a pronoun is followed by an appositive, choose the case of the pronoun that would be correct if the appositive were omitted.

We actors have fun at the Drama Club rehearsals. (*We* instead of *us* is the correct form because *we* is the subject of the sentence.)

Uncle Rex sent the package to **us nephews.** (*Us* instead of *we* is the correct form because *us* is the object of the preposition *to.*)

In incomplete adverb clauses using *than* and *as,* choose the case of the pronoun that you would use if the missing words were present.

Amanda finished her sundae more quickly than **she.** (The nominative pronoun *she* is the subject of the incomplete adverb clause *than she finished her sundae.*)

The comedy amused Robert and Boyd as much as **him.** (The objective pronoun *him* is the direct object of the incomplete adverb clause *as much as it amused him.*)

▶ **Exercise 1** **Underline the correct pronoun. Identify the case by writing *nom.* (nominative) or *obj.* (objective) in the blank.**

_**obj.**___ Mom offered the tickets to her friends, Sally and (<u>her</u>, she).

_____ **1.** Pablo saw two people, Anita and (I, me), at the movies.

_____ **2.** We spoke to the artists, Mr. Santiago and (him, he), about their work.

_____ **3.** Tell the co-captains, Robin and (she, her), what you learned about the equipment.

_____ **4.** Hakim did more work for the recycling project than (her, she).

_____ **5.** (Us, We) Salazar sisters always stick together when things get tough!

_____ 6. The two girls, Becca and (she, her), asked if they could give their presentation first.

_____ 7. Stand between your friends, David and (him, he).

_____ 8. Please call one of the organizers, Sandra or (I, me), if you won't be able to come to the pizza party.

_____ 9. The man's constant talking during the movie bothered everyone else as much as (me, I).

_____ 10. The magazine story was about the young scientists who made the discovery, Marcus Hamilton and (they, them).

_____ 11. The winners of the award are the best players on the volleyball team, Nikki and (her, she).

_____ 12. The boy cheerleaders lifted the girls, Darlene, Tracey, and (I, me), into the air.

_____ 13. Both of the musicians, Yuri and (he, him), received the highest marks at the district competition.

_____ 14. The lawyer offered his clients, Ms. Constable and (her, she), some useful advice about their legal problem.

_____ 15. The subjects of the book were two great photographers, Matthew Brady and (he, him).

_____ 16. At the assembly be sure to sit with (we, us) drama club members.

_____ 17. Sandra sent cards to her favorite teachers, Ms. Fukuzawa and (he, him).

_____ 18. The gorilla watched the zoo visitors, (we, us), carefully.

_____ 19. Club members, Carlos, Jalen, and (he, him) share many of the same interests.

_____ 20. Jay's teasing bothers his friends, Rey and (I, me).

_____ 21. The president and vice president of the class for next year will be two of my friends, Shawn and (she, her).

_____ 22. The zookeeper's presentation about carnivores impressed me as much as (them, they).

_____ 23. Bring the typists, Brian and (he, him), your manuscript as soon as you can.

_____ 24. The detective noticed the strangers, the tall one and (he, him), standing by the door ready to run away.

_____ 25. The people standing by the popcorn machine are Michael's cousins, Lillian, Whitney, and (him, he).

_____ 26. The senators from our state, Mr. Ortiz and (her, she), will be appearing together on election night.

Lesson 54
Who and *Whom* in Questions and Subordinate Clauses

Use the nominative pronoun *who* for subjects of sentences and clauses.

Who answered the door? (*Who* is the subject.)

Tell me **who** will give the speech. (*Who* is the subject of the noun clause *who will give the speech.*)

The person **who** took the cupcake ran out the back door. (*Who* is the subject of the adjective clause *who took the cupcake.*)

Use the objective pronoun *whom* for the direct or indirect object of a verb or verbal or for the object of a preposition.

To **whom** are you writing? (*Whom* is the object of the preposition *To.*)

Mr. Kim wondered **whom** we had seen at the library. (*Whom* is the direct object of the verb *had seen* in the noun clause *whom we had seen at the library.*)

Joaquin wondered to **whom** the letter was addressed. (*Whom* is the object of the preposition *to* in the noun clause *to whom the letter was addressed.*)

▶ **Exercise 1** **Complete each sentence by adding *who* or *whom,* whichever is correct.**

Do you know anyone _____who_____ has traveled around the world?

1. _____ hasn't dreamed of traveling around the world?

2. Is there anyone to _____ the life of a traveler doesn't sound appealing?

3. A woman about _____ few people have heard made this dream come true.

4. Ida Pfeiffer, _____ many consider to have been the first female professional traveler, was born in Vienna, Austria, in 1797.

5. The few women of her time _____ did travel were usually wives of diplomats or missionaries.

6. The thought of an ordinary woman _____ simply went wherever she wanted to go was preposterous!

7. Ida Pfeiffer, _____ grew up in a large family with six brothers, was brave and determined from the very beginning.

8. Ida's father, _____ had progressive ideas for his time, felt she should receive the same education as her brothers.

9. Ida, to _____ the long petticoats and skirts that girls wore were a bother, often preferred boys' trousers.

10. When she was twenty-two, Ida married a man _____ was much older than she.

11. Her husband, _____ was a government official, lost his job because of political tensions.

Grammar

12. Ida and her husband, _____ moved to a small town, separated in 1835.

13. _____ could have guessed what lay in store for this amazing woman?

14. Her friends, to _____ she confided her plans, were shocked.

15. They wondered _____ she thought she was to harbor such ambitions!

16. Ida, _____ had conceived a plan to visit the Holy Land, described her trip to friends.

17. Most people _____ she told agreed that a religious trip was less scandalous for a single woman.

18. However, Ida, _____ kept quiet about her other plans, was also heading to Egypt.

19. _____ among her friends didn't shake their heads when she claimed, "Privation and discomfort had no terrors for me"?

20. Ida, _____ knew that Egypt was a dangerous place, made out her will before she left.

21. Many travelers _____ had explored Egypt had never returned.

22. Ida, _____ spent nine months on her first voyage, did return.

23. Her adventures included an argument with a camel driver _____ she was certain had cheated her.

24. Friends _____ read the diary she kept urged her to publish it.

25. When Ida, _____ sold her book to a publisher in 1846, received money, she embarked on a second trip to Iceland.

26. No one knows from _____ Ida got her next idea for a trip.

27. Ida, _____ was now becoming well known as a traveler, set sail for South America in 1846, the first stop on her round-the-world trip.

28. Ida, _____ carried a pair of pistols for protection, went from South America to China, India, and the Middle East.

29. Those _____ read her book *A Lady's Voyage Around the World* learned of her fearless attitude and unquenchable curiosity.

30. Readers with _____ she shared her amazing journeys admired her sense of adventure, even if they did not dare duplicate her feats.

▶ **Writing Link** **Write a brief paragraph about someone you know who has traveled to another state or country. Use *who* or *whom* in at least two of your sentences.**

_____

_____

_____

_____

Lesson 55
Pronoun-Antecedent Agreement: Number and Gender

Grammar

An **antecedent** is the word or group of words to which a pronoun refers or that a pronoun replaces. A pronoun must agree with its antecedent in number (singular or plural) and gender (masculine, feminine, or neuter).

Edna O'Brien published **her** book *The Lonely Girl* in 1962. (singular feminine pronoun)

Gabriel García Marquéz published **his** novel *Love in the Time of Cholera* in 1985. (singular masculine pronoun)

Edna O'Brien and **Gabriel García Marquéz** have sold many copies of **their** books in the United States. (plural pronoun)

The old saying about never judging a **book** by **its** cover contains a lot of truth! (singular neuter pronoun)

▶ **Exercise 1** Complete each sentence by adding a personal pronoun that agrees with the antecedent. Underline the antecedent.

<u>Cats</u> often give birth to _____**their**_____ kittens in secluded places.

1. Did your grandparents tell you all about _____ trip to Hawaii?

2. A girl on the soccer team has to buy _____ own soccer shoes.

3. The large sugar maple in the park by the school lost one of _____ limbs in the storm last night.

4. Soldiers are expected to obey _____ commanding officer's orders.

5. My father is going to _____ twenty-fifth high school reunion this Saturday.

6. Beavers and buffalo were hunted for _____ pelts in the last century.

7. A student in Ms. Archibald's class has to be ready to do _____ best work.

8. My dog Ellie takes very good care of _____ six new puppies.

9. This computer has something wrong with _____ disk drive.

10. Uncle Dwight told us about _____ tour of duty in Vietnam.

11. Ms. Sunjoo said you could take _____ aerobic exercise class.

12. The members of the Chess Club want to bring _____ own chess boards and pieces.

13. A person who plans to join the military has to make sure _____ grades are good.

14. A police officer must maintain _____ weight at a certain level.

15. Are Jon and Kyle going to give _____ multimedia presentation today?

16. Ask your mother if she'll let you borrow _____ tennis racquet.

17. Do you think this robot can do _____ job as well as a person?

18. If a singer wants to try out for the choir, _____ name has to be on the sign-up sheet by this afternoon.

19. A professional football player spends much of _____ time in training.

20. Our next-door neighbors asked me to water _____ plants while they are in Chicago.

21. The people who live in that house spend a lot of time working in _____ garden.

22. Did you tell me that Tina had _____ job application accepted?

23. Walnut is a favorite wood, prized for _____ deep brown color.

24. Evergreens don't lose _____ leaves in the fall the way deciduous trees do.

25. Susan's father broke _____ arm playing rugby.

26. A professional dancer has to work very hard on _____ flexibility and strength.

27. Don't let the children lose _____ gloves at the playground.

28. The mother bird returned to _____ nest with a fat worm.

29. Allan and Margaret asked if I had seen _____ paintings in the art show.

30. Janice's car hit a pothole in the road and lost _____ muffler.

31. My little sister Louisa took _____ first step on my birthday.

32. The race cars revved _____ engines at the starting line.

33. Mr. Lopez and Ms. Tyler take what _____ students say very seriously.

34. We wanted to play soccer on Saturday, but the ball had lost all _____ air.

35. The new blouse that we bought for Cassandra was _____ favorite color.

36. Paula and Jerome were looking for new homes for _____ pets.

37. We enjoyed the movie you recommended, but we had trouble understanding _____ plot.

38. My stepfather likes _____ new job at the branch bank.

39. Australia is famous for _____ beautiful coral reefs and unusual animals.

40. Can you return the jacket and hat to _____ rightful owner?

Lesson 56
Pronoun-Antecedent Agreement: Person

Grammar

A pronoun must agree in person with its antecedent. When a pronoun has another pronoun as its antecedent, the two pronouns should agree in person. Be sure not to refer to an antecedent in the third person by using the second-person pronoun *you*. Use either an appropriate third-person pronoun or a suitable noun.

POOR   Sal and Jarrod are going to a lake where **you** can catch **your** limit of bass.
BETTER   Sal and Jarrod are going to a lake where **they** can catch **their** limit of bass.

▶ **Exercise 1** **Complete each sentence with the correct personal pronoun.**

Dawn carefully hung _____**her**_____ new jacket in the closet.

1. Two of the most famous American travelers were Fanny Bullock Workman and _____ husband William Workman.

2. For twenty-five years they traveled together, _____ relationship based on equality.

3. Fanny was born into a well-to-do family in Massachusetts, where _____ father was governor.

4. In 1881 Fanny Bullock met _____ partner for life and married the doctor William Workman.

5. Several years later Dr. Workman decided to give up _____ medical practice because of his poor health.

6. You should hope that _____ health is as "poor" as Dr. Workman's.

7. He lived for another forty-eight years after _____ retirement!

8. After William and Fanny moved to Germany, _____ soon took up an active outdoor life.

9. The Bullocks spent some of _____ time mountain climbing in Norway and Sweden.

10. Fanny showed off _____ skills when she became one of the first women to climb the Matterhorn in Switzerland.

11. Soon the Workmans were ready to abandon _____ ordinary life.

12. Placing their daughter Rachel in a boarding school, _____ began a bicycle trip through North Africa and Spain.

13. At about this time in _____ life, Fanny became involved in women's rights issues.

14. Her own life, _____ believed, proved that women were just as capable as men.

15. On their next trip, _____ took their bicycles to India, Burma, Java, Cambodia, and Sri Lanka, then known as Ceylon.

16. In northern India they saw the Himalayan Mountains, with _____ majestic peaks and inaccessible villages.

17. Setting aside their bicycles, the Workmans decided to take up mountaineering in the

    Himalayan Range and _____ companion, the Karakoram Range.

18. Fanny's desire to accomplish things no woman ever had, led _____ to climb Mt. Koser Gunge, setting a world record for women mountaineers.

19. Fanny continued to set climbing records throughout _____ life.

20. William Workman was always supportive of Fanny's exploits and praised _____ wife for her "courage, endurance, and enthusiasm."

▶ **Exercise 2** Underline each personal pronoun and its antecedent.

    I am excited about taking <u>my</u> first trip to New York.

1. Traveling is fun and interesting, but it can also be quite exhausting.

2. When Randall and I visited New York City, we must have walked twenty miles!

3. When Randall packed for the trip, he only put in one pair of shoes.

4. I could have used at least three pairs during my trip!

5. When my parents were in college, they went on backpacking trips.

6. Mom and Dad carried up to fifty pounds in their packs.

7. Many travelers might choose bicycling as one of their favorite methods of transportation.

8. A touring bike has its handlebars twisted low, away from the rider.

9. Handlebars in this shape help a rider use his or her energy more efficiently.

10. The bicycles the Workmans rode across North Africa, however, were very different from their

    modern counterparts.

11. Where would you like to go on your dream trip?

12. I am interested in seeing China, where my parents were born.

13. When my grandfather retired, he took a trip to Hawaii with a friend.

14. Hawaii, with its warm climate, fascinating culture, and gorgeous scenery, is a favorite tourist

    destination.

15. I also find that Alaska appeals to me very much.

16. You can make your way up the western coast of Canada on a boat.

Lesson 57

Pronoun-Antecedent Agreement: Indefinite Pronoun Antecedents

In general, use a **singular personal pronoun** when the antecedent is a singular indefinite pronoun such as *anybody, anyone, anything, each, either, everybody, everyone, everything, much, neither, nobody, no one, nothing, one, other, somebody, someone,* or *something.*

Neither of the girls gave **her** report on Tuesday.

Use a **plural personal pronoun** when the antecedent is a plural indefinite pronoun like *several, both, few,* and *many.*

Both of the boys presented **their** essays on Friday.

Some **indefinite pronouns**, such as *all, any, enough, more, most, none, plenty,* and *some,* can be singular or plural depending on the sentence.

Most of the tigers in the exhibit had finished **their** meals.
Most of the cornmeal had spilled out of **its** box.

▶ **Exercise 1** Complete each sentence by inserting a personal pronoun that agrees with the antecedent. Underline the indefinite pronoun antecedent.

<u>Each</u> of the tigers looked at ease in _____ its _____ cage.

1. Does anyone in the Computer Club have _____ own computer?

2. All of the players on the college basketball team earned _____ degrees.

3. Something has left _____ scent on the tent, and I think it might be a skunk!

4. Someone made a big mistake, and I hope _____ corrects it right away.

5. If there is any of that juice left in the container, could you please drink _____?

6. Only a few of the soldiers returned from _____ attack on the fort.

7. All of the water had leaked out of _____ container.

8. Neither of the pine trees reached _____ full height.

9. No one should feel that _____ work is finished until the clean-up is complete.

10. If enough of the citizens cast _____ votes for her, she will win the election.

11. If everyone keeps _____ composure, I'm sure we can resolve this difficult situation.

12. Most of the people in the community lost _____ homes in the disastrous flooding.

13. Either of the cars seems to be well worth _____ price.

14. I hope everybody remembers to take _____ geometry book to class.

15. Both of the orangutans seem to have recovered from _____ illness.

16. Several of the students who took the test earned _____ best grades ever.

17. Everybody on the team agreed to do _____ best.

18. Each of the attendees at the conference received _____ copy of the speaker's book.

19. If anybody would like to help with the homecoming committee, _____ should

contact the chairperson.

20. Neither of the boys brought _____ calculator to school.

▶ **Exercise 2** Place a check (✔) beside each sentence in which the pronoun and antecedent
are in agreement.

_____   Everybody needs to bring their softball glove to practice.

_____ **1.** Several of the play's cast members have performed their roles before.

_____ **2.** Judith couldn't find anyone who would finish their homework early and then go

play tennis.

_____ **3.** One of the churches in the village lost its steeple in the windstorm.

_____ **4.** Somebody wrote their name on the sign-up sheet without writing a telephone number.

_____ **5.** Few of the people knew how much they had done to improve the situation.

_____ **6.** Dad and Mom were sure we had plenty of gas in the car, but we ran out of them near

El Paso.

_____ **7.** Both Paul and Lawrence hoped they would be considered for the role.

_____ **8.** Nobody should exit a computer file without saving, unless they want to risk losing

their work.

_____ **9.** Neither of the teachers could recall anything so odd ever happening in her class.

_____ **10.** Much of this newly painted fence has fingerprints on them.

_____ **11.** There was no one left in the cafeteria to finish their meal.

_____ **12.** Enough of the cake mix had gotten wet to make it unusable.

_____ **13.** Every book by that author has a picture of white horses on their cover.

_____ **14.** Everybody will just have to wait their turn!

_____ **15.** Would either of the foreign exchange students please raise their hand?

_____ **16.** Each of the tapirs at the zoo put their nose in the air and sniffed.

Lesson 58
Clear Pronoun Reference

Make sure that the antecedent of a pronoun is clear and that a pronoun cannot possibly refer to more than one antecedent. Do not use the pronouns *this, that, which,* or *it* without a clearly stated antecedent.

VAGUE   Todd is a good writer, and **that** was something that he was proud of.
CLEAR   Todd is a good writer, and **his writing ability** was something he was proud of.

If a pronoun seems to refer to more than one antecedent, either reword the sentence to make the antecedent clear or eliminate the pronoun.

VAGUE   After the planes unloaded the passengers, **they** left the terminal.
CLEAR   After **they** were unloaded from the plane, the passengers left the terminal.

Avoid the indefinite use of the pronouns *you* and *they*.

VAGUE   At most zoos, **they** feed the animals tons of fresh vegetables.
CLEAR   At most zoos, the zookeepers feed the animals tons of fresh vegetables.

▶ **Exercise 1 Replace the italicized pronoun in each sentence with a word or phrase that makes the meaning more clear.**

Joon does sit-ups every day because *it* is important to her.

staying healthy _____

1. When the trees are full of apples, *they* begin falling to the ground.

_____

2. In some countries *they* do not allow people to own guns.

_____

3. Indira's cat had died, and *it* showed in her expression.

_____

4. When Craig opened the door to the cage, *he* got away.

_____

5. The Golden Bears met the Yellow Jackets in the first game, and *they* won easily.

_____

6. He said he was sorry about the accident, but *it* was too late.

_____

7. She opened the windows and yelled for help, and *that* made the fire spread.

_____

8. When the sun goes behind the clouds, *it* gets dark.

_____

9. On the radio *they* said to leave your home and move to higher ground.

_____

10. Meryl wants to go to college like her sister, because *that* can help you get a good job.

_____

11. Because of the new law, *you* can't construct a building without a permit.

_____

12. If you expect to win, you need to enter before *it* is over.

_____

13. Both computers had color graphics, and *they* were state-of-the-art.

_____

14. Amir wants to be a photographer because he likes *it*.

_____

15. In some restaurants *they* won't bring the check unless you ask.

_____

16. Michael was a wonderful person and artist, and *this* was obvious when you saw his paintings.

_____

17. She wanted to see her favorite musician, but *it* seemed hopeless.

_____

18. When poachers in Africa hunt elephants, *they* are slaughtered for their ivory.

_____

19. Kim thought about getting a job because *it* would help her pay her expenses.

_____

20. When traveling in space, *you* weigh less because of a lack of gravity.

_____

✓ Unit 8 Review

▶ **Exercise 1** Underline the pronoun in parentheses that correctly completes each sentence.

The two best bowlers in my class, Michael and (<u>he</u>, him), tied for the first place trophy.

1. When Alena and (I, me) finished our science project, we had a great feeling of accomplishment.

2. My grandmother is a person for (who, whom) I would do anything.

3. Gymnasts have to spend a lot of time working on (his, their) balance and coordination.

4. While waiting for the bus, I saw your friends, Jamal and (she, her).

5. All of the choir members had to prepare (his, their) audition numbers.

6. Most of the critics felt that the female lead in the play did a better acting job than (he, him).

7. The tomato, because of (its, their) versatility, is found in cuisines from many different parts of the world.

8. The president of the Drama Club reminded everyone to bring (his, their) contribution to the bake sale.

9. In some European countries, (they, students) go to school on Saturday mornings.

10. At summer camp last year, (he, him) and his cabinmates went fishing almost every day.

11. Excuse me, could you tell us (who, whom) to contact about swimming pool memberships?

12. Neither of the puppies would venture far away from (its, their) mother.

13. The poem made a greater impression on Rose than (I, me).

14. Some of the musicians had neglected to learn (her, their) parts by heart.

15. (Who, Whom) is going to be the first to volunteer for the decorations committee?

16. Someone hiking for the first time in the White Mountains has to watch out for (herself, themselves).

17. The assistant principal congratulated (we, us) sophomores on our homecoming float.

18. Sachi and Shannon went to a music store where (you, they) could find the new CD.

19. (Who, Whom) did Thomas say won first prize in the speech contest?

20. The folder lying on the table is (theirs, their's).

21. Would somebody please raise (her, their) hand and offer to help with the aluminum can drive?

22. Two of the league all-stars are players on our team, Roberto and (he, him).

Cumulative Review: Units 1–8

▶ **Exercise 1 Draw a line under the correct word in parentheses.**

The mother was proud of her children, for (who, <u>whom</u>) she had sacrificed much.

1. Will you help Addie and (I, me)?

2. The highest producers, Rafael and (he, him), were treated to lunch.

3. The president of the school board (himself, hisself) visited the class.

4. Blame the sophomores rather than (we, us).

5. Anita got (her, herself) a new pair of shoes for the party.

6. Mr. Taylor, (who, whom) he had trusted, proved to be unreliable.

7. In speech class, the class told about (its, their) hobbies.

8. The Millers go to the lake often where (you, they) can relax and revitalize themselves.

9. Anyone who wants to participate must have (his, their) physical exam by next week.

10. I bought bouquets for Karin and (she, her).

11. Give this to the first-chair flutist, (she, her).

12. Ariel, as well as (he, him), was late for the ball-game.

13. To finance their banquet, the members of the French Club raised two hundred dollars for (them, themselves).

14. Juanita called Kareem, (who, whom) is the chairman of the committee.

15. Each member of the volleyball team received (its, her) award at the dinner.

16. Because (you, he) can wear old clothes all the time, Yoshin loves to go camping.

17. Many of our class (is, are) involved in some type of community service program.

18. I can't tell (who, whom) wrote this.

19. The army (is, are) an important part of our nation's defense.

20. Because she is new, Mr. Alvaraz gave Jenny a written copy of (his, her) duties.

▶ **Exercise 2** Identify the italicized verb. Write *pres.* if the verb is in present tense, *past* if it is in past, *pres. perf.* if it is present perfect, *past perf.* if it is past perfect, *pres. prog.* if it is present progressive, and *past prog.* if it is past progressive.

_____past_____   The lion *roared.*

_____   **1.** The surfer carefully *balanced* herself.

_____   **2.** The drivers *revved* up their cars' engines.

_____   **3.** Our teacher *has assigned* a new lesson.

_____   **4.** The elephant *is eating* the fresh hay.

_____   **5.** The king *had passed* the law before he died.

_____   **6.** Some clouds *have come* out of the west.

_____   **7.** Paula *is reading* her speech.

_____   **8.** By what time *had* you *finished* it?

_____   **9.** That type of paint *dries* slowly.

_____   **10.** We *are leaving* for Peru on Tuesday.

_____   **11.** I *am* late for school!

_____   **12.** They *have* already *left* for the lake.

_____   **13.** She *is going* to the park this afternoon.

_____   **14.** I *have* never *read* that book.

_____   **15.** The kite *is tumbling* out of control.

_____   **16.** *Have* you *heard* the latest about the picnic?

_____   **17.** Coach told us we *had played* well.

_____   **18.** We *have worked* on this puzzle far too long.

_____   **19.** Peggy *was getting* the pizza, wasn't she?

_____   **20.** Really, I thought you said you *did* it already.

_____   **21.** I *am watching* television downstairs.

_____   **22.** The sun *is shining* without a cloud in the sky.

_____   **23.** We always *sit* in the porch swing on summer evenings.

_____   **24.** I *love* the way the ocean sounds on the beach.

_____   **25.** The fossil *was* beautifully delicate and fragile.

▶ **Exercise 3** Write the part of speech of each italicized word in the blank. Use these abbreviations: *N* (noun), *V* (verb), *pro.* (pronoun), *adj.* (adjective), *adv.* (adverb), *prep.* (preposition), *conj.* (conjunction), and *int.* (interjection).

_____adj._____ The *antique* vase was filled with yellow roses.

_____ 1. Pamela searched *frantically* for the missing diamond ring.

_____ 2. Yesterday *we* learned how to prepare Italian beef sandwiches.

_____ 3. The library was filled with dedicated *patrons*.

_____ 4. Three comedians *performed* at the annual talent show.

_____ 5. Sal always places a cherry on top *of* each ice cream sundae.

_____ 6. *Wow!* This amusement park has amazing rides.

_____ 7. *Either* Tom *or* Steve will be selected drum major.

_____ 8. Every April the trees *on* our street produce beautiful blossoms.

_____ 9. Tamara saw a *fascinating* play at the local theater.

_____ 10. Jay *and* Ruth are planning another ski trip.

_____ 11. Sylvia suggested we try the new *Spanish* restaurant.

_____ 12. Using a more powerful telescope, *Curt* could see stars he had never seen before.

_____ 13. A neighborhood lumberyard is *donating* materials for our clubhouse.

_____ 14. *Help!* I can't resist the cherry cheesecake.

_____ 15. The player *in* the blue uniform forgot to bring his white jersey.

_____ 16. Mom *often* asks my opinion of her decorating choices.

_____ 17. The novel was long *but* interesting.

_____ 18. *Anyone* who dislikes pizza has never tried Antonio's.

_____ 19. Hannah had *never* been to the symphony before.

_____ 20. I was shocked to discover a *quiet* brook behind the wood.

_____ 21. *Neither* Carol *nor* Jim will be able to go to the hockey game tonight.

_____ 22. Dorothy watched the hot-air *balloon* float up to the sky.

_____ 23. Dad *examined* the used car thoroughly before buying it.

_____ 24. Sheep grazed contentedly in the meadow *beside* the road.

_____ 25. *Well,* what did you expect to happen?

Unit 9: Using Modifiers Correctly

Lesson 59
Modifiers: Three Degrees of Comparison

Most adjectives and adverbs have three degrees or forms: positive, comparative, and superlative. The **positive degree** of a modifier is the basic form found in the dictionary and is not used to make a comparison. The **comparative degree** of a modifier is used to show comparison between two things. The **superlative degree** of a modifier is used to show comparison among three or more things.

For most short (one-syllable and two-syllable) modifiers, add -*er* to the positive degree to form the comparative and -*est* to form the superlative. Some words change spelling when -*er* or -*est* is added. If the modifier ends in *e*, drop the final *e* before adding -*er* or -*est*. If the modifier ends in *y* preceded by a consonant, change the *y* to an *i*. Double a final consonant after a vowel that is short in sound.

dark, dark**er**, dark**est**   sure, sur**er**, sur**est**
angry, angr**ier**, angr**iest**   wet, wet**ter**, wet**test**

Some short modifiers, all modifiers of three or more syllables, and all adverbs ending in -*ly* use *more* and *most* instead of -*er* and -*est* to form the comparative and superlative forms.

often, **more** often, **most** often
tasteless, **more** tasteless, **most** tasteless
brightly, **more** brightly, **most** brightly

Less and *least* can be used with most modifiers to show negative comparison.

dull, **less** dull, **least** dull   obvious, **less** obvious, **least** obvious

▶ **Exercise 1** Complete each sentence by writing the correct comparative or superlative form of the modifier indicated in parentheses.

English grammar is my _____easiest_____ subject. (easy)

1. Robert is _____ than I am. (angry)

2. This year is the _____ one on record. (wet)

3. The glass in the bathroom window is _____. (opaque)

4. Volunteering for the teen suicide hotline is one of my _____ _____ experiences. (satisfying)

5. Any of these sweatshirts can be ordered in a _____ size. (large)

6. This house is built on a slab of _____ limestone. (solid)

7. Angela has been very _____ lately. (secretive)

8. The new subway trains travel _____ than the old ones did. (rapidly)

9. Ethan has the _____ appetite in the family. (voracious)

10. A ride in Fred's antique car is _____ than a drive in our new car. (jerky)

11. I know Mr. Sposoto _____ than I know Mr. Iozzo. (personally)

12. Gladys gets good grades _____ this year than last year. (often)

13. Of the five children Deanna behaved the _____. (politely)

14. After therapy Tazu could move _____ than before. (easily)

15. These are the _____ facts I have ever encountered. (unusual)

16. The second suspect was _____ followed than the first. (closely)

17. Mark appeared _____ that any other player. (fast)

18. In our house, Mom is always up _____ of all. (early)

19. Your motives are _____ than they were before. (transparent)

20. Of the two, Mrs. Strube is our _____ benefactor. (generous)

▶ **Exercise 2 Complete each sentence by writing the correct form of the modifier indicated in parentheses.**

I will try to be ___**more understanding**___. (*understanding*, comparative)

1. The Solomons have the _____ baby. (*cute*, superlative)

2. Andrea's performance seemed _____ than life. (*large*, comparative)

3. Computer glitches are so _____. (*frustrating*, positive)

4. I find some of Kristen's attitudes _____. (*puzzling*, positive)

5. Try to cheer _____ than the others. (*loudly*, comparative)

6. Gerard is becoming _____ every day. (*polite*, comparative)

7. _____ I read *A Tale of Two Cities*. (*recently*, superlative)

8. Our _____ neighbors moved in yesterday. (*new*, superlative)

9. I feel _____ today. (*depressed*, positive)

10. Attack the problem _____. (*vigorously*, positive)

11. Angelica is _____ than ever. (*attentive*, negative comparative)

12. You are _____ today than you were yesterday. (*irritating*, comparative)

13. This spring has the _____ natural water around. (*pure*, superlative)

14. My headaches occur _____ now than before. (*randomly*, comparative)

Lesson 60
Modifiers: Irregular Comparisons

Some modifiers have irregular comparative and superlative forms.

IRREGULAR ADJECTIVES

POSITIVE	COMPARATIVE	SUPERLATIVE
good	better	best
bad	worse	worst
far (distance only)	farther	farthest
far (degree, time)	further	furthest
little (amount)	less	least
many	more	most
much	more	most

IRREGULAR ADVERBS

POSITIVE	COMPARATIVE	SUPERLATIVE
badly	worse	worst
ill	worse	worst
well	better	best

▶ **Exercise 1** Complete each sentence by writing the correct form of the modifier indicated in the parentheses.

This is just the _____ **worst** _____ thing that could happen to me. (bad)

1. I have _____ free time this morning than this afternoon. (little)

2. Can you think of a time that I performed _____ than I did today? (badly)

3. Mia's aim is improving. Today she threw _____ she has ever thrown. (well)

4. How _____ yards of material do you need for the costumes? (many)

5. Mr. Zimmerman was rather sore after his surgery, but now he is feeling _____.

   (well)

6. Give me _____ ice cream than you gave Jason. (little)

7. _____ I have traveled by car is from Maine to Florida. (far)

8. Sheila needs time to think _____ on this issue. (far)

9. Go back _____ in time to the first thing you can remember. (far)

10. We need _____ help in the morning than in the afternoon. (much)

11. When it comes to praise for a job well done, Jordan deserves _____ of all. (much)

12. Karen received a special award for being the one volunteer who contributed _____ hours this year. (many)

13. That movie was rather _____. (bad)

14. The ice on the ski slope was _____ tonight than last night. (bad)

15. Even though Briana was nervous, she did very _____ on stage. (well)

16. Sean didn't think _____ of our tactics. (much)

17. I worked _____ hours than Sandra this week. (many)

18. Truly, a vacation is _____ thing from my mind. (far)

19. Don't go too _____ with that argument. (far)

20. Concerning this particular topic, Mollie seemed _____ interested student in the class. (little)

▶ **Exercise 2 Write the indicated form of the modifier.**

	comparative	far (degree, time)	_____further_____
1.	comparative	far (distance)	_____
2.	comparative	well	_____
3.	superlative	far (degree, time)	_____
4.	superlative	badly	_____
5.	comparative	ill	_____
6.	superlative	many	_____
7.	comparative	far (distance)	_____
8.	comparative	little (amount)	_____
9.	superlative	ill	_____
10.	comparative	much	_____
11.	superlative	good	_____
12.	superlative	well	_____
13.	superlative	bad	_____
14.	comparative	badly	_____
15.	comparative	many	_____
16.	superlative	far (distance)	_____

Lesson 61
Modifiers: Double and Incomplete Comparisons

Grammar

Do not make a double comparison by using *more* or *most* before modifiers ending in *-er* or *-est*.

INCORRECT: Mount Everest is the **most tallest** mountain in the world.

CORRECT: Mount Everest is the **tallest** mountain in the world.

Avoid incomplete or unclear comparisons. Include *other* or *else* when comparing one member of a group with another. Compare like things.

UNCLEAR: The fit of hiking boots is more important than the fit of shoes.

CLEAR: The fit of hiking boots is more important than the fit of **other** shoes.

INCOMPLETE: Climbing mountains is more dangerous than hills.

COMPLETE: Climbing mountains is more dangerous than **climbing** hills.

▶ **Exercise 1 Edit each sentence. Use the delete symbol (⅄) to eliminate double comparisons.**

If they had stayed on the peak ~~more~~ longer, their oxygen might have run out.

1. In May 1953, Edmund Hillary and Tenzing Norgay were the first people to reach the summit of Mount Everest, the most tallest mountain in the world.

2. The top of the mountain is more higher than the clouds.

3. Everest is one of the most coldest places on Earth, with temperatures as low as −40°F, even in the summer.

4. The risks were great, but the two men knew that this would be their bestest chance to reach the summit.

5. Weather at other times of the year would make the ascent more difficulter.

6. Hillary and Tenzing joined an expedition, organized by the British, with fourteen of the world's most finest climbers.

7. Many people had tried to reach the peak, but Hillary and Tenzing had the most strongest start.

8. While two team members tried unsuccessfully to climb to the top, the remaining men moved the camp more farther up the mountain.

9. They pitched their tents five miles above sea level, more higher than anyone had ever camped before.

10. The higher the final camp, the more likelier the men could reach the summit before their oxygen ran out.

11. The higher one climbs, the lesser oxygen there is in the air.

12. They had more fewer canisters of oxygen than they would have liked.

13. Oxygen tanks are heavy, and the climb is more harder with them than without them.

14. They had the most lightest tanks available.

15. Since the temperature was seventeen degrees Fahrenheit below zero when they left the tent, the two men wore their most warmest clothing.

16. Though they had worked for eight months to get where they were, the two men still faced the most greatest obstacles of the expedition.

17. Their packs grew more heavier with every step.

18. Loose snow made the ridge route more dangerouser than the face route.

19. An even more greater barrier was a giant rock, forty feet high, blocking the ridge.

20. Despite the many challenges, the two men reached the summit of Mount Everest, the most grandest mountain in the world.

▶ **Exercise 2** Edit each sentence to eliminate any incomplete comparison.

hiking
Hiking in a group is safer than alone.
^

1. Backpacking in cold climates is more difficult than temperate climates.

2. It is better to start backpacking in mild weather.

3. Leather hiking boots will last longer than fabric with suede reinforcements.

4. Day hikes are easier to organize than sleeping overnight.

5. On your first hike, don't try to hike farther than anyone.

6. Sleeping in a tent is better than outdoors.

7. Because you need to carry more equipment when you stay overnight, overnight backpacks are much larger and sturdier than day hikes.

8. Backpacks with flexible internal frames are becoming more popular than external frames.

Lesson 62
Using *Good* and *Well; Bad* and *Badly*

Good is an adjective. Use *good* to modify nouns or pronouns or to serve as a predicate adjective. *Well* may be used as an adverb of manner to tell how ably something is done or as an adjective meaning "in good health."

Aaron is a **good** writer. (adjective describing a noun)
All the news seems **good**. (predicate adjective)
Sadie performed **well** in yesterday's rehearsal. (adverb of manner)
The vet said Kirby is **well** again. (adjective meaning "in good health")

Bad is an adjective. Use *bad* to modify nouns or pronouns or as a predicate adjective. Use *badly* as an adverb to modify an action verb.

Put all the **bad** paper in the recycling bin. (adjective)
Those colors look **bad** together. (predicate adjective)
Ben thinks he ran **badly** in the race. (adverb modifying an action verb)

▶ **Exercise 1** Write *good, well, bad,* or *badly* in the space provided to complete each sentence correctly

It helps to give a _____ good _____ first impression.

1. I have a _____ idea.

2. That fresh bread smells so _____.

3. Steve performs _____ under pressure.

4. Does Agnes feel _____ today?

5. Kate gets very _____ headaches when she is in the bright sunshine.

6. Hold that thought! It's not half _____!

7. I was angry because he behaved so _____.

8. Garth performed _____, perhaps better than anyone else.

9. Julie has fully recovered and feels _____ now.

10. You are such a _____ friend; I hope we remain friends forever.

11. The editor said my article was written _____ and needed no editing.

12. Does the news seem as _____ as it did when you first heard it?

13. Erin's voice projects _____, so she probably won't get a lead in the play.

14. Jeremy feels _____ now, even though he's had several bouts of the flu.

15. My definition of a _____ job is one that pays well and teaches me something.

16. My little sister behaves so _____ that we don't know how to help her anymore.

17. The hiking trails at the park are _____ for riding bikes.

18. Everything at the restaurant tasted so _____.

19. You look really _____ in that color.

20. The news appears _____, but perhaps everything will look better tomorrow.

▶ **Exercise 2** **Draw a line under the word in parentheses that correctly completes each sentence.**

He promised me a raise if I do my job (good, <u>well</u>).

1. Performing an act of kindness each day helps me feel (good, well) about myself.

2. Nothing can be that (bad, badly).

3. I think that this is a really (bad, badly) idea.

4. Nathan handled the emergency situation very (good, well).

5. The rash on her face looks (bad, badly). Is she (good, well)?

6. People unaccustomed to winter weather often drive (bad, badly) in snow.

7. Eat a (good, well) breakfast every morning.

8. Although she was sick enough to miss three days of school, Maggie is (good, well) today.

9. If we carry the ball (good, well), we will win the game.

10. Ramon is such a (good, well) team player.

11. At first glance your grade appears (bad, badly).

12. (Bad, Badly) weather is expected tonight and tomorrow.

13. The first reports are promising, so your prospects look (good, well).

14. Norma is (good, well) at what she does.

15. The car skidded (bad, badly) before it left the road.

16. Cloie felt (bad, badly) when she realized she might not be able to go to college right away.

17. The good news became (bad, badly) when we heard the details.

18. I have heard that Mr. Eberst is a really (good, well) teacher.

19. This subject is so interesting, I don't think anyone could present it (bad, badly).

20. Irene does everything (good, well).

Lesson 63
Double Negatives

In general, do not use two negative words in the same clause to convey a negative idea.
To correct a double negative, delete one of the negative words. Before deleting a word,
decide which word most accurately conveys the intended meaning.

INCORRECT: Henry says he never did nothing wrong.
CORRECT: Henry says he never did anything wrong.
CORRECT: Henry says he did nothing wrong.

▶ **Exercise 1 Correct each sentence by eliminating the double negative. Most sentences can be
corrected in more than one way.**

No one at the dinner ordered no dessert.

1. Sometimes it seems Barbra can't do no wrong.

2. I hardly never see Jeremy any more.

3. The Johnsons say they don't need no help from us.

4. Zoli says he doesn't have no homework tonight.

5. Really, I didn't do nothing wrong.

6. Don't use no double negatives.

7. Nothing couldn't make me do that!

8. Nobody said nothing after Lydia dropped that bombshell.

9. No one here never heard of Mr. Talltree.

10. I couldn't hardly see through the driving rain.

11. Mom said I can't go nowhere until my homework is done.

12. Really, Mom, I wouldn't never take the car out without your permission.

13. Zach told his little sisters that they shouldn't never tell a lie.

14. No one never learned that lesson better than Benjamin.

15. Couldn't no one pick me up after school on Thursday?

Grammar

16. Penelope scarcely never thinks before she opens her mouth to speak.

17. John hadn't barely started his morning jog when the heavy rain started.

18. I won't never take this ring off my finger.

19. Never tell no one the combination to your locker.

20. Denise hadn't scarcely settled into her chair when the phone rang.

▶ **Exercise 2** Draw a line under the word that completes the sentence without creating a double negative.

I couldn't get (anybody, nobody) to help.

1. Doesn't that sound bother (anybody, nobody) but me?

2. Can't you find (somebody, nobody) who can help you with the play?

3. I can't go (anywhere, nowhere) until my mom gets home from work.

4. Shannon has grown so much this year, that none of these clothes fit her (anymore, no more).

5. Nothing (ever, never) startled me quite that much.

6. Don't (ever, never) take his word for it.

7. I (can, can't) hardly believe my own ears!

8. None of my friends (ever, never) let me down.

9. I know (anywhere, nowhere) better to go when I need help.

10. You must believe me when I say that I have not done (anything, nothing) wrong.

11. There is no way that they will let us in without (any, no) tickets.

12. Scarcely (anything, nothing) fazes Georgina anymore.

13. Since I hadn't seen Uncle Michael in ten years, I (could, couldn't) hardly recognize him.

14. Mrs. Sullivan didn't like (any, none) of my topics for my term paper.

15. Can't you (ever, never) think positively?

16. Though he spent time looking for it, Justin could find the report (anywhere, nowhere).

17. The sign said they did not allow (any, no) pets.

18. No one (ever, never) believes anything I say.

19. Do not eat (nothing, anything) before you swim your laps.

20. I didn't go (anywhere, nowhere) after school.

Lesson 64
Misplaced and Dangling Modifiers

Modifiers should be placed as close as possible to the words they modify. **Misplaced modifiers** are modifiers (words, phrases, or clauses) that cause confusion because they modify the wrong word or seem to modify more than one word in a sentence. To make the meaning of the sentence clear, move the modifier as close as possible to the word it modifies.

MISPLACED: Interested in a compromise, the mediator's suggestions appealed to both parties.

CLEAR: The mediator's suggestions appealed to both parties interested in a compromise.

Dangling modifiers are modifiers that do not logically modify any word in the sentence. A sentence with a dangling modifier often can be rewritten correctly by supplying the words that are implied.

DANGLING: After trying for many years to locate my birth mother, she lives in Tucson.

CLEAR: After trying for many years to locate my birth mother, I found her living in Tucson.

In most cases, place the adverb *only* before the word or group of words it modifies. The meaning of a sentence may be unclear if *only* is positioned incorrectly.

UNCLEAR: **Only Nickie** wears gloves in the dead of winter. (Nickie is the only person who wears gloves.)

UNCLEAR: Nickie **wears only gloves** in the dead of winter. (Nickie is probably rather chilly because she isn't wearing anything but gloves.)

CLEAR: Nickie wears gloves **only in the dead of winter.** (Nickie doesn't wear gloves in warm weather.)

▶ **Exercise 1** Above the italicized word or group of words write *M* for a misplaced modifier, *D* for a dangling modifier, or *C* for a modifier that is correctly placed.

      D
Trying to get to practice on time, the coach started without me.

1. *Taxiing on the runway,* the radio tower was in contact with the pilot.

2. *Carefully choosing the words to use,* it was time to make my speech.

3. *Without much hope of success,* Adam struggled to learn the vocabulary before the test.

4. *Studying all weekend,* the television never was on.

5. *Particularly interested in history,* the development of American industry seemed an attractive topic to me.

6. The model sashayed down the runway *with the red and white mini skirt.*

7. There was faint hope that the journey would be over *soon after it began.*

8. I want to sing with the symphony *in the worst way.*

9. *Missing my family,* the dormitory seemed like a lonely place.

10. The water was too rough for surfing *with its high waves.*

11. The driveway, covered *with a thin coat of ice and a foot of snow,* proved to be very treacherous.

12. *Watching in horror as the building burned,* Pedro and I were busy caring for the stunned survivors.

13. *Standing at the top of the Sears Tower,* the city of Chicago looked like a picture postcard.

14. The computer program crashed *with all of my data* and forced me to stop work for the day.

15. *While eating breakfast,* the diner car lurched forward and spilled my food.

16. The bookshelves swayed *with the weight of their load.*

17. The Shillings, *destroyed by fire,* built a new home within a year.

18. *Feeling anxious,* holding still was difficult.

19. *Listening attentively,* only Paul was able to follow the complicated story line.

20. *Cooperating with each other,* Jane and Trevi were able to finish the project in record time.

▶ **Exercise 2 Draw a line under the dangling or misplaced modifier in each sentence.**

<u>Taking my time</u>, we arrived late to the party.

1. Giggling, the movie obviously pleased the two girls.

2. Before leaving for school, breakfast is a good thing.

3. Carefully watering the garden, the plants bloomed profusely.

4. After it scored the winning touchdown, the crowd cheered the home team.

5. Watching from the river bank, the rafters floated through the white water and past us.

6. Slipping on the ice, the sidewalk had no traction.

7. Horatius, a Roman soldier, defended the Wooden Bridge, courageous and defiant.

8. He opened the door, mustering all of his courage.

9. Swimming in our very best form, the trophy was richly deserved.

10. Driving for hours, the trip was almost at an end.

11. Roasting meat and baking bread, the smells coming from the kitchen were most enticing.

12. Jerome's team, with a broken rudder, manned the winning boat.

13. Finishing first in the race, the Olympic Committee presented her with a medal.

14. After working in the yard all afternoon, the tall glass of lemonade was very refreshing.

15. When peeling onions, my eyes water profusely.

16. The United States uses 30 percent of the world's energy with only 5 percent of the world's population.

17. Dark and threatening, the artist studied the stormy sky.

18. Singing all morning, the muscles of my mouth were rather sore.

19. The gurgle of the creek almost invites waders with its clear, cool water.

20. Film critics did not seem to enjoy the movie unlike the general public.

21. The darkest night can be made as bright as the day with electricity.

22. Including the Matterhorn and Mount Blanc, Lucy Walker climbed almost one hundred high mountains.

23. Relaxing with nothing to do, the sunny afternoon made me sleepy.

24. Working long hours for low pay, the job defeated Janine.

25. A fine athletic talent, Pedro's name is well known in the league.

▶ **Exercise 3 Draw an arrow from *only* to the word or words it modifies.**

Stephen reads only one weekly magazine.

1. In our family only Harold lived in San Francisco.

2. Maude likes only pistachio ice cream.

3. I have trouble seeing, but only at night.

4. Jerry shoveled the driveway only.

5. I only bought food for dinner tonight.

6. Ryan played only football in high school.

7. Send only one request per envelope.

8. The newspaper is delivered only to the front door.

9. That box fits only in that particular space.

10. The feel of the winter uniform annoys only me.

11. Sheila watches only television comedies.

12. Henry studies only the languages that interest him.

13. I told only Sook that we'd be late.

14. Mr. Tibbs, our cat, will eat only one brand of cat food.

15. Teresa Vitale is the only author whom I know personally.

16. Only I had the courage to walk into Mr. Henderson's office.

17. Lee knew that only Gary and Abby were coming to his birthday party.

18. Miles backpacks only in the spring and fall.

19. Surely the only form of transportation slower than a bicycle is walking.

20. The only review of the new musical published in this morning's paper is the least favorable of

them all.

21. Only the caterer seemed only worried about the weather.

22. Coreen served only one hitch in the army.

▶ **Writing Link** **Write a paragraph that contains dangling and misplaced modifiers. Exchange
papers with a classmate and edit each other's paragraph.**

_____

_____

_____

_____

_____

_____

_____

_____

_____

☑️ Unit 9 **Review**

Grammar

▶ **Exercise 1** Edit each sentence to make it correct. Each sentence contains one error in the use of modifiers.

I only have one chance in ten of getting the part.

1. We must address this issue most aggressively than we have in the past.

2. In order to join the expedition, Miguel traveled further than Simon.

3. Uncle Bert, this dinner looks so well it makes my mouth water!

4. Doesn't nobody care enough to ask what happened last night?

5. With vivid imaginations, the movie frightened the children.

6. We saw a bear driving in Yellowstone Park.

7. Read this chapter good, and be ready for a discussion tomorrow.

8. Since his tape player needs repair, Matt only buys compact discs now.

9. This down comforter is more warmer than the other comforter.

10. Driving carefully on city streets is just as important as highways.

11. Tonight was your bestest performance ever.

12. Of all my extracurricular activities, I've enjoyed being in the musicals more than anything.

13. Does the weather appear that badly?

14. Have you ever read an article that was more duller?

15. The height of Mt. Everest is greater than Mt. Hood.

16. David, I was embarrassed that you behaved so bad today.

17. Nobody got no tickets for the game, and now there are no more.

18. I did good on my math exam.

Copyright © by Glencoe/McGraw-Hill

Cumulative Review: Units 1–9

▶ **Exercise 1** Identify the type of phrase italicized in each sentence. Write *prep.* for prepositional, *part.* for participial, *G* for gerund, and *I* for infinitive above each phrase.

       G
    Fishing alone is my dad's favorite pastime.

1. *Exploring the possibilities,* I found three scholarships for which I qualify.

2. She dreams *of a better life.*

3. *Avoiding the conflict* rarely solves the problem.

4. We must design the sets this week if we want *to finish on time.*

5. *Helping other people* was their goal.

6. *Deeply sleeping,* he was oblivious to the activity in the room.

7. Go *past the barber shop,* and turn right.

8. Kitty wants *to pass her driving test.*

9. *Trying my best,* I was able to place fourth in the competition.

10. *Balancing too many containers,* Nelson spilled a quart of orange juice.

11. *Choosing a college* will be an important decision in your life.

12. George no longer plans *to work after ten on school nights.*

13. *Sharing some time with children,* Jason found a sense of worth.

14. Fully one fourth of the school was absent *during the flu epidemic.*

15. The creaking in the board *on the third step* annoys Gertrude.

16. *Exercising regularly* is essential if you want to be healthy.

17. Amy has succeeded *beyond her wildest expectations.*

18. *Dealing with uncertainty* is a challenge for most high school seniors.

19. Try *to eliminate all careless errors.*

20. If I knew how *to stabilize the vertical boards,* the project would be almost complete.

▶ **Exercise 2** Identify each sentence as *simple,* *compound,* *complex,* or *compound-complex.*

_____simple_____ Abraham Lincoln, the sixteenth president of the United States, was elected first in 1860 and again in 1864.

_____ 1. Canoeing has been an Olympic event since 1936.

_____ 2. Strategy is crucial, but patience is important also.

_____ **3.** My dad served in the navy when it was an all-male institution.

_____ **4.** Study French if you like, but I plan to take four years of Latin.

_____ **5.** Kenyon College in Gambier, Ohio, initiated the concept of advanced placement credit for high school studies.

_____ **6.** Almost half of the oil pumped each year is used to fuel the world's motor vehicles.

_____ **7.** Would you rather come with me, or should I go alone?

_____ **8.** Frank Lloyd Wright actually designed and built a home in western Pennsylvania over a small waterfall.

_____ **9.** Now I like to be called Martha, but when I was younger everyone called me Marty.

_____ **10.** When the phone rang, I answered it.

_____ **11.** Omelets can be high in calories and cholesterol but are good sources of protein and iron.

_____ **12.** Choose a topic, and begin to write.

_____ **13.** We can begin by agreeing on a topic, or we can each choose one independently.

_____ **14.** You can practice with me on Friday, or you can just appear at the audition on Saturday morning if you want.

_____ **15.** *Pride and Prejudice* is a book that I recommend for serious students of British literature.

_____ **16.** The CD-ROM demands a surprising amount of memory even when it is not engaged.

_____ **17.** Nick traveled whenever he wanted, but he was always home for the holidays.

_____ **18.** Tropical cyclones are usually born in the summer or fall.

_____ **19.** Paris is known as "the City of Lights," but Rome is called "the Eternal City."

_____ **20.** Norton works three evenings a week, and he volunteers at the art center whenever he can.

▶ **Exercise 3** Edit each sentence to make it correct. Some sentences contain errors in the use of modifiers.

          we left behind
Reluctantly, the house that had been our home for ten years ~~was left behind~~.

1. I only have eyes for you!

2. In all their majestic snow-capped splendor, my visitors spent time enjoying the Rockies.

3. Located on Fifth Avenue at 34th Street, the Empire State Building used to be taller than any building in the city.

4. We organized the hall closet since there wasn't no more room for coats.

5. Without any fear of heights, the mountains were still somewhat daunting.

6. Ever since he made varsity soccer, Bradley feels well about himself.

7. I like American History more better than I imagined I would.

8. Adriana answered the questions more intelligently of all.

9. In your opinion, which is the most interesting country, France or China?

10. Mark only wears a blue striped suit and a paisley tie on Sunday.

11. Choose the better of the lot, and throw the rest away.

12. Are the trends in women's fashion more fickle than men's clothing?

13. Do your job good, and you will achieve a sense of satisfaction.

14. Just try more harder the next time, and perhaps you will succeed.

15. I can't hardly stand all the tension in this room!

16. Everyone in the cast agrees Simone looks more foolish in that role.

17. Out of control, the radio tower guided the damaged plane to a safe landing.

18. Looking away for just an instant, the accident occurred at that time.

19. Julia only put away the silverware.

20. The population of Los Angeles is greater than St. Louis.

*U*sage Glossary

. . . .

Unit 10: Usage Glossary

Lesson 65

Usage: *a* to *altogether*

Words that are similar are sometimes misused.

a, an Use *a* before words that begin with a consonant and before words that begin with a "*yew*" sound. Use *an* before words that begin with a vowel or an unsounded *h*.

a basketball   **a h**eart   **a u**nit   **an a**rticle   **an h**our   **an u**mbrella

a lot *A lot* means "a large amount" and is always two words. It is best to avoid this expression. When possible, replace it with *much, many,* or a specific number.

He brought **a lot** of movies to the party.   He brought **eight** movies to the party.

a while, awhile The expression *a while* is formed by the article *a* and the noun *while*. It is used after a preposition. *Awhile* is one word and is an adverb.

We went to the arcade for **a while**. We played **awhile** before we went to the movie.

accept, except *Accept* is a verb that means "to receive" or "to agree to." *Except* is usually a preposition and means "but" or "other than."

Will he **accept** the assignment? Everything is finished **except** the paperwork.

affect, effect *Affect* is a verb that means "to cause a change in; to influence." *Effect* is usually a noun and means "a result; that which has been brought about." Less often, *effect* can be a verb meaning "to bring about or accomplish."

The referee's call will **affect** the score.
The referee's call has an **effect** on the score.
The referee's call will **effect** a change in the score.

ain't Avoid this expression unless it is part of a direct quote.

▶ **Exercise 1** Underline the word or words in parentheses that best complete each sentence.

All of us (except, accept) Alex are going out for pizza.

1. My little brother rode (a, <u>an</u>) elephant at the zoo.

2. We ate (alot, <u>a lot</u>) of candy.

3. Let me rest (a while, <u>awhile</u>) before we walk farther.

4. Please (<u>accept</u>, except) charges for the phone call.

5. Did yesterday's rain (<u>affect</u>, effect) the traffic?

6. Pedro (<u>isn't</u>, ain't) going to attend the orientation.

Usage

7. Janice will probably attend (a, an) university in her home state.

8. I finished my science report (except, accept) for the bibliography.

9. The (affect, effect) of the rain was to erode our garden.

10. We'll have lunch after (a while, awhile).

---

all ready, already As two words, *all ready* means "completely ready." As one word, *already* is an adverb meaning "before or by this time."

We are **all ready** for the class party.   Spring has **already** arrived.

all right *All right* is always two words.

My teacher said it would be **all right** to hand in my report tomorrow.

all the farther, all the faster These are informal expressions. Instead, use *as far as* and *as fast as*.

I've gone **as far as** I can.   She drives **as fast as** she can.

all together, altogether *All together* means "in a group." *Altogether* is an adverb meaning "completely" or "on the whole."

We put the tools **all together**.   **Altogether**, it was an interesting day.

▶ **Exercise 2** Correct the word or words in italics. If the sentence is correct, write *C* in the blank.

_____already_____ He has *all ready* been accepted for the training program.

all together 1. Please file the computer chips *altogether*.

all ready 2. Kai was so excited about the trip that she was *already* by ten o'clock.

as far as 3. Alfonso jogged two miles, but that was *all the farther* he could go.

____C____ 4. The speech was *altogether* too long.

all right 5. My audition went *alright*, but I don't know if I'll get a part.

____C____ 6. Julie walked *as fast as* she could around the track.

altogether 7. The hedge clippers we bought were *all together* useless.

____C____ 8. Is it *all right* to feed a cat ice cream?

already / C 9. The choir members were *all ready* in their robes when the director arrived.

all together 10. The basketball team rode *altogether* on one bus.

Lesson 66
Usage: *amount* to *could of*

amount , number Both words refer to quantity, but *number* refers to nouns that can be counted and *amount* refers to nouns that cannot be counted.

A small **amount** of rain fell yesterday.
A **number** of raindrops dotted the patio.

being as , being that Avoid these expressions in formal writing and speaking. Replace them with *because* or *since*.

We were late to the concert **because** we had a flat tire.
Since Mark made the team, we seldom see him.

beside , besides *Beside* is a preposition meaning "located at the side of." *Besides* is usually an adverb meaning "in addition to."

We spent several days **beside** the ocean.
Besides the two pencils, you will need a pen.

between , among *Between* shows the relationship of one person or thing to another. *Among* shows the relationship of more than two persons or things.

A friendship developed **between** Buzz and William.
Friendship **among** team members usually improves performance.

▶ **Exercise 1** Underline the word or words that best complete each sentence.

(Being that, Because) we were late, we missed the train.

1. There was little difference (between, among) the ten proposals submitted.

2. The (amount, number) of fat in your diet can be important to your health.

3. (Being as, Since) the movie started at three o'clock, we decided not to go.

4. There are four years (between, among) Marcus and his younger brother.

5. Did you buy anything (beside, besides) a new shirt?

6. A large (number, amount) of people enrolled in the new computer course.

7. The body builder ate five chicken breasts for dinner (being that, because) he had a competition the next day.

8. Gina put her new sweater (besides, beside) the skirt to see if they would match.

9. No (amount, number) of encouragement would convince me to sing a solo!

10. The staff of our school paper took a poll (between, among) the students to learn how many would prefer changing the school's hours.

bring, **take** *Bring* means "to carry from a distant place to a closer one." *Take* means "to carry from a nearby place to a more distant one."

Please **bring** potato salad to our picnic.
Joe will **take** his car when he visits his aunt.

can, **may** *Can* implies the ability to do something. *May* implies permission to do it. *May* also means "might."

How many pounds **can** you lift?
May I go with you to the gym?
I **may** go tonight.

can't hardly, **can't scarcely** These terms are double negatives since *hardly* and *scarcely* are negatives by themselves. Use *can hardly* and *can scarcely*.

I **can hardly** remember that old movie.
I **can scarcely** get to my neighbor's house in time to pick up the paper.

could of, **might of**, **must of**, **should of**, **would of** In these expressions, the helping verb *have* should follow *could, might, must, should,* and *would.*

I **should have** remembered you were leaving early this morning.

▶ **Exercise 2** Correct the word or words in italics. If the sentence is correct, write *C* in the blank.

_____may_____ Of course, you *can* borrow my book.

can hardly 1. I *can't hardly* believe you didn't do well on the test.

bring 2. Please *take* all your records when you come to your appointment after school.

must have 3. The delivery person *must of* misplaced the address.

_C_ 4. I *can* do twenty push-ups if I try really hard.

take 5. Kenji, will you *bring* the trash out to the garage?

would have 6. Moira *would of* watched the basketball play-offs, but she had an exam the next day.

can 7. Zinc *may* be combined with other metals to form alloys such as brass or bronze.

_C_ 8. The Drama Club *should have* put up posters in the community to advertise the school play.

can scarcely 9. I *can't scarcely* believe that the American eagle is an endangered species!

may 10. *Can* I go to the restroom, Mrs. Moore?

Lesson 67
Usage: *different from* to *regardless*

---

different from, **different than** *Different from* is preferable to *different than*.

Whales are very **different from** fish.

doesn't, **don't** *Doesn't* is a contraction of *does not* and is used with all singular nouns and the pronouns *he, she,* and *it. Don't* is a contraction of *do not* and is used with all plural nouns and the pronouns *I, you, we,* and *they.*

I **don't** believe I've met your cousin. **Doesn't** Mother have an appointment?

emigrate, **immigrate** *Emigrate* means "to move from one country to another." *Immigrate* means "to enter a country in order to live there."

Sanjay **emigrated** from India three years ago.
He **immigrated** to the United States.

farther, **further** *Farther* refers to physical distance. *Further* refers to degree or time.

Miami is **farther** than Orlando.
There was a **further** development in the detective's case.

fewer, **less** *Fewer* usually refers to things that can be counted, while *less* refers to things that cannot be counted. *Less* is sometimes used with figures that express single amounts or quantities.

There are **fewer** people and **less** air on Mars than on Earth.

hanged, **hung** Use *hung* unless the meaning is "to put to death by hanging."

Outlaws were **hanged** for their evil deeds. She **hung** the coats in the closet.

in, **into** *In* indicates a location "inside" or "within" a place. *Into* indicates movement or direction from outside to inside.

Kevin had a role **in** the movie. Victor dived **into** the pool.

irregardless, **regardless** *Regardless* is the correct term. The suffix *-less* and the prefix *ir-* both indicate negatives, so the word *irregardless* is really a double negative.

Please enter through the door on the right, **regardless** of the sign.

▶ **Exercise 1 Correct the word in parentheses. If the word is correct, write *C* in the blank.**

<u>**different from**</u> Ernest Hemingway's novels were (different than) other novels of his time.

<u>in</u> 1. Hemingway was born in 1899 (into) Oak Park, Illinois.

<u>C</u> 2. Hemingway began his career as a journalist (in) Kansas City at the *Star.*

C 3. (Regardless) of his budding career, he went to Italy and worked as an ambulance driver in World War I.

further 4. Due to his wartime experiences, his writings delved (farther) into themes of violence and the need for courage.

different from 5. Hemingway went to Paris where he met American authors such as F. Scott Fitzgerald and Gertrude Stein who were not so (different than) himself.

hung 6. They (hanged) around together and encouraged each other to write.

C 7. One of his most famous novels, *The Sun Also Rises,* was about a group of disillusioned Americans, not (different from) those he met while in Paris.

C 8. *A Farewell to Arms,* while set in World War I Italy, was (less) a war story than a love story.

doesn't 9. *For Whom the Bell Tolls* (don't) take place in Italy, but in Spain during the Spanish Civil War.

fewer 10. During the 1950s Hemingway wrote (less) books.

C 11. He did, however, (further) his career with the successful 1952 novel, *The Old Man and the Sea.*

fewer 12. Developing an interest in fishing, he wrote (less) novels but created characters who seem to live.

C 13. For example, the reader (doesn't) forget Santiago from *The Old Man and the Sea.*

further less 14. Santiago is an aged Cuban fisherman who takes his boat into the ocean (further) than is safe.

C 15. Although he was once a respected fisherman, Santiago's long streak of bad luck means people (don't) have faith in him.

regardless 16. He wants to hook the marlin and bring it in (irregardless) of what happens to himself.

fewer 17. He spends (less) days following the fish to catch it than he does to bring it back.

in 18. By the time Santiago beaches the marlin (into) the village, the sharks have eaten everything but the skeleton.

C 19. Most of Hemingway's stories (hung) on the outdoors and heavily masculine themes.

Regardless 20. (Irregardless) of personal and physical problems, he was the personification of courage, which he defined in one of his books as "grace under pressure."

Usage

Lesson 68
Usage: *this kind* to *reason is because*

---

this kind, **these kinds** *This kind* is singular and is used with singular words. *These kinds* is plural and is used with plural words.

This kind of drama is my favorite.   **These kinds** of papers are hard to read.

lay, **lie** *Lay* means "to place" or "to put" and always takes a direct object. *Lie* means "to recline" or "to be positioned" and does not take an object. The principal parts of the verbs are as follows: *Lay*—laying, laid, laid; *Lie*—lying, lay, lain.

Will you **lay** the book on her desk?   I like to **lie** in the sun.

learn, **teach** *Learn* means "to gain knowledge." *Teach* means "to instruct" or "to give knowledge to."

I like to **learn** new things.   Who will **teach** eighth grade next year?

leave, **let** *Leave* means "to go away; to depart." *Let* means "to allow; to permit."

We'll need to **leave** home at six o'clock.
Will your mother **let** you go to the concert?

like, **as** *Like* is a preposition and introduces a prepositional phrase. *As* is a subordinating conjunction and introduces a subordinate clause.

The kite flew **like** a bird.   The kite flew freely **as** it should.

▶ **Exercise 1** Underline the word or words in parentheses that best complete each sentence.

Juan asked his dad to (teach, learn) him how to play racquetball.

1. Few persons know as much about American history (like, as) Dr. Deever does.

2. (This kind, These kinds) of report is not usually based on fact.

3. I hope you will (leave, let) the bulletin board display as it is for another week.

4. My dog loves to (lay, lie) in front of the fireplace.

5. Ted, a sophomore, will (learn, teach) how to drive this summer.

6. (This kind, These kinds) of flowers do well in the shade.

7. Jonas had to (leave, let) for his baby-sitting job at seven o'clock.

8. Please (lay, lie) my tennis trophy on the mantel.

9. My little sister has a dress just (like, as) her doll's dress.

10. Last Saturday morning I (laid, lay) in bed until noon.

Usage

loose, lose *Loose* is an adjective meaning "free," or "not fitting tightly."
Lose is a verb meaning "to have no longer, to misplace; to fail to win."

The old chair leg is **loose**.   If I **lose** my key, I can't get into my house.

passed, past Use *passed* only as the past tense of the verb *pass*. *Past* can be a noun, an adjective, a preposition, or an adverb.

The boy **passed** the library.   The Wild West is in the **past**.
It is **past** time for extra reading.   The guard goes **past** once an hour.

precede, proceed *Precede* means "to go or come before." *Proceed* means "to continue" or "to move along."

The band will **precede** the floats in the parade.
The parade will **proceed** down Main Street.

raise, rise The transitive verb *raise* means "to cause to move up." *Rise* is an intransitive verb meaning "to get up" or "to move up."

Raise the flag on the Fourth of July.   When the president appears, we will **rise**.

reason is because Use either *reason is that* or *because*.

The **reason** Grandma called **is that** today is Micah's birthday.
Grandma called **because** today is Micah's birthday.

Usage

▶ **Exercise 2** Correct the word in italics. If the word is correct, write *C* in the blank.

___raise___   If you know the answer, *rise* your hand.

___loose___   **1.** When I get home from school, I let the dog *lose* so it can get some exercise.

___C___   **2.** Helen's dad hoped his boss would *raise* his salary.

___past___   **3.** I'm certainly glad that our argument is in the *passed*.

___proceed___   **4.** If you're driving in the snow, you must *precede* with caution.

___passed___   **5.** Enrique *past* through the grocery store on his way home from school.

___reason is that___   **6.** The *reason* we recycle paper *is because* we want to save the trees.

___precede___   **7.** The information boxes *proceed* the exercises in this workbook.

___C___   **8.** Did my candidate *lose* the election?

___C___   **9.** My mom *rises* early each day to go to the gym before work.

___loose___   **10.** Amed and Héroko are working together to fix the *lose* knob on the stereo.

Lesson 69
Usage: *respectfully* to *where at*

---

respectfully, respectively *Respectfully* means "with respect." *Respectively* means "in the order named."

Dishya always speaks **respectfully**.
Please mark the three drawers "oils," "chalk," and "watercolors," **respectively**.

says, said *Says* is the third person singular of the verb *say*. *Said* is the past tense of *say*.

He **says** the trip will be an interesting one.
Yesterday he **said** only five people had signed up.

sit, set *Sit* means "to be seated." *Set* means "to put" or "to place."

I like to **sit** in that chair.   **Set** the bowl on the shelf.

than, then *Than* is a conjunction used in comparisons. *Then* is an adverb used to refer to time.

I am taller **than** my brother.   The bell clanged and **then** was silent.

this here, that there Avoid using *here* and *there* after *this* and *that*.

This bowl is for the fresh fruit.   **That** towel needs washing.

where at Avoid using *at* after *where*.

Where are the test papers?

▶ **Exercise 1** Underline the word in parentheses that best completes each sentence.

After standing at my after-school job, I need to (set, <u>sit</u>) for a while.

1. Carlos, Pete, and Hillman are eight, ten, and fourteen, (respectfully, <u>respectively</u>).

2. You can do better (<u>than</u>, then) that!

3. (This here, <u>This</u>) coat is my favorite.

4. Yesterday, my teacher (says, <u>said</u>) I could make up the test.

5. Please (<u>sit</u>, set) quietly while the speaker is introduced.

6. If you must point out his errors, please do it (<u>respectfully</u>, respectively).

7. (Where at, <u>Where</u>) are the maps we will need for our trip?

8. (That there, <u>That</u>) constellation can be seen only in the Southern Hemisphere.

9. Everyone (<u>says</u>, said) this has been the best year yet.

10. (Sit, <u>Set</u>) the procedure and follow it each time to prevent confusion.

11. Yesterday the art teacher (say, said) "Who would like to exhibit a project at the public library?"

12. Endangered species, such as the California condor, are more (than, then) just threatened.

13. In 1940 tensions rose between the United States and Japan, and (than, then) on December 7, 1941, Japan attacked Pearl Harbor.

14. Do you know (where, where at) the original Constitution of the United States is kept?

15. Claudio (respectfully, respectively) asked his grandma if he could have another piece of her homemade apple pie.

▶ **Exercise 2** **Correct the word in italics. If the word is correct, write *C* in the blank.**

_____than_____   Jennifer's dog is more obedient *then* Jason's dog.

_____where_____   1. Do you know *where* the posters are *at?*

_____respectively_____   2. Phil and Jennifer received a B and an A, *respectfully.*

_____that_____   3. *That there* salad looks delicious.

_____C_____   4. The financial report was *respectfully* submitted by the club's treasurer.

_____set_____   5. *Sit* the vase of flowers on the dining room table.

_____C_____   6. Then Keisha *said* that we should add milk to the dry mixture.

_____C_____   7. First Jerome rode his horse across the field; *then* he guided it back to the stable.

_____said_____   8. Last week a reporter *says* the dam was ready to burst.

_____this_____   9. *This here* plan is the best of the architect's designs.

_____C_____   10. The girl in the red sweater and the one in the blue dress are Jan and Jean, *respectively.*

_____sit_____   11. Would you like to *set* beside the window, or would you prefer an aisle seat?

_____C_____   12. Tonight's dinner is less spicy *than* last night's dinner.

_____where_____   13. *Where* are the musical videos *at?*

_____says_____   14. At the moment Glenda *said* the plans are still in progress.

_____C_____   15. Is *this* the right amount of glue to hold the boards together?

_____than_____   16. This plastic sheet is as pliable as, or more pliable *then,* that hard rubber one.

_____set_____   17. Gary Lee *sat* up the folding chairs and then sat in one.

_____said_____   18. Stuart *says* to thank you for sending him a get-well card.

✓ Unit 10 **Review**

▶ **Exercise 1** **Correct the word or words in italics. If the sentence is correct, write _C_ in the blank.**

_____*Since*_____   *Being as* I was feeling sick, the nurse sent me home.

_____*a lot*_____ **1.** Marcy eats *alot* of popcorn when she goes to the movies.

_____*effect*_____ **2.** The sun shone and the *affect* on our spirits was amazing.

_____*C*_____ **3.** I ate *altogether* too much for lunch.

_____*beside*_____ **4.** I was pleased to have my father walk *besides* me.

_____*C*_____ **5.** Share the book *among* the three of you.

_____*take*_____ **6.** Would you *bring* a copy of my book report when you go to class?

_____*C*_____ **7.** *Can* you play the piano?

_____*could have*_____ **8.** I *could of* taken geometry, but I decided to wait until next year.

_____*can hardly*_____ **9.** Brian *can't hardly* reach the top shelf in the closet.

_____*different from*_____ **10.** Aerobics is *different than* anything I've ever done.

_____*between*_____ **11.** It is difficult to tell the difference *among* the twins.

_____*farther*_____ **12.** The farmhouse you see across the valley is *further* than the main highway.

_____*may*_____ **13.** Did your mother say you *can* go along with us?

_____*fewer*_____ **14.** I volunteer *less* hours at the hospital this year than last.

_____*should have*_____ **15.** You *should of* told me you didn't want to see this movie.

_____*this*_____ **16.** Do you like *this here* museum as much as I do?

_____*sit*_____ **17.** *Set* here beside me so we can look at the recipes together.

_____*Regardless*_____ **18.** *Irregardless* of your decision, we want you to know how much we appreciate your friendship.

_____*C*_____ **19.** *This kind* of exercise is good for the heart.

_____*lay*_____ **20.** The cloth *laid* on the picnic table in a wrinkled mess.

_____*let*_____ **21.** Will you *leave* Maureen go to the party with me?

_____*C*_____ **22.** You are fortunate to *learn* another language so easily.

Usage

Cumulative Review: Units 1–10

▶ **Exercise 1** Identify the part of speech of each italicized word: *N* (noun), *pro.* (pronoun), *V* (verb), *adj.* (adjective), or *adv.* (adverb).

<u>adj.</u>   The *lovely* vase was filled with lilies and ferns.

pro **1.** *Who* do you suppose the winner of the sportsmanship award will be?

adv **2.** Sue *avidly* studied the report to learn as much as she could.

prep **3.** *Beyond* the white, sandy beach lay beautiful dunes.

_V_ **4.** This is the song I was *telling* you about.

_n_ **5.** As soon as we walked into the *building,* the lights went out.

adv **6.** Yani turned *quickly* when he heard the footsteps behind him.

adj **7.** Please take the *empty* seat beside me.

adv **8.** *Yesterday* I spent several hours with my friend.

_n_ **9.** What kind of *shortening* does the recipe call for?

pro **10.** Has *anyone* registered for the karate class?

adv **11.** Five people stood *up* when the principal entered the classroom.

_n_ **12.** The rain fell in *torrents* causing our basement to flood.

_V_ **13.** Please *let* Uncle Joe and Aunt Marie use my apartment.

adj **14.** The senator took *excellent* notes at the environmental meeting.

_n_ **15.** Mechanical toys were the *predecessors* of robots.

_V_ **16.** Our family *loves* to vacation in the mountains.

adj **17.** The *jazz* band gave no concerts last week.

_V_ **18.** Of course you may *borrow* my compass!

pro **19.** Is *this* your locker for the semester?

adj **20.** The *park* attendant will help us find a picnic table.

adv **21.** The picnickers waited *impatiently* for the rain to stop.

adj **22.** The *young* joggers splashed happily through the mud puddles in their path.

_V_ **23.** The voyagers who *survived* the shipwreck tell a thrilling story.

pro **24.** Does *anyone* know where I left my scissors?

_n_ **25.** In the doorway appeared a long, bent *shadow.*

▶ **Exercise 2** Write the correct form (comparative or superlative) of the modifier in parentheses.

This movie is the __most *or* least interesting__ one I have seen all year. (interesting)

1. The third contestant sounded the _____ as far as I was concerned. (truthful)

2. Garth arrived for the marathon _____ than his brother Logan. (early)

3. I know the route to Chicago _____ than the one to Dallas. (well)

4. You can develop that idea _____ than you have done so far. (far)

5. Five inches of snow is the _____ we ever get in this part of the country. (much)

6. She is the _____ dancer I have ever seen. (graceful)

7. In our family, artistic ability is _____ esteemed than in many other families. (highly)

8. The crowd cheered that star _____. (loudly)

9. Charles caught the _____ fish that had ever been caught in his village. (large)

10. We made the requested changes _____ than she expected. (cheerfully)

11. The department store manager was _____ to help us than her employee was. (eager)

12. That was the _____ service we have had in a long time. (good)

13. As a doctor, Aaron was _____ than his brother. (successful)

14. Of all the neighbors, he speaks _____ with Mrs. Andrews. (often)

15. The path was winding and _____ toward the top of the hill. (narrow)

16. I have never experienced anything _____ than the riverbank that morning. (peaceful)

17. Catherine said she was _____ that day than she had ever been before. (angry)

18. Of all the campers, Jack approached the animal _____. (cautiously)

19. There was _____ preparation for the party than we expected. (little)

20. The fog is _____ today than yesterday. (dense)

21. Manny has been elected class treasurer _____ than anyone else in the school's history. (times)

22. I can run _____ than my older sister Alta. (fast)

23. After breaking a statuette, the clerk handled the china _____. (careful)

24. I'm the _____ person in my family. (impatient)

25. Surely the only form of transportation _____ _____ than a bicycle is walking. (slow)

Usage

▶ **Exercise 3** Underline the word in parentheses that best completes each sentence.

Don't forget to take (a, <u>an</u>) umbrella with you.

1. There were not as many people at the game (like, <u>as</u>) we expected.

2. On the way home from school, we go (passed, <u>past</u>) the library.

3. It's a good idea to (<u>precede</u>, proceed) each speech with a few deep breaths.

4. I would rather walk in the woods (<u>than</u>, then) play ball.

5. I didn't mind waiting, but I certainly got tired of (<u>sitting</u>, setting) still.

6. I'm afraid I'll (loose, <u>lose</u>) the combination for the lock.

7. The director waited (a while, <u>awhile</u>) before asking the orchestra to tune their instruments.

8. I received the invitation, but I must (<u>respectfully</u>, respectively) decline.

9. All the flowers were in bloom (accept, <u>except</u>) the dahlias.

10. Please excuse the interruption and (precede, <u>proceed</u>) with what you were doing.

11. I dropped the cassette tape, but it was (<u>all right</u>, alright).

12. Maia wants to form a writer's group whenever we (<u>can</u>, may) get together.

13. He (<u>doesn't</u>, don't) believe the car can be repaired.

14. We rowed the canoe (<u>farther</u>, further) upriver than we had ever gone before.

15. We'll do our homework and (than, <u>then</u>) we'll go to the park.

16. Would everyone please move (in, <u>into</u>) the study hall?

17. The warm weather will (affect, <u>effect</u>) the candy we are planning to make.

18. Even though he's very young, Roger has (all ready, <u>already</u>) become a good cook.

19. Father had the porch repaired because the railing was (<u>loose</u>, lose).

20. Juan is the best person to (<u>raise</u>, rise) the issue.

21. Too full from the main course, I (<u>passed</u>, past) on having dessert.

22. (Precede, <u>Proceed</u>) with caution.

23. Oscar's, Justin's, and Gary's favorite activities, (respectfully, <u>respectively</u>), are riding horses, playing volleyball on the beach, and lying in a hammock at the end of the day.

24. Pick some vegetables from the garden, and (than, <u>then</u>) fix a salad for lunch.

25. Dad, (can, <u>may</u>) I carve another pumpkin for the front steps?

26. I know I've lost weight; my jeans are too (<u>loose</u>, lose).

Usage

Mechanics

Unit 11: Capitalization

Lesson 70
Capitalization of Sentences

Capitalize the first word of a sentence.

The movie we saw was a classic.

Capitalize the first word of a direct quotation that is a complete sentence.

John F. Kennedy said, "**A**sk not what your country can do for you; ask what you can do for your country."

Do not capitalize the first word of a quotation that cannot stand as a complete sentence.

The reporter characterized the scene as one of "**c**omplete, absolute chaos."

Capitalize the first word of a complete sentence that stands by itself in parentheses. Do not capitalize a sentence in parentheses if it is within another sentence.

(**T**he experiment should take five minutes.)
Set out your lab equipment (**t**he experiment should take five minutes) and work with your partner.

▶ **Exercise 1** Draw three lines under each lowercase letter that should be capitalized.

<u>t</u>raining a dog can be a difficult job.

1. monica said, "there is no reason we cannot finish the project today."

2. the recipe calls for butter. (margarine may also be used.)

3. principal Steadman described the test scores as "encouraging."

4. Send your entry in before the deadline. (the address is listed at the bottom.)

5. Thomas Paine wrote, "these are the times that try men's souls."

6. sign up to participate in the band concert (if you haven't already).

7. our youth group is selling magazines (they are for a good cause) this month..

8. Swimming class is held Monday through Thursday (fridays are optional.)

9. mr. Johnson said, "the resources you'll need are available in the library."

10. she earns money by baby-sitting on the weekends.

11. the firefighters gave helpful suggestions. (for example, it is a good idea to have home fire drills.)

12. we usually have pizza on Friday nights.

Mechanics

13. "you are all invited to join the Physics Club," Mrs. McCann said.

14. sharon was a bridesmaid in her sister's wedding.

15. new inventions were on display at the fair.

16. the presidential candidate said that reducing the national deficit was "of primary concern."

17. Arturo whispered the instructions to me. (talking loudly is not permitted in study hall.)

18. The photographer said, "please move to your left."

19. the flu epidemic reduced class attendance last week.

20. jazz music is Danielle's favorite. (her father is a jazz musician.)

▶ **Exercise 2** Draw three lines under each lowercase letter that should be capitalized. Draw a slash (/) through each capitalized letter that should be lowercase.

antibiotics (Usually derived from bacteria or molds) can be used to treat many diseases.

1. the speaker encouraged us to "Treat everyone with equal respect."

2. The rules say You should not leave the school grounds for lunch.

3. several members of the basketball team intend to play basketball in college.

4. the children (Especially the younger ones) were restless during the program.

5. City law states That it is illegal to park in that area.

6. "my friend is waiting for me," Janet said, "But I can spare a few minutes."

7. her paintings (Including the mural in the lobby) have brought Mika much recognition.

8. jerod bought himself a new computer game with the money he earned.

9. we walked to the library to do research for our English papers.

10. It was January (Not February) when we last saw our cousin.

11. "did you remember to feed the fish?" asked Mom.

12. Carlos said that He needed a ride to the game.

13. jim forgot his notebook. (later he realized he had left it in his locker.)

14. the school newspaper ran an article on recycling.

15. Experiments (We performed one today) are important in scientific investigation.

16. The choir director said, "rise slowly together and exit to the right."

17. astronaut Neil Armstrong said, "that's one small step for man, one giant leap for mankind."

18. Water skiing (Along with swimming and bike riding) is our favorite summer activity.

Lesson 71
Capitalization of Proper Nouns

Proper nouns should be capitalized. A **proper noun** names a specific person, place, or thing. In proper nouns composed of several words, do not capitalize articles, coordinating conjunctions, or prepositions of fewer than five letters unless they are the first or last word of a title.

Aunt Nancy	Christmas	General Colin Powell	Lake Ontario
Harvard Law School	Spain	Biology 101	Middle East
the South	the Big Dipper	"America the Beautiful"	Steinway piano

In general, capitalize a title that describes a relative only when it is used with or in place of a proper name. Do not capitilize a title that follows an article or a possessive.

Ask **M**om to call me.   My **m**om has to work today.

▶ **Exercise 1** Draw three lines under each lowercase letter that should be capitalized.

William <u>shakespeare</u> was born in <u>stratford</u>, <u>england</u>, in 1564.

1. william shakespeare authored some of the world's best-known plays, sonnets, and poems.

2. Many of his memorable plays were tragedies, such as *julius caesar, hamlet,* and *othello.*

3. shakespeare also wrote many comedies.

4. *the merchant of venice* is one of the most popular Shakespearean comedies.

5. It was based on a story by Italian writer giovanni fiorentino.

6. It deals with the predicament faced by antonio, a merchant in debt.

7. The play takes place in italy and has a theme of mercy over malice.

8. Shakespeare deals with a complicated series of plots in *a midsummer night's dream.*

9. This story shows shakespeare's talent for interweaving plots and characters.

10. The comedy *much ado about nothing* is similar in some ways.

11. It describes the relationship between two persons, benedick and beatrice.

12. In the comedy *as you like it,* shakespeare lets audiences choose their own meaning for the play.

13. In this play, rightful ruler duke senior is banished by duke frederick.

14. duke senior is sent to the forest of arden, a place apart from the realities of the world.

15. *twelfth night* deals with classic twists and turns in romance.

16. Characters viola and sebastian find love.

Mechanics

17. Through the power of their love for each other, characters olivia and orsino rid themselves of self-love.

18. Many of Shakespeare's plays are built around historic figures such as julius caesar.

19. Several of them focus on the kings of england.

20. William Shakespeare is considered one of the most famous writers of the renaissance.

▶ **Exercise 2** Draw three lines under each lowercase letter that should be capitalized. If the capitalization is correct, write *C* in the blank.

_____ shakespeare's writing took place during a period in literature known as the Elizabethan Age.

_____ 1. This was the name given to the time during the reign of queen elizabeth I.

_____ 2. The Elizabethan movement in literature took place from the mid-1500s to the early 1600s.

_____ 3. It has been regarded as one of the greatest periods in the history of england.

_____ 4. During the Elizabethan Age, there was a sharing of old and new ideas.

_____ 5. Along with shakespeare, poets such as edmund spenser produced Elizabethan poetry.

_____ 6. The Romantic period in literature began in the nineteenth century.

_____ 7. Romantic literature showed an appreciation of the romances of the middle ages.

_____ 8. Two of the most famous poets of the period were william wordsworth and john keats.

_____ 9. Percy b. shelley also wrote poems in this period, such as *ode to the west wind* and *to a Skylark.*

_____ 10. The Victorian period in literature is named for the reign of Queen Victoria.

_____ 11. The Victorian period lasted from the 1830s to the 1860s.

_____ 12. Writing of the Victorian period reflected the changing society in london and the rest of england.

_____ 13. Famous novelists of this era included charles dickens and charlotte brontë.

_____ 14. Dickens wrote such classics as *the pickwick papers, oliver twist, a tale of two cities,* and *great expectations.*

_____ 15. charlotte brontë's *jane eyre* describes a woman's struggle for independence and love.

Mechanics

Lesson 72
Capitalization of Proper Adjectives

Capitalize proper adjectives (adjectives formed from proper nouns). These include persons' names, place names, and names of national, ethnic, and religious groups used as adjectives.

Members of the **C**linton administration attended the dinner.
Terry read a book on how to do **J**apanese origami.

▶ **Exercise 1** Draw three lines under each lowercase letter that should be capitalized.

Inali is an alaskan native who spent many years in the canadian Rockies before moving here.

1. For breakfast I had canadian bacon on an english muffin.

2. We always try to attend the annual italian festival.

3. There are many legends in native american folklore.

4. Our family gets a christmas tree on christmas eve.

5. The art museum downtown has a renoir exhibit.

6. In the algerian Revolution, Muslim Algerians fought against french rule.

7. Jason has an english sheep dog and an irish setter.

8. The Yamaguchis live in the victorian house on the corner.

9. We learned much about american history on our easter vacation.

10. My friend Maryam teaches me all about islamic customs.

11. Rachel enjoys elizabethan poetry.

12. We studied french culture and history.

13. The american dollar is accepted in many foreign countries.

14. There are many wild animals living in the african jungles.

15. *Moby Dick* is a classic american novel about the sea.

16. Cody wants to play for the miami Dolphins someday.

17. The building on the corner was formerly a jewish synagogue.

18. Ancient egyptian persons developed elaborate and colossal structures.

19. My mother's prized possession is a grecian urn that she found at a local auction.

20. The president of the United States lives on pennsylvania avenue.

Mechanics

21. Lena and I are going to a halloween party.

22. In ancient Rome, Pompey the Great and Julius Caesar fought for power in the roman republic.

23. The cathedral in Paris called Notre-Dame is an example of gothic architecture.

24. The weather forecaster predicted stormy weather for the great plains region of the country.

25. The hispanic population of the United States has grown considerably.

26. Our english class spent two weeks discussing greek mythology.

27. Chad's father works in the north american office of a worldwide corporation.

28. Li-Ching is the only other asian girl in my class besides me.

29. parisian fashions often set trends for the rest of the world.

30. Appalachia is a region that gets its name from the appalachian Mountains that run through it.

31. Although Teresa enjoys indian food, she prefers chinese food.

32. While visiting Austria, we quickly adapted to austrian customs.

33. My great-grandfather fought in many german battles.

34. The spanish quiz was a difficult one.

35. Aunt Pauline has a west highland white terrier.

36. My jewish friends have learned to speak the hebrew language.

37. My uncle explored the australian outback many years ago.

38. Sonia is proud of her puerto rican heritage.

39. The leaders were concerned with middle eastern politics.

40. Our favorite game is chinese checkers.

41. The class paused for a long time at the monet exhibit.

42. One freudian concept is the influence of the unconscious mind on conscious thoughts.

43. During the sacred observance of Ramadan, many muslim persons fast.

44. american auto makers often compete for sales with japanese auto makers.

45. The alaskan pipeline runs from the Arctic Ocean to a port on the Gulf of Alaska.

Mechanics

✓ Unit 11 **Review**

▶ **Exercise 1** Draw three lines under each lowercase letter that should be capitalized.

the geometry tests were easy. (the final exam was much more difficult.)

1. When my uncle met aunt carol, he knew he would marry her one day.

2. Ricardo volunteered to help the democrats with their campaign.

3. tara enjoys listening to contemporary music.

4. On our trip to washington, d.c., we visited the jefferson memorial.

5. The minards take their annual vacation in july.

6. In the spring the drama club will perform *cheaper by the dozen.*

7. Our teacher explained that newtonian physics deals with principles formulated by sir isaac newton.

8. "choose any puppy you wish," said uncle paul. "there are plenty."

9. On a clear night David can see cassiopeia with his telescope.

10. The advanced biology class will be dissecting this week. (supplies are in the lab.)

11. general norman schwarzkopf was the commander of u.s. forces in the persian gulf war.

12. All of the neighbors (including the martins) were having a barbecue.

13. Mrs. Danbury, the principal, said she would speak to superintendent wilson about funding.

14. We attended the ceremony when cousin meg graduated from penn state.

15. traditional african art consists of many religious masks, figures, and decorative objects.

16. our grandparents came to this country from italy.

17. the building on the corner of lake street and green avenue is called the columbus environmental center.

18. We traveled west (it's our first family vacation) to yellowstone national park.

19. For mother's day, we got mom tickets to see the boston symphony orchestra.

20. The california condor is one of the rarest north american birds.

Mechanics

Name _____ Class _____ Date _____

Cumulative Review: Units 1–11

Exercise 1 Write *col.* above each collective noun, *con.* above each concrete noun, and *abst.* above each abstract noun. Draw two lines under the verb in each sentence.

    col.   con.   abst.

The choir is often winning awards for excellence.

1. The old car was making strange noises.

2. Our team seems ready to face the opponent.

3. Adolescence is a difficult time for many kids.

4. Without my glasses, the chalkboard is hard to see.

5. Cindy's necklace looks expensive.

Exercise 2 Underline each adjective, including possessives and articles, and circle each adverb.

Doug fell (asleep) (immediately) when his head hit the soft pillow.

1. Rolonda never misses afternoon practice.

2. When Erica finally received her college degree, she was very happy.

3. Because she's a fast runner, individuals constantly tell Andrea to audition for the track team.

4. Jane did extremely well on the driving test.

5. Kenji chose a complex topic for his term paper.

Exercise 3 Draw a vertical line between the subject and predicate in each sentence.

A team of paramedics | demonstrated CPR for the class.

1. Many of the students wore the school colors on Friday.

2. The flood waters were held back by sandbags.

3. Rhode Island is the smallest state in the United States.

4. Coach Jackson and his assistant led the team to victory.

5. The bus stalled several times before starting.

6. Barbecued ribs and corn on the cob were served at the picnic.

7. Florida has many family vacation spots.

8. The dinosaur exhibit was interesting for adults as well as children.

9. Several inches of snow fell within an hour.

Mechanics

Copyright © by Glencoe/McGraw-Hill

242 *Grammar and Language Workbook, Grade 10*

10. The chemical explosion caused damage to many buildings.

▶ **Exercise 4** Underline each prepositional phrase and circle each appositive phrase.

Craig, (my best friend,) dove off the diving board and hit the water with a splash.

1. Sarah is at Community Hospital, the city's finest cardiac care facility.

2. The Big Dipper, a group of seven stars, is part of the constellation Ursa Major.

3. Keiko had a cast on her arm as a result of her fall.

4. The dance marathon, an event held to raise money for charity, was a big success.

5. Behind the curtain the cast waited to bow for the audience.

6. Brad looked under the hood to see what was wrong with the car.

7. Laurie poured the solution into the beaker.

8. The Astrodome, an indoor stadium, is where the Houston Astros play.

9. Marilyn, Cathy's sister, is a camp counselor.

10. The letter from Kimiko made Jenny happy for the rest of the day.

▶ **Exercise 5** Label each italicized phrase *ger.* for gerund, *part.* for participial, or *inf.* for infinitive.

part.
Smiling at the clown, the little boy accepted the balloon.

1. *Daily practicing* improved Joel's backstroke.

2. Miguel likes *to take pictures at athletic events*.

3. The general wore a uniform *decorated with many medals*.

4. Dad set the timer *to turn on the lights at sundown*.

5. We saw one stingray *swimming among the fish*.

▶ **Exercise 6** Label each italicized clause *adj.* for adjective, *N* for noun, or *adv.* for adverb.

adv.
We returned to our seats *after we got some popcorn*.

1. *What I couldn't understand* was the concept of geometric theorems.

2. The students *who play in the band* were excused early.

3. *Because she studies hard*, Beatriz gets good grades.

4. Beth would not tell *who won the contest*.

Mechanics

5. Hiroko, *whose parents speak little English*, is adjusting well to the United States.

▶ **Exercise 7** Write in the blank the tense of each italicized verb: *present, past, future, past perf., present perf.*, or *future perf.*

<u>**future perf.**</u>   After I finish Dad's car, I *will have washed* three cars.

_____ **1.** The Booster Club *supports* the football team.

_____ **2.** Roberto *had learned* about go-cart racing from his uncle.

_____ **3.** The drama coach *will give* us a pep talk before the performance.

_____ **4.** Andre *earns* money by delivering newspapers.

_____ **5.** I *have performed* with my dance troupe every year.

_____ **6.** Derek *attends* soccer camp every summer.

_____ **7.** An ankle injury *had kept* Austin from playing hockey.

_____ **8.** He *has collected* model trains since he was a child.

_____ **9.** Chad and Rafael *joined* us for a game of tennis.

_____ **10.** By tomorrow, we *will have missed* three days of school due to snowy weather.

▶ **Exercise 8** Draw three lines under each lowercase letter that should be capitalized.

A picture of <u>e</u>lvis <u>p</u>resley appeared on a <u>u</u>.<u>s</u>. postage stamp.

1. My dad made mexican food for dinner.

2. Mrs. aviles asked, "does everyone have a pencil for the aptitude test?"

3. The invitation was for a party on saturday. (a map to the house was included.)

4. The fireworks (usually held on the fourth of july) were postponed due to rain.

5. "caroline is waiting for you," mother called from the stairs.

6. Dr. williams reminded us to "eat well and take vitamins."

7. The site near our house was evaluated by the environmental protection agency.

8. the united states fought great britain in the war of 1812.

9. grandfather's new truck was made by the ford motor company.

10. The president of the United States flew in from china on *air force one.*

Mechanics

Unit 12: Punctuation, Abbreviations, and Numbers

Lesson 73
End-of-Sentence Punctuation

Use a period at the end of a declarative sentence and at the end of a polite command.

The trees are swaying in the wind. (declarative sentence)
Please pass the pepper. (polite command)

Use an exclamation point to show strong feeling and to indicate a forceful command.

What a beautiful shawl this is! (exclamation)
Listen to me! (strong imperative)

Use a question mark to indicate a direction question.

How do bishops move in chess?

Do not place a question mark after a declarative sentence that contains an indirect question.

Brian asked how bishops move in chess.

▶ **Exercise 1 Add a period, question mark, or exclamation point at the end of each sentence.**

Do you know who Andrew Johnson was ?

1. Andrew Johnson became president after the assassination of Abraham Lincoln

2. Like Lincoln he had grown up in a poor family

3. Johnson started out his adult life as a tailor, but he had a talent for public speaking and soon got involved in politics

4. He became governor, congressman, and senator in Tennessee, his home state

5. Johnson was a Democrat and a slave owner

6. Are you wondering what side he took in the Civil War

7. Although Tennessee seceded with the other Southern states, Johnson (a senator at the time) remained loyal to the Union

8. During the war, Lincoln made him military governor of Tennessee

9. Before the war ended, Lincoln, a Republican, asked him to be his vice president

Mechanics

10. Although Johnson was a Democrat, Lincoln believed he could help bring the North and South together again

11. Johnson had shown great courage as military governor, a post that often put him in danger

12. What other traits did he have

13. He was extremely stubborn and uncompromising

14. Many questioned these traits, saying he would be a poor leader during Reconstruction

15. Right after the war Johnson created the Freedmen's Bureau

16. The bureau offered food, clothing, and shelter and began opening schools for former slaves

17. At the same time, however, leaders in the Southern states passed laws that discriminated against African Americans

18. They also did nothing to stop outbreaks of violence against former slaves

19. What outrage this caused among the leaders of Congress

20. These leaders, known as Radical Republicans, passed a Civil Rights Act to guarantee the rights of African Americans in the South

21. What did Johnson do that illustrated he did not believe in equality

22. He vetoed the civil rights law, but Congress was able to override his veto

23. Congress also passed the Fourteenth Amendment, which said no state could take away any person's rights

24. How Johnson hated the powerful radicals

25. His hatred for his political enemies made him very unpopular

26. By refusing to bend on the issue of states' rights, he alienated Northerners, African Americans in both the South and the North, and moderate Southerners

27. Senator Thaddeus Stevens, the leader of the Radical Republicans, and many citizens believed that Johnson had betrayed the Union

28. Many cried, "Impeach him "

29. If two thirds of the Senate vote to convict a president, the president can be removed from office

30. At Johnson's impeachment trial the Senate failed to convict the president by only one vote

31. Was Johnson really tried for "high crimes" as the Constitution allows

32. Many historians believe he was actually tried because of his ideas and opinions

Mechanics

Lesson 74
Colons

Use a colon to introduce a list, especially after a statement that uses words such as *these, the following,* or *as follows.*

The new parents considered **these** three names for their baby daughter: Penelope, Priscilla, and Patricia.

Do not use a colon to introduce a list if the list immediately follows a verb or a preposition.

The meal **includes** salad, soup, a main course, and dessert.
I went to the movie **with** Carmen, Celeste, and Carol.

Use a colon to introduce material that illustrates, explains, or restates the preceding material. The complete sentence after the colon is generally lowercased.

Marvin had mixed feelings about the event: it made him feel sad and happy at the same time.

Use a colon to introduce a long or formal quotation. A formal quotation is often preceded by words such as *this, these, the following,* or *as follows.*

Arman's speech ended with **this** quotation from Chief Joseph of the Nez Percé: "Hear me my chiefs! I am tired; my heart is sick and sad. From where the sun now stands I will fight no more forever."

Use a colon between the hour and the minute of the precise time, between the chapter and the verse in biblical references, and after the salutation of a business letter.

3:32 A.M.   Genesis 1:1–31   Dear Ms. Elanko:

▶ **Exercise 1 Insert a colon where necessary. If the sentence is correct, write *C* in the blank.**

_____   Assemble these materials: newspaper, marking pens, and masking tape.

_____ **1.** You can pick up the package between 800 and 830.

_____ **2.** "To every thing there is a season" is a quotation from Ecclesiastes 3:1.

_____ **3.** So you see my predicament: if I say yes, I will feel selfish, and if I say no, I will feel I have missed an opportunity.

_____ **4.** Marissa greatly admires the work of the following modern artists Henry Moore, Louise Nevelson, and Willem de Kooning.

_____ **5.** Many enlistment posters for World War I had this caption: "Uncle Sam wants you!"

Mechanics

_____ **6.** In order, the first three presidents of the United States were George Washington, John Adams, and Thomas Jefferson.

_____ **7.** Abyssinia's national costume consisted of a plum-colored silk shirt, a gray flannel skirt, and a handwoven wool vest.

_____ **8.** Before you cross a railroad track, always do this stop, look both ways, and listen.

_____ **9.** To begin the sermon, the minister read Mark 4:14–25.

_____ **10.** Last summer Keshia read these works by Mark Twain *Life on the Mississippi, Huckleberry Finn, The Prince and the Pauper,* and *Tom Sawyer.*

_____ **11.** After class is over, I would like to meet with Pam, Erin, and Rosa.

_____ **12.** The mournful tune began with this line "Yesterday is but a sweet memory."

_____ **13.** At the Chinese restaurant we ordered these appetizers steamed dumplings, fried won ton, and egg rolls.

_____ **14.** Three clues suggested that the thief was in a hurry the open window, the muddy footprints on the rug, and a broken vase next to the table.

_____ **15.** The main characters in Louisa May Alcott's novel *Little Women* are four sisters: Amy, Beth, Meg, and Jo.

_____ **16.** Every morning I try to do the following chores (1) make my bed, (2) pick up my clothes, and (3) rinse my breakfast dishes.

_____ **17.** I have to get up early tomorrow to catch the 7:00 A.M. bus.

_____ **18.** When a thunderstorm is coming, follow these steps to avoid damage to your personal computer (1) turn off the computer, (2) turn off the surge protector, and (3) unplug the system at the wall.

_____ **19.** The following items can be picked up in the lost-and-found-room a red umbrella, a pair of gray mittens, and a leather key case.

_____ **20.** The words echoed in my mind: "Do not hurry. Do take a rest."

_____ **21.** Imamu's list of places to visit in New York City included Ellis Island, the Museum of Modern Art, and the New York Stock Exchange.

_____ **22.** Alan began his letter with "Dear Sir or Madam:" because he didn't know if the president of the company was a man or a woman.

Mechanics

Lesson 75
Semicolons

Use a semicolon to separate main clauses that are not joined by a coordinating conjunction *(and, but, or, nor, yet,* or *for).*

Evelyn is the youngest daughter, and Elizabeth is the oldest.
Evelyn is the youngest daughter; Elizabeth is the oldest.

Use a semicolon to separate main clauses joined by a conjunctive adverb (such as *however, therefore, nevertheless, moreover, furthermore,* and *consequently*) or by an expression such as *for example* or *that is.* Usually, a conjunctive adverb or an expression such as *for example* is followed by a comma.

Ohio has produced several presidents; for example, Harrison, Grant, Hayes, McKinley, Taft, and Harding were all from Ohio.

Use a semicolon to separate the items in a series when the items contain commas.

This picture shows Sheryl, my best friend, in the front row; Sam, the class president, in the second row; and Evita, the exchange student, standing behind Sam.

Use a semicolon to separate two main clauses joined by a coordinating conjunction when such clauses already contain several commas.

Many people who come to the library, including Effie, leave with a bag full of books; but just as many people leave with videos and CDs, which have become very popular since the audiovisual department expanded.

▶ **Exercise 1** Write *C* in the blank if the sentence is correctly punctuated.

___C___   One of my favorite actors is Tom Hanks; I especially liked his performance in the movie *Forrest Gump.*

_____   **1.** Jim isn't here now, and he hasn't been here all day.

_____   **2.** We stepped into the dark theater; then we waited a moment for our eyes to adjust before looking for a seat.

_____   **3.** Arthur Ashe had outstanding leadership qualities and a special talent for playing tennis his talents have made him a role model among young people.

_____   **4.** Many pets; for example, my cat Nellie, are treated like members of the family.

_____   **5.** Kareem loves to play ice hockey, however, he does not own his own equipment.

_____   **6.** Among the works of T.S. Eliot are *The Wasteland*, a long poem published as a book; *Murder in the Cathedral*, a play; and *Old Possum's Book of Practical Cats*, a children's book that later became the inspiration for the musical *Cats.*

_____   **7.** The old house badly needed a coat of paint; furthermore, the gutters were sagging and the porch railing was broken.

_____ **8.** When you pack for the trip to England, be sure to include a plastic rain parka because it rains frequently there and you should also pack a warm sweater because the weather can be chilly.

_____ **9.** It sprinkled on and off at the picnic; nevertheless, we still had a good time.

_____ **10.** Hakeem attended the soccer game; but his brother did not.

_____ **11.** Thomas Edison was a gifted inventor; and he also improved on the inventions of others.

_____ **12.** Angela came in first in the cross-country race; Rayann came in second.

_____ **13.** I have a marching band rehearsal on Saturday morning however, I'll be free by 11:00.

_____ **14.** The crowd included people from Columbus, Georgia, Columbus, Indiana, and Columbus, Ohio.

_____ **15.** This CD-ROM encyclopedia includes short video sequences; for example, if you click on this line, you can view the crash of the *Hindenburg*, an early airship.

_____ **16.** Anna plays the oboe, an instrument I like; but I decided to take up the flute because, as many people will tell you, it has such a beautiful sound.

_____ **17.** Several branches of the old tree were rubbing against the telephone wires, therefore, the telephone company sent someone to trim the branches.

_____ **18.** At the mall Enrique bought a pair of shoes, and Fred bought a tropical fish.

_____ **19.** Miguel's pirate costume, complete with an eye patch, a long dark moustache, and a large black hat, was wonderful; he had even trained his pet parrot to ride on his shoulder.

_____ **20.** I can't go to the concert because I have to baby-sit; moreover, I don't have any extra money right now.

_____ **21.** Many species of worms are marine, that is, they live in the oceans.

_____ **22.** Allow me to introduce my grandmother, Mrs. Dice; my mother, Mrs. Morgan; and my sister, Lorraine Morgan.

▶ **Writing Link** **Write a brief paragraph describing your favorite type of music and your favorite musical performers. Use semicolons in at least half of your sentences.**

_____
_____
_____
_____
_____
_____
_____

Mechanics

Lesson 76
Commas: Compound Sentences

Use commas between the main clauses in a compound sentence. Place a comma before a coordinating conjunction *(and, but, or, nor, yet,* or *for)* that joins two main clauses.

Today we visited the battlefield at Gettysburg, and tomorrow we will drive to Antietam.

You may omit the comma between very short main clauses that are connected by a coordinating conjunction, unless the comma is needed to avoid confusion.

Tomaka opened the window and a bird flew in. (clear)
Hank petted the dog and the cat meowed. (confusing)
Hank petted the dog, and the cat meowed. (clear)

▶ **Exercise 1** **Add commas where needed. Write *C* in the blank if the sentence uses commas correctly.**

_____ Susan's school performed *Tom Sawyer*, and she played Becky Thatcher.

_____ 1. The much-admired writer Mark Twain was born in a small frontier settlement in Missouri and he grew up in Hannibal, Missouri.

_____ 2. Hannibal was a quiet town on the banks of the Mississippi, but the town became lively when a riverboat appeared.

_____ 3. Like many young boys, Twain admired the riverboat pilots and longed to become one someday.

_____ 4. The pilot always had to be aware of the depth of the water for riverboats could get stuck in shallow water.

_____ 5. Twain's real name was Samuel Clemens, but he is best known by his pen name.

_____ 6. Riverboat workers called out "mark twain" when the water was two fathoms (12 feet) deep and a pilot hearing this call knew that the water was safe to cross.

_____ 7. Twain had several jobs but he started out as an apprentice to a printer, his older brother.

_____ 8. Twain didn't always get along with his brother but he did learn the printing trade.

_____ 9. Twain then took a series of printing jobs in different parts of the country, and he also began to write humorous stories.

_____ 10. In 1857 he began an apprenticeship as a riverboat pilot, and his experiences on the river led him to write a series of sketches called *Life on the Mississippi*.

Mechanics

_____ **11.** Twain tried to become a silver prospector in Nevada and there he experienced the "wild" West.

_____ **12.** He did not strike it rich as a prospector, yet he did find rich subject matter for his novel *Roughing It.*

_____ **13.** Next he headed for San Francisco, and there he took a job as a newspaper reporter and met other western writers.

_____ **14.** One of Twain's most famous stories was written there in 1865; it is about a jumping frog.

_____ **15.** Twain's stories made people laugh but the stories often had a serious point.

_____ **16.** He might satirize the excesses of the very rich or he might point out human cruelty and injustice.

_____ **17.** Mark Twain and writer Charles Dudley Warner both thought the emphasis on making money after the Civil War was causing people to neglect democratic ideals, and they named these years the "Gilded Age."

_____ **18.** The novel *Huckleberry Finn* is an adventure story about how a boy and a runaway slave search for freedom but it is also a story about friendship.

_____ **19.** *Tom Sawyer* is a book that many readers enjoy, for it paints a charming picture of the simple pleasures of boyhood in a Mississippi river town.

_____ **20.** Twain had a wide experience of America and Americans, and this experience is reflected in his novels.

_____ **21.** Twain also had an ear for dialects and he was the first great writer to use this everyday speech of Americans in novels and stories.

_____ **22.** In his later life, Twain took a very dark view of human nature and his pessimism is reflected in works such as *The Mysterious Stranger.*

_____ **23.** Mark Twain was born in a year in which Halley's comet was visible from Earth, and he predicted that his death would coincide with the comet's return.

_____ **24.** Halley's comet returns to Earth about every seventy-six years and it did so in 1910, the year of Mark Twain's death.

_____ **25.** I have not yet read Twain's *Tom Sawyer* nor have I read *A Connecticut Yankee in King Arthur's Court.*

Lesson 77
Commas: Series and Coordinate Adjectives

Use commas to separate three or more words, phrases, or clauses in a series.

Snakes, lizards, and crocodiles are all reptiles.
The snake crawled over the log, through the grass, and into the stream.

No commas are necessary when all of the items are connected by conjunctions.

Celia has a boa constrictor and an iguana and a chameleon.

Nouns that are used in pairs (salt and pepper, thunder and lightning, red beans and rice) are usually considered single units and should not be separated by commas. If such pairs appear with other nouns or groups of nouns in a series, they must be set off from the other items in the series.

Will you have ranch dressing, Italian dressing, or oil and vinegar on your salad?

Place a comma between coordinate adjectives that precede a noun. Coordinate adjectives modify a noun equally. To tell whether adjectives are coordinate, try to reverse their order or put the word *and* between them. If the sentence still sounds right, the adjectives are coordinate.

The short, dark-haired, handsome hero saved the day.
I tore off a piece of fragrant, crusty French bread.
The children played with a large red rubber ball.

▶ **Exercise 1 Add commas where necessary. Cross out incorrect commas using the delete symbol (ϒ).**

Students, teachers, and staff attended the special,⁄Environmental Day ceremonies.

1. Allegra gathered old newspapers, magazines and catalogs to take to the recycling center.

2. We spread the picnic blanket under a large, silver, beech tree.

3. Shawn has received letters for basketball soccer and track.

4. For breakfast Lek ate fresh grapefruit, ham, and eggs, and whole wheat toast.

5. Eliza got into bed set the alarm and turned out the light.

6. The roses in my grandmother's garden are pink, and yellow and red.

7. Kuniko wore a lovely, pink and green Japanese kimono to the tea ceremony.

8. On the table was a small tray of condiments including salt and pepper, relish and packets of sugar.

9. Soto raked the leaves onto the old sheet gathered up the corners and swung the big bundle over his shoulder.

10. Like most summer camps, this one offers swimming canoeing and hiking.

11. The airplane stopped in Atlanta, refueled and then flew to Luxembourg, Belgium.

12. Ahmed looked for his notebook at home, at school and on the bus.

13. In his speech the president spoke about health care the federal budget and trade with Mexico and Japan.

14. Monday was a cold, and damp, and dreary day.

15. In the North American habitat at the zoo, the class saw mountain lions wolves, coyotes and badgers.

16. As Jeanette walked down the block she passed the shoe repair the laundromat, and the bakery.

17. Snow, and sleet, and fog delayed us on our drive through New York state.

18. Leah, Seth and Tom are collaborating on a mural depicting the lives of African Americans just after the Civil War.

19. The crazy cat raced around the room out the front door and up a tree.

20. Chet didn't know who the lady was, what she wanted or where she lived.

21. Matt opened his backpack and took out a tiny lantern, a cook kit and a waterproof container of matches.

22. Heat the skillet over moderate heat add the hamburger patties and cook them for five minutes on each side.

23. The editorial said that the 200-year-old trees are valuable irreplaceable, natural resources.

24. On Saturday morning I need to mow the lawn, pull the weeds and sweep the front porch.

25. My brother is training for a triathlon that includes swimming, bicycling and running.

26. Yvonne enjoyed the movie because it starred her favorite actor, it was set in a small town like her own and it accurately portrayed high school life.

27. When we went on the owl walk, we took a flashlight, a tape recorder and a notebook.

28. Tess shrieked when she saw the long coiled hissing snake.

29. This summer Inez plans to spend time reading mysteries playing tennis, and helping her father build a canoe.

30. At the flea market Reggie found an old, wooden bucket, and a tattered, faded, red and white quilt.

Mechanics

Lesson 78
Commas: Nonessential Elements

Use commas to set off participles, infinitives, and their phrases if they are not essential to the meaning of the sentence. Nonessential elements can be removed without changing the meaning of the sentence.

Garrett, **wearing a necktie for the occasion,** accepted the award. (nonessential participle)
The player **wearing the number 20** is the one to watch. (essential participle)
Number 20 is worth watching, **to be sure.** (nonessential infinitive)
The player **to watch** is number 20. (essential infinitive)

Use commas to set off a nonessential adjective clause.

Zora Neal Hurston, **who was born around 1901,** is a well-known writer of the Harlem Renaissance. (nonessential clause)
The writer **who has made the greatest impression on me** is Ernest Hemingway. (essential clause)

Use commas to set off an appositive if it is not essential to the meaning of a sentence.

I read an essay by the writer **Virginia Woolf.** (essential appositive)
John Steinbeck, **a writer I admire,** wrote *The Grapes of Wrath.* (nonessential appositive)

▶ **Exercise 1** Write *C* in the blank if the sentence uses commas correctly.

C   Land and earth art, an especially interesting form of modern art, stresses landscape or the earth itself.

_____ **1.** Land and earth artists are those, who work with rock, soil, turf, and other natural elements.

_____ **2.** These artists generally do not create a traditional art object, something you can see in an art gallery.

_____ **3.** Their works are often impermanent, existing for only a few days or a few weeks.

_____ **4.** Christo, who uses only his first name, is probably the best-known land artist.

_____ **5.** In 1976 Christo built a running fence made of white nylon fabric.

_____ **6.** The fence, which was 18 feet high and 24 miles long, stretched across two hilly counties in northern California.

_____ **7.** Christo said he wanted to present something that people had never seen before.

_____ **8.** This "something" to quote him exactly would be "not an image but a real thing like the pyramids in Egypt or the Great Wall of China."

_____ **9.** The nylon fence, billowing in the wind like a long, taut sail, was a striking sight as it snaked across the rolling countryside.

Mechanics

_____ **10.** For the artist Christo the mechanics of setting up the fence and the impact on the landscape and its human neighbors were also important parts of the art work.

_____ **11.** Richard Long another land artist works with the land in a different way.

_____ **12.** Long, who was born in 1945, takes long and difficult journeys on foot in different parts of the world.

_____ **13.** In lonely locations, such as a plain in Tibet, he makes some mark, to show his presence.

_____ **14.** For example, he might walk back and forth continuously over the ground to create a line on the ground or heap nearby stones into a neat pile.

_____ **15.** The artist takes a photograph of each mark or construction to document the work.

_____ **16.** Richard Long's works, which may or may not be long-lasting, have an air of mystery.

_____ **17.** Their mystery is something like that, associated with prehistoric sites, such as Stonehenge.

_____ **18.** Long's works seem to get people thinking about human permanence and impermanence on Earth.

_____ **19.** Robert Smithson's most famous work, *Spiral Jetty*, was created in the Great Salt Lake in Utah.

_____ **20.** A jetty is a structure that projects into a body of water, to protect a harbor or influence water flow.

_____ **21.** Smithson's construction, which does not have a practical purpose, was created by bulldozers.

_____ **22.** The jetty measuring over 1,500 feet and resembling a coiled question mark is made of black basalt, limestone, earth and native red algae.

_____ **23.** You would need to fly over the desolate Great Salt Lake, to get a good view of this work of art.

_____ **24.** The spiral jetty soon began to decay.

▶ **Writing Link** Write a paragraph about an artist you admire. Use at least one nonessential **participle, clause, and appositive.**

_____

_____

_____

_____

_____

_____

_____

Mechanics

Lesson 79
Commas: Interjections, Parenthetical Expressions, and Conjunctive Adverbs

Use commas to set off interjections (such as *oh* and *well*), parenthetical expressions (such as *on the contrary, on the other hand*, *in fact, by the way, to be exact*, and *after all*), and conjunctive adverbs (such as *however, moreover*, and *consequently*).

Yes, I'd like to try riding a camel.
This train depot, **by the way,** was built in 1888.
Joshua loves snow skiing; **however,** he has never tried water skiing.

▶ **Exercise 1** **Insert commas where necessary. Some sentences may be correct.**

So, you want to go to college.

1. The living world might seem to be made up of only plants and animals; however there are at least five major groups of living things.

2. To be more exact biologists divide living things into different groups, called kingdoms.

3. Yes I have heard of these five basic kingdoms: plants, animals, bacteria, fungi, and protists.

4. Protists by the way are single-celled organisms, such as amoebas.

5. Indeed the protist kingdom is a sort of "catch-all" group for organisms that do not clearly fit into the other kingdoms.

6. Some biologists put protists into the kingdom protoctists; therefore you may come across this name in your reading.

7. In fact, there are some single-celled organisms in the other major kingdoms.

8. A yeast is a single-celled animal of course, and some species of algae are single-celled.

9. Bacteria exist in huge numbers in many habitats; indeed, many kinds of bacteria live in the human body.

10. *E. coli* is normally found in the human digestive tract in fact.

11. Some bacteria are harmful and cause disease; nevertheless many other kinds of bacteria are useful.

12. Many fungi grow out of the earth; consequently they are often discussed in books about plants.

13. Fungi however are an entirely separate group.

14. They have a very different life cycle from plants; moreover their internal structure is nothing like that of plants.

15. Besides fungi do not use sunlight to make their own food as plants do.

16. Instead they make food from the remains of plants and animals, or they live as parasites on living plants or animals.

17. Some fungi, on the other hand, prey on live animals; one type of fungi lives in pond mud and traps amoebae.

18. Also some fungi form close and mutually beneficial associations with living plants.

19. These fungi often grow on the roots of plants; as a result the fungi channel nutrients to the plants, and the plants supply the fungi with sugar for energy.

20. *Sym* means "together" and *bio* means "life"; therefore, *symbiosis* is an appropriate word for this kind of association between plant and fungus.

21. All members of the plant kingdom have complex cells; moreover they all produce sugar, as food, with the help of sunlight.

22. This kingdom, however, can be divided into vascular and nonvascular plants.

23. Many plants do not have internal structures for carrying water and nutrients from one part of the plant to another; therefore they are called nonvascular plants.

24. Seaweeds do not have vascular structures; likewise mosses and liverworts lack these structures.

25. Yes nonvascular plants grow only where it is wet.

▶ **Writing Link** **Write a paragraph about how something in your house, such as an appliance, works. Use interjections, parenthetical expressions, and conjunctive adverbs in your sentences.**

_____

_____

_____

_____

_____

_____

_____

_____

Mechanics

Lesson 80
Commas: Introductory Phrases, Adverb Clauses, and Antithetical Phrases

Use a comma after a short introductory prepositional phrase only if the sentence would be misread without it.

Before the election, results of the primaries were discussed in the news.

Use a comma after a long prepositional phrase or after the final phrase in a series of phrases. Do not use a comma if the phrase is immediately followed by a verb.

On the crest of the ridge to the left of the lookout tower, we could see fire.
On the mantel between the two pewter candlesticks sat an unusual figurine.

Use a comma to set off introductory participles and participial phrases.

Grinning, Lamont handed me a letter.
Steering to the left, Georgia guided the boat close to the pier.

Use a comma to set off an introductory adverb clause. Use commas to set off internal adverb clauses that interrupt the flow of the sentence. In general, do not set off an ending adverb clause unless the clause is parenthetical.

Because we are identical twins, people frequently confuse our names.
The house, even though it is more than two hundred years old, is in good condition.
Jerry will wash his car unless it rains.
Young children can be trying sometimes, if you know what I mean. (parenthetical)

Use commas to set off an antithetical phrase. In an antithetical phrase, a word such as *not* or *unlike* qualifies what comes before it.

Austria, unlike many European nations, is a landlocked country.

▶ **Exercise 1 Write *C* in the blank if the sentence is correctly punctuated.**

__C__   In the first leg of the four-hundred-meter relay, Kelley ran a little slowly.

_____ **1.** On top of the bookshelf in my room, you'll find my Spanish dictionary.

_____ **2.** Although Marvin loves to fish he seldom gets the chance.

_____ **3.** On Friday before the big game, I had trouble concentrating on my school work.

_____ **4.** Although you can skip a day every now and then it's best to floss your teeth every day.

_____ **5.** On our trip to the Badlands of South Dakota, we frequently saw jackrabbits.

_____ **6.** This field unlike all the others is planted in sunflowers.

_____ **7.** Over the summer Atepa plans to visit her grandmother in Taos, New Mexico.

_____ **8.** Using sign language, Nora related her vacation experiences.

_____ **9.** On Friday night I'd like to ride with you to the basketball game.

_____ **10.** Wearing a wool cap with earflaps and a big muffler Hank protected his face from the biting wind.

_____ **11.** This book, although it's long, can be read quickly.

_____ **12.** Analyzing the neat rows of holes in the tree, Reba guessed that a sapsucker had been there.

_____ **13.** Among the video games, was one that simulates a cattle drive in the Old West.

_____ **14.** In the upper stands at the baseball game was a large group wearing blue caps and waving Yankee pennants.

_____ **15.** Roberto, even though he's only fifteen is a skilled horseman.

_____ **16.** After the opening notes, Nguyen recognized the piece as Beethoven's Fifth Symphony.

_____ **17.** In the dim light houses that were white appeared gray.

_____ **18.** At the art museum the class viewed paintings by Monet and other Impressionists.

_____ **19.** Before you get into the boat, be sure to put on your life jacket.

_____ **20.** At the beginning of the novel, the boy is lonely because he lives on a remote ranch, in the outback of Australia.

_____ **21.** In my opinion the meeting, unlike the lecture, was a waste of time.

_____ **22.** Sealed tightly with some sort of wax, the box was impossible to open.

_____ **23.** Taking a deep breath Monique began to tell the story of how she had come to the United States.

_____ **24.** After thirty push-ups, Kyle's arms were quivering.

_____ **25.** The Cape of Good Hope is at the tip of Africa, not South America.

_____ **26.** In the middle of the summer here it doesn't get completely dark until about 9:00.

_____ **27.** On a bike tour through southern Wisconsin Rick saw countless black and white cows.

_____ **28.** Rushing to the net, the tennis player surprised his opponent with a delicate drop shot.

Mechanics

Lesson 81
Commas: Titles, Addresses, and Numbers

Use commas to set off titles when they follow a person's name.

Carlos Ramirez, M.D.
Christine Whitman, governor of New Jersey
Roberta Shipley, R.N., will demonstrate how to take a blood sample.

Use commas to separate the various parts of an address, a geographical term, or a date.

The Millers' farm is at 11699 Pleasant Valley Road, Mount Vernon, Ohio.
The new summer camp in Greenwich, Connecticut, opens on Monday, June 6, 1996.

In a letter use commas as follows:

142 Logan Avenue
Stanford, KY 40484
May 3, 1995

Do not use commas if only the month and day or only the month and year are given.

November 20   October 1987

Use commas to set off the parts of a reference that direct the reader to the exact source.

The quotation is from Herman Melville's *Moby-Dick*, page 1.
Act II, scene iii, of the play opens with a busy street scene.

▶ **Exercise 1 Add commas where necessary. Cross out commas used incorrectly by using the delete symbol (⟨). Some sentences may be correct.**

Mark's brother is attending college in Beloit, Wisconsin.

1. The package is addressed to Roger Moore, 453 Crystal Circle, Salinas CA, 93901.

2. Abraham Lincoln was assassinated on April 14 1865 just five days after the Civil War ended.

3. Walt Whitman's poem *When Lilacs Last in the Dooryard Bloom'd,* stanza 6, describes how Americans mourned President Lincoln's death.

4. Do you know why December 7, 1941 is an important date in the history of the United States?

5. This story about Crispus Attucks is from Virginia Hamilton's *Many Thousand Gone* pages 20–22.

6. My dental appointment is on Thursday, March 17.

7. I wrote to the publisher at 2460 Kerper Boulevard Dubuque IA 52001.

8. The Greensboro, North Carolina company produces modular computer furniture.

9. Summer vacation begins this year on June, 10.

10. Dr. Cesar Jimenez, M.D. gave expert testimony at the trial.

11. Annela is a foreign exchange student from Helsinki Finland.

12. In April, 1917 the United States entered World War I.

13. According to the application, January 26, 1980, is Jenny's date of birth.

14. The article was written by Marian Otting Ph.D. an expert on the Jewish religion.

15. Angie read aloud the opening lines of act I, scene ii, of Shakespeare's *Julius Caesar.*

16. Ted Kennedy, senator from Massachusetts, was a sponsor of the bill.

17. This catalog just arrived from a video game company in Rochester New York.

18. Garrett won't be eligible to take his driver's test until May, 1996.

19. At the rehearsal tonight our drama teacher wants us to read through Act Two, of *Our Town.*

20. Our route takes us from Biloxi, Mississippi to Chattanooga, Tennessee.

21. In the atlas the location for Washington, Pennsylvania, is given as page 36, A-2.

22. Send your postcards with the correct answer to Geo Quiz, 346 First Street, Denver, CO 80217.

23. The deadline for the writing contest is September 26 1994.

24. Holmes County Ohio, has the largest Amish population outside Pennsylvania.

25. You must register for the painting and drawing classes at the cultural arts center by

    January 5 1995.

26. The sporting goods company has moved to 7676 Carondelet Avenue St. Louis MO, 63105.

27. At the Winter Festival in Montreal, Canada, you can see huge snow sculptures.

28. This year Emily will be attending cheerleading camp from July 28 to August 2.

29. Currently Jenny Farmer is, mayor of Two Forks, Tennessee.

30. A letter dated February 2 1882 fell out of the dusty old book.

31. The footnote cited *Guide to Owl Watching in North America* page 35, as the source for the map

    of owl territories.

32. The news reporter gave her report live from Tokyo, Japan.

Mechanics

Lesson 82
Commas: Direct Address, Tag Questions, and Letters

Use commas to set off words or names used in direct address.

Will you be able to pick me up on Thursday, Danielle?
Have a seat, Felicia, and I'll be right with you.
Ladies and gentlemen, may I present Maestro Santini.

Use commas to set off a tag question. A tag question (such as *do you?* or *can I?*) emphasizes an implied answer to the statement preceding it.

You've never played golf before, have you?
He does know the curfew is ten o'clock, doesn't he?

Place a comma after the salutation of an informal letter and after the closing of all letters.

Dear Marianne,
Yours truly,

▶ **Exercise 1** Add commas where necessary. Write *C* in the blank if the sentence is correct as written.

_____ Denise, could you call me tonight to discuss our biology project?

_____ 1. So, Fredericka you've decided to go out for track.

_____ 2. He does know how to get here, doesn't he?

_____ 3. Dear Julie

_____ 4. Good evening ladies and gentlemen.

_____ 5. Cranberry juice tastes better than grape juice don't you think?

_____ 6. Listen to me, Mickey.

_____ 7. You won't give away my secret, will you?

_____ 8. This is Mr. Freeman's office isn't it?

_____ 9. You will read one of your poems for us won't you?

_____ 10. Excuse me ma'am.

_____ 11. With best wishes, Manuel

_____ 12. Tell me my good friend, how do you intend to reach your goal?

_____ 13. Way to go Michelle!

_____ 14. Dear Amber and Elaine

_____ 15. I couldn't very well leave him there at the bus stop could I?

_____ **16.** Tom, you'll find the plates and bowls in the cupboard over the sink.

_____ **17.** Come on, team! Defense!

_____ **18.** This is flight 663 to Los Angeles, isn't it?

_____ **19.** No Irene I've never met Lynne before today.

_____ **20.** You did remember the tickets didn't you?

_____ **21.** Dear Mother and Father

_____ **22.** He doesn't have a spare key, does he?

_____ **23.** This is not funny Vanida!

_____ **24.** Yes Mrs. Lorenzo I'll drop off your groceries by three o'clock.

_____ **25.** Rover come and get your squeeze toy.

_____ **26.** Yes, Mr. President, all the cabinet members are present.

_____ **27.** Good evening folks; I'm running for county commissioner.

_____ **28.** You know Sunnee I'm not sure I'm good enough to make the football team.

_____ **29.** Certainly, sir I have three recommendations from people I've worked for.

_____ **30.** Cordially yours,

_____ **31.** Company, halt!

_____ **32.** Mrs. Suzuki I'd like you to meet Amy and John Locke.

_____ **33.** Those are your muddy boots on the back porch, aren't they?

_____ **34.** I hope Mom that you'll be able to come to our concert.

_____ **35.** We did a fine job didn't we?

▶ **Writing Link** **Write a short conversation you might have with a friend. Use direct address and tag questions.**

_____

_____

_____

_____

_____

_____

_____

Mechanics

Lesson 83
Commas in Review

▶ **Exercise 1** Add commas where necessary. Delete commas used incorrectly using the delete symbol (γ).

To make matters worse, the snow had turned to freezing rain.

1. Holding the puppy inside her coat Virginia waited to surprise her young cousins.

2. During deer-hunting season, each hunter in our state is allowed to take two deer.

3. Philip Yaeger Ph.D. is a civil engineer who specializes in constructing earthquake-resistant buildings and bridges.

4. Martin washed the car and I watched him.

5. Kirsty wearing a black skirt and purple tights that matched her beret sang several French songs at the talent show.

6. The knights mounted their horses, grabbed their lances and prepared for the joust.

7. After reading this chapter on the Middle Ages, I can tell you the meaning of *fief,* and *vassal,* and *fealty.*

8. I don't want to spend all morning painting the living room nor do I want to spend all afternoon washing windows.

9. No we will not be dissecting frogs in this class, but we will dissect a worm.

10. Many tourists visit Italy in late summer and fall but few people go there in the winter.

11. Last night about an hour after sunset Dan heard the haunting call of a screech owl from the woods across the field.

12. The bus carrying the basketball team was delayed by a snowstorm; consequently the game was canceled.

13. Our snack was simple fare: fruit, bread and butter and cheese.

14. Hazard County Kentucky has a long history of coal-mining.

15. Unlike most owls the small saw-whet owl is quite tame.

16. Charlemagne, the first Holy Roman Emperor, encouraged scholarship; however he himself never learned to write.

17. Your mother volunteers at the homeless shelter doesn't she?

Mechanics

18. To always tell the truth, is a good rule to live by.

19. This morning Ezio watched a man carve a fabulous outdoor, ice sculpture.

20. Mario on the other hand does not share his father's love for woodworking.

21. Hey could you give me a hand with this?

22. My subscription to *Sports Illustrated* runs out in June, 1996.

23. During his job interview at the supermarket Ross asked if his hours would be flexible.

24. This house by the way was a stop on the Underground Railroad before the Civil War.

25. To tell you the truth I never learned how to ride a bicycle.

26. The small, red, pickup truck had an extended bed and new tires.

27. Kanya baked the bread and the cookies were made by Henry.

28. That was a great shot Nathaniel.

29. Mrs. Drum who is a skilled photographer is giving a slide show of Greek and Roman ruins today.

30. At the workshop, Paul and Sumalee learned to make natural dyes from plants.

31. Attention all passengers for flight 1102, we are now boarding at gate B-1.

32. Leonardo da Vinci one of the greatest figures of the Renaissance was not only a master painter but an innovative scientific thinker.

33. Among the inventions, that he sketched in his notebooks, were a flying machine, a horseless carriage, and a parachute.

34. At the all-day picnic, we threw horseshoes, played badminton and had a tug-of-war.

35. The choir had rehearsed their music diligently and the director beamed with pride at their performance on Saturday night.

36. Marissa is eager to learn how to spin but she doesn't own a spinning wheel.

37. The Hambrechts' forwarding address was stamped on the envelope: 181 Clinton Heights, Milwaukee, WI, 53201.

38. The varied scenery included rocky cliffs lush forests and gently rolling fields.

Mechanics

Lesson 84
Dashes to Signal Change and to Emphasize

Use a dash to indicate an abrupt break or change in thought within a sentence.

I was happy—no, I was ecstatic—about being selected to work on an actual television show.

Use a dash to set off and emphasize supplemental information or parenthetical comments.

The thin dog—as thin as a sliver he was—nosed around in the garbage for a scrap of food.

I'm saving for a really warm coat—you know, one that's filled with goose down and comes down below the knees.

▶ **Exercise 1** Insert a dash or dashes where necessary.

I just heard a strange noise—shush, there it is again.

1. The poster offered a huge reward I think it was $500 for finding the lost show horse.

2. My father has typical middle-class values he believes in hard work, family life, education, and property ownership although he was born very poor.

3. It was either 1990 or 1991 I can't remember exactly when I first set eyes on the Pacific Ocean.

4. Grab a handful of those marbles say, about fifteen or twenty of them.

5. To top it off you won't believe this he said he had actually spoken to Michael Jordan!

6. We have more than a thousand envelopes to address not all in one day, of course.

7. The girl I met at summer camp I think her name is Darla is in my homeroom at school.

8. Elena shares whatever she has she's just that kind of person.

9. When it comes to strength and endurance, too Sachel is an incredible athlete.

10. Nora's last name something like Schultz or Schmidt is frequently misspelled by others.

11. The main character in the story knew he must have always known that he was descended from an African prince.

12. I think Cody's behavior if you'll allow me to be frank was extremely selfish.

13. The hikers' next task and this was critical was to find some sort of shelter from the cold, driving rain.

14. There was nothing in the barren Arctic landscape just pure emptiness.

Mechanics

15. I am telling the truth cross my heart.

16. Time after time even in near darkness Maggie's arrow struck the bull's-eye of the target.

17. It takes a keen eye actually it takes two to be a good archer.

18. Hear what I have to say just a few words if you please.

19. At her new school in Germany, Dale is taking Latin, German, English, math, physics, and biology; and if you can believe it! she plays soccer and takes oboe lessons!

20. They all agreed every one of them.

21. Lucy squandered much of her time too much of it, probably trying to guess what the future would bring.

22. I got a letter it was ten pages long! from my sister in Taiwan!

23. There's just one more thing something I've never told anyone before.

24. Beyond that log on the trail, it looks like no, it can't be a timber rattler!

25. The new student about the same age as Leo but a foot taller had a good chance of making the basketball team.

26. The raft was made of six-inch timbers lashed together with stout rope a very solid craft.

27. Bonita had nothing to say nothing at all.

28. He was a good friend more like a brother than a friend and I will miss him very much.

29. The trainer held the white rabbit in his hand, and then with the turn of his head it was gone!

30. Walk this way mind your head on that low door to the castle dungeon.

31. Nicki everyone else calls her Nicole is the first person I've ever met who speaks two languages fluently.

32. I intend to graduate from high school or should I say I hope to do so? with a *B* average.

33. If I know William and I think I do he'll be the first one to volunteer for the clean-up project.

34. Jackie broke the school record in the long jump and she did it not once, but twice.

35. A beautiful cat its fur thick and shiny was lying on my pink bedspread!

Mechanics

Lesson 85
Parentheses

Use parentheses to set off supplemental material that is not intended to be a part of the main statement.

An amoeba (the plural is amoebae) is a single-celled organism without a fixed shape.

If a complete sentence in parentheses is contained within another sentence, it is not capitalized and needs no period. If a complete sentence stands by itself within parentheses, both a capital letter and a period are needed.

Only one president, Andrew Johnson, has ever been impeached (for more information on impeachment, see page 184).

The Constitution allows Congress to impeach, or bring to trial, federal officials accused of "treason, bribery, or other high crimes and misdemeanors." (The impeachment process is borrowed from the English system of government.)

Place a comma, semicolon, or colon after the closing parenthesis if it is needed in the sentence.

Roughly a third of registered voters (35 percent), and even less in our state, turned out to vote in the last congressional election.

Place a question mark or an exclamation point inside the parentheses if it is part of the parenthetical expression.

Barely decipherable on the old gravestone was the name Moses (or was it Moser?).

▶ **Exercise 1 Add parentheses or a single parenthesis where necessary. Underline three times (≡) each letter that should be capitalized. Draw a slash (/) through each letter that should be lowercased.**

After the Civil War, longhorn cattle (a tough breed named for their long horns) were abundant on the Texas plains.

1. These longhorns they were descended from cattle brought to America by Columbus and the Spaniards ran loose on the range.

2. Beef was in great demand in the East (And demanded high prices).

3. A man named Jesse Chisholm who was half Cherokee and half Scot drove a herd of cattle from Texas north to Abilene, Kansas.

4. Chisholm made a map of his route. This was important because the route had to have grass and water so the cattle would fatten on the journey.

Mechanics

5. In Abilene a businessman named Joe McCoy then shipped the longhorns east to Chicago on the Kansas Pacific Railroad. (in 1867 this was one of the southernmost of the major western railroads.)

6. Chisholm could buy a longhorn for about $5 in Texas, and McCoy paid $40 A great deal of money in those days per head for cattle.

7. Both the cattle owner and the cattle buyer could make a substantial profit, and McCoy who may be the source for the expression "the real McCoy" became both rich and famous.

8. Most of the cattle were shipped to Chicago, which became the meatpacking center of the country. (the invention of the refrigerated railroad car made this possible.)

9. For twenty years cowboys they were paid $90 or less for the two- or three-month journey drove cattle north on the Chisholm Trail.

10. The cowboys had to contend with many dangers and hardships: blistering heat, blizzards, cattle rustlers, and stampedes the most common danger.

11. Ever watchful over their wandering "dogies" Cowboy slang for stray or motherless calves, cowboys worked long, hard days.

12. About a dozen cowboys looked after a large herd Two or three thousand cattle in one herd was quite common.

13. Cowboys were white, Mexican, and African American Nat Love, known as the great cowboy Deadwood Dick, was an African American from Tennessee); some were part Native American, and some were women.

14. Elizabeth E. Johnson she was a former schoolteacher! bought a herd in Texas and drove it up the Chisholm Trail in 1879.

15. Did you know that many cowboy terms (*rodeo, ranch,* and *lariat* are three examples) come from Spanish words?

16. Many articles of cowboy clothing their leather chaps, open vests, and broad-brimmed hats also reflect a Spanish influence.

17. Think about the cowboy's lonely life. Can you imagine seeing nothing else for three months but cattle, open prairie, and a few fellow cowhands?

18. Think about the physical hardship and the boredom no wonder cowboys sang songs and told tall tales to liven things up.

Lesson 86
Quotation Marks for Direct Quotations

Use quotation marks to enclose a direct quotation. Set off introductory or explanatory remarks from the quotation with a comma. Do not use a comma after a quotation that ends with an exclamation point or a question mark.

The Fourteenth Amendment states in part, "No State shall deprive any person of life, liberty, or property, without due process of law."
"Just what is freedom?" the teacher asked the class.

When a quotation is interrupted by explanatory words such as *he said*, use two sets of quotation marks.

"This train," said the ticket taker, "stops at 125th Street and 42nd Street."

Do not use quotation marks in an indirect quotation.

"Beware of all enterprises that require new clothes," said Henry David Thoreau.
Thoreau said we should be wary of enterprises that require new clothes.

Use single quotation marks around a quotation within a quotation.

Mary said, "I heard the conductor say, 'Next stop, Greenwich.'"

▶ **Exercise 1** Write *C* in the blank next to each sentence that is punctuated correctly.

___C___   After the Civil War, most legislators opposed female suffrage; as one legislator put it, "Woman can't engage in politics without losing her virtue."

_____   1. Even the well-known abolitionist newspaperman Horace Greeley commented, "The best women I know do not want to vote.

_____   2. Some women did declare that they were against female suffrage.

_____   3. A leader of the United Daughters of the Confederacy said that "woman's suffrage comes from women who do not believe in states' rights and who want to see black women using the ballot."

_____   4. In 1869 no law anywhere said that women had the right to vote.

_____   5. A Wyoming woman named Esther Morris met with William H. Bright, a candidate for the state senate, and asked him to promise to support female suffrage if he was elected.

_____   6. Bright said "I will," and after his election he introduced a bill to give Wyoming women the vote.

_____   7. The bill passed, although one newspaper reporter wrote of woman's suffrage, "It's a kind of wild train on a single track, and we've got to keep our eyes peeled or we'll get into the ditch."

Mechanics

_____ 8. When it appeared that woman's suffrage might keep Wyoming from becoming a state, Wyoming men said "they would rather stay out of the Union than join without the women."

_____ 9. Susan B. Anthony continued to campaign for the right to vote; "Men their rights and nothing more; women their rights and nothing less!", she demanded.

_____ 10. Anthony, like Elizabeth Cady Stanton, Lucy Stone, and Sojourner Truth, had worked tirelessly to abolish slavery; these woman argued that women's rights and abolition were two sides of the same coin.

_____ 11. At a women's rights convention in Akron, Ohio, Sojourner Truth declared, I have ploughed, and planted, and gathered into barns, and no man could head me. And ain't I a woman?

_____ 12. "The right of the citizens of the United States to vote," the Fifth Amendment states, shall not be denied or abridged by the United States or by any state on account of race, color, or previous condition of servitude."

_____ 13. Before it was passed, Anthony and Stanton urged Congress to change the wording of the amendment to read race, color, sex, or previous condition of servitude."

_____ 14. Sympathetic congressmen "explained that this wording would make the amendment even more difficult to pass," but the amendment did become law in 1870.

_____ 15. The law stated that all citizens could vote; so Susan B. Anthony asked "Is a woman a citizen?"

_____ 16. After all, women were taxed as citizens, and "the founders had declared, no taxation without representation."

_____ 17. Anthony and fifteen other women said that they would test the issue by voting in the 1872 election.

_____ 18. Anthony was arrested; the warrant said she had violated an act of Congress.

_____ 19. Bypassing the jury in what was an unfair trial, the judge declared "Anthony guilty, although she was never required to pay her fine or go to jail."

_____ 20. In 1776 John Adams said that talk about political representation would continue for years to come, and he predicted, "New claims will arise; women will demand a vote."

_____ 21. Referring to the Constitution, Anthony asserted, "'We, the people' does not mean 'We, the male citizens.'"

_____ 22. Susan B. Anthony had made a claim for women, but it would be another fifty years before the nation said "yes to woman's suffrage."

Lesson 87
Quotation Marks with Titles of Short Works, Unusual Expressions, and with Other Marks of Punctuation

Use quotation marks to enclose titles of short works, such as stories, poems, essays, newspaper and magazine articles, book chapters, and songs.

"Concord Hymn" (poem)   "The Legend of Sleepy Hollow" (short story)

Use quotation marks to enclose unfamiliar slang terms and unusual expressions.

An old nickname for the Missouri River is "Big Muddy."

Place a comma or a period inside closing quotation marks. Place a colon or semicolon outside closing quotation marks.

Our group is studying Walt Whitman's poem "Song of Myself"; in fact, we'd like to perform it as a readers' theater for the class.

Place a question mark or an exclamation point inside the closing quotation marks when it is part of the quotation. Place a question mark or an exclamation point outside the closing quotation marks when it is not a part of the quotation.

Are you sure she said, "The note will be on the back door"?
Lindsay asked me, "Is your mom feeling better?"

▶ **Exercise 1** Add or delete quotation marks and punctuation where necessary. Some sentences may be correct.

In the 1870s the Central Plains began to produce so much wheat that the region was called the nation's "bread basket."

1. Did you know that "Ring-Around-the-Rosie," the familiar children's rhyme, originated during the Middle Ages?

2. For tomorrow, please read chapter 11, The Renaissance in Northern Europe.

3. Susan B. Anthony sometimes spoke of the hateful oligarchy of sex"; she was saying half of the people (men) ruled the other half (women).

4. Have you ever heard this familiar saying: "All the world's a stage"

5. Everyone stood as they played The Star Spangled Banner.

6. Yesterday Natalie read The Celebrated Jumping Frog of Calaveras County, a very funny short story by Mark Twain.

7. It was first published in a California newspaper under the title Jim Smiley and His Jumping Frog.

Mechanics

8. The song Home on the Range began as a poem written by a Pennsylvania doctor who became a homesteader in Kansas; the title of his poem was The Western Home.

9. The farmer explained that in a flock of sheep the male parent of a lamb is called the sire and the female parent is the dam.

10. Before I read the essay "How to Look at Modern Art," I was puzzled by abstract paintings and sculptures.

11. Do you know the first line of Robert Frost's poem The Road Not Taken"?

12. The Basenji is sometimes called the barkless dog"; although it growls and whines like other dogs, its bark has a hoarse, hollow sound.

13. Did you see the article Who's Middle Class? in today's paper?

14. During the English Civil War in the mid-1600s, Puritan supporters of parliamentary government were nicknamed Roundheads because of their close-cropped hair.

15. Erma Bombeck writes a humor column called At Wit's End.

16. Do you know how to say How much does this cost in French?

17. The first line in the article about attending college asked the question, "Why is college important?"

18. Have you read Joyce Kilmer's poem "Trees"

19. The Audience, by C. Walter Hoges, is a story that recreates Columbus's appearance before the king and queen of Spain.

20. My British cousin uses the word bumbershoot when she is referring to an umbrella.

21. My little brother loves to recite Humpty Dumpty, Jack and Jill, and Mary Had a Little Lamb.

22. My first article as an environmental reporter was entitled "Recycled Products Save Landfill Space.

▶ **Writing Link** Write a paragraph for an adult explaining the meaning of at least three slang words that you use. Use quotation marks correctly.

_____

_____

_____

_____

_____

Lesson 88
Italics (Underlining)

Italic type slants upward and to the right. (*This is printed in italics.*) In typing or in handwriting, indicate italics by underlining. (This is <u>underlined</u>.)

Italicize (underline) titles of books, lengthy poems, plays, films and television series, paintings and sculptures, and long musical compositions. Also italicize (underline) the names of newspapers and magazines, ships, trains, airplanes, and spacecraft. Italicize (underline) and capitalize articles (*a, an, the*) at the beginning of a title only when they are part of the title itself. Do not italicize (underline) the article preceding the title of a newspaper or magazine.

The Secret Garden (book)   the *Chicago Tribune* (newspaper)
Sports Illustrated (magazine)   *King Lear* (play)
Star Trek (television series)   *Dances with Wolves* (film)
The Odyssey (long poem)   *Nighthawks* (painting)
Spirit of St. Louis (airplane)   *Queen Elizabeth* (ship)

Italicize (underline) foreign words and expressions that are not used frequently in English. Do not italicize (underline) words or phrases commonly used in English.

The poem captures the decade's ***zeitgeist,*** or spirit of the times.
With a heavy heart, we say aloha to the beautiful island of Hawaii.

Italicize (underline) words, letters, and numerals used to represent themselves.

It's annoying that this typewriter doesn't have a ***4*** or an ***h.***
I like how the poet uses the word ***prepare*** instead of ***fix.***

▶ **Exercise 1** **Underline each word or phrase that should be italicized. If the sentence is correct, write *C* in the blank.**

_____ The president waved to reporters as he boarded <u>Air Force One</u> on the runway.

_____ 1. For many readers, Middlemarch, by George Eliot, is the greatest novel ever written in English.

_____ 2. George Eliot is a nom de plume, or pen name, for a woman named Mary Anne Evans who lived from 1819 to 1880.

_____ 3. Mary Anne Evans grew up in rural England, the daughter of a farm manager.

_____ 4. Her first literary work was the translation of a German work on religion, Das Leben Jesu.

_____ 5. Mary Anne moved to London and became assistant editor of the Westminster Review, a magazine devoted to literature and the arts.

_____ 6. Another translation, Ethics, by the seventeenth-century Dutch philosopher Baruch Spinoza, and book reviews took up much of her time after her move to London.

Mechanics

_____ 7. After falling in love with George Henry Lewes, a writer and historian, Mary Anne Evans turned to writing fiction.

_____ 8. Her first book, published in Blackwood's magazine in 1857, was Scenes of Clerical Life.

_____ 9. Her first book recalled her childhood in rural Warwickshire at the beginning of the nineteenth century.

_____ 10. Adam Bede is also a novel that portrays rural and small town life in provincial England.

_____ 11. The Mill on the Floss, along with its heroine Maggie Tulliver, contains much that is autobiographical.

_____ 12. Many critics consider this novel to be a bildungsroman, a German term for a novel about a young person's development and education.

_____ 13. Some readers feel that the flood of the river Floss that forms the climax of the book is unrealistic and improbable.

_____ 14. Such a plot device, called a deus ex machina, Latin for "god from a machine," comes from a tradition in ancient Greek drama in which a god suddenly appears and solves all the characters' problems.

_____ 15. Still, the book's portrayal of what the author called "old-fashioned family life on the banks of the Floss" has given it lasting popularity.

_____ 16. After this book George Eliot wrote Silas Marner, the tale of a lonely weaver who adopts a baby girl.

_____ 17. In this novel she was much influenced by the poet William Wordsworth, whose short poems "Simon Lee" and "Goody Blake and Harry Gill" describe rural life.

_____ 18. George Eliot also completed a long narrative poem called The Spanish Gypsy.

_____ 19. George Eliot's early novels offer a smorgasbord of delights to those who want to learn more about the human heart and mind.

_____ 20. Her greatest work, however, which is often compared with Tolstoy's War and Peace, was yet to come.

_____ 21. This masterpiece, Middlemarch: A Study of Provincial Life, contains many complex characters.

_____ 22. Her last novel, Daniel Deronda, offered a warm portrait of its heroine, Gwendolen Harleth.

Mechanics

Lesson 89
The Apostrophe

Use an apostrophe and *-s* for the possessive of a singular indefinite pronoun.

one**'s** coat *but* his sleeping bag

Use an apostrophe and *-s* to form the possessive of a singular noun, even one that ends in *-s.*

The dress**'s** fabric   Charles Addams**'s** cartoons   the dog**'s** collar

Use an apostrophe alone to form the possessive of a plural noun that ends in *-s.*

the girls**'** meeting   the hats**'** sizes   the bats**'** habits

Use an apostrophe and *-s* to form the possessive of a plural noun that does not end in *-s.*

the women**'s** department   the sheep**'s** pasture   the children**'s** hour

Put only the last word of a compound noun in the possessive form.

her father-in-law**'s** car   the attorney general**'s** office

If two or more persons possess something jointly, use the possessive form for the last person named. If two or more persons (or companies) possess an item individually, put each one's name in the possessive form.

Uncle Dan and Aunt Susan**'s** house   Procter and Gamble**'s** soaps
Bach**'s** and Handel**'s** music   Tom Cruise**'s** and Julia Roberts**'s** films

Use an apostrophe in place of letters omitted in contractions (words formed from two words that have been combined by omitting one or more letters).

I + am = I**'m**   could + not = couldn**'t**   Linda + is = Linda**'s**

Use an apostrophe in place of the omitted numerals of a particular year.

the Super Bowl of **'**94   the rebellion of **'**98   the winter of **'**77

Use an apostrophe and *-s* to form the plural of letters, numerals, symbols, and words used to represent themselves.

*9***'s**   *7***'s**   *@***'s**   *&***'s**

▶ **Exercise 1 Add apostrophes where needed. Cross out apostrophes used incorrectly using the delete (⟨) symbol. If the sentence is correct, write *C* in the blank.**

_____   Aunt Elizabeth's dog had to have it's broken leg set by a veterinarian.

_____ **1.** Perhap's youve marveled at the incredible gymnastic ability of various primate's.

_____ **2.** Their abilities' are on display in zoos, animal parks, and, for a few lucky people, in the

animals natural habitats.

Mechanics

_____ 3. Primate's include lemurs, monkeys, and apes.

_____ 4. Consider, for example, the graceful gibbons, which live in southeast Asia.

_____ 5. With it's long, muscular arms and legs, a gibbon has no trouble spending two hours a

day swinging through the tree's.

_____ 6. Using a method of movement known to zoologist's as brachiation, the gibbon swings

first with one arm and then the other.

_____ 7. A gibbons ability to stand upright is second only to that of humans.

_____ 8. These beautiful creature's have a distinctive ring of white fur around their faces.

_____ 9. Some lemur's, a group of about 23 species that live on the African island of Madagascar,

hop quickly along the ground with their' arms' waving.

_____ 10. Their peculiar movement makes them look like little ballet dancer's.

_____ 11. Most lemurs are very skilled at leaping great distances from tree to tree.

_____ 12. The sportive lemur jumps from tree trunk to tree trunk with it's body vertical.

_____ 13. Perhaps the most gymnastic primates, however, are the South American monkeys,

whose athletic feats are legendary.

_____ 14. Large monkeys such as the spider monkeys and woolly monkeys possess one great

advantage over other primate specie's.

_____ 15. These monkeys tails are prehensile, which means they are able to grasp limbs and

branches.

▶ **Exercise 2 Write in the blank the form of the word or phrase indicated.**

Sharon (possessive) _Sharon's_____

1. anyone (possessive) _____   9. will not (contraction) _____

2. you are (contraction) _____   10. snakes (possessive) _____

3. son-in-law (possessive) _____   11. secretary of defense (possessive)

4. *8* (plural) _____   _____

5. oxen (possessive) _____   12. Barnum and Bailey (possessive)

6. she is (contraction) _____   _____

7. does not (contraction) _____   13. I am (contraction) _____

8. Twentieth Century-Fox (possessive)   14. it (possessive) _____

_____   15. gorillas (possessive) _____

Mechanics

Lesson 90
The Hyphen

Use a hyphen after any prefix joined to a proper noun or proper adjective. Use a hyphen after the prefixes *all-*, *ex-*, and *self-* joined to any noun or adjective. Use a hyphen after the prefix *anti-* when it joins a word beginning with *i*. Also use a hyphen after the prefix *vice-*, except in *vice president*.

anti-British   all-state   ex-senator   self-employed   anti-inflationary   vice-principal

Use a hyphen in a compound adjective that precedes a noun, but not when it follows a noun.

a fifteen-year-old dog   the dog was fifteen years old
a well-written article   the article was well written

Use a hyphen to avoid confusion between words beginning with *re-* that look alike but are different in meaning and pronunciation.

re-lay the carpet   relay the message

Do not hyphenate an expression made up of an adverb ending in *-ly* and an adjective.

a surprisingly good movie   an oddly beautiful song

Hyphenate any spelled-out cardinal or ordinal numbers up to ninety-nine or ninety-ninth. Hyphenate a fraction used as an adjective (but not one used as a noun).

sixty-seven   thirty-second   two-thirds vote   two thirds of the voters

Divide a word at the end of a line between syllables or pronounceable parts. In general, if a word contains two consonants occurring between two vowels or if it contains a double consonant, divide the word between the two consonants. If a suffix has been added to a complete word that ends in two consonants, divide the word after the two consonants.

sig-nificant   rep-resent   statis-tic   stall-ing   grand-est

▶ **Exercise 1** **Add hyphens where needed. If the sentence is correct, write *C* in the blank.**

_____   Herbert Hoover was the thirty-first president of the United States.

_____ **1.** To ensure a reply, Juan sent a self-addressed, stamped envelope.

_____ **2.** Virginia is remarkably well traveled for a fourteen year old girl.

_____ **3.** The theme of the professor's talk was that the country is currently experiencing an

           antiintellectual period.

_____ **4.** PreColumbian refers to the time period before Columbus arrived in the Americas.

_____ **5.** Rogan's mother came in fifty first out of ninety nine runners in her age class in the

           marathon last week.

Mechanics

_____ **6.** Mr. Gillespie has a well trained golden retriever that can jump up and put letters in the mailbox.

_____ **7.** The election was a tie, so we had to recount the votes.

_____ **8.** If the bill passes, a two thirds majority will be needed to raise taxes in this state.

_____ **9.** Queen Victoria, perhaps Britain's greatest monarch, ruled for sixty four years, from 1837–1901.

_____ **10.** The Chos' new car is mostly red with a tan interior and white racing stripe on the side.

_____ **11.** One half of a liter is about the same amount as one half quart.

_____ **12.** The judge's far reaching decision was likely to affect thousands of people in many parts of the country.

_____ **13.** In government class, we studied the beginnings of the antipoverty programs of President Lyndon Johnson in the 1960s.

_____ **14.** Sarah's eighty five year old great-grandmother was happily married to her husband for sixty one years.

_____ **15.** Be sure to include a well written letter with your job application.

_____ **16.** Because the waiter dropped the tray with our dinners, he was forced to re serve the entire meal!

_____ **17.** Jessica's dad and step-mom are thirty two and thirty four.

_____ **18.** Nicole was surprised at how tiny a two week old baby is.

_____ **19.** The news show offered a wide ranging review of the week's important stories.

_____ **20.** Because he suffers from hay fever and other allergies, my uncle has to take antihistamines often.

▶ **Exercise 2 Indicate where each word would be divided at the end of a line.**

rich|est   wash|able   rus|tic   rap|per

1. strolling

2. darkness

3. flimsy

4. teacher

5. rampage

6. vulture

7. scolding

8. hurting

9. contest

10. member

Mechanics

Lesson 91
Abbreviations

Use only one period if an abbreviation occurs at the end of a sentence. If an abbreviation occurs at the end of a sentence that ends with a question mark or an exclamation point, use the period *and* the second mark of punctuation.

The scheduled speaker was Marissa Long, Ph. D.
Did Jorge say to meet him at 7:00 P.M.or at 7:00 A.M.?

Capitalize abbreviations of proper nouns and abbreviations related to historical dates.Words that refer to streets, such as *Boulevard, Lane, Court,* and *Road,* can be abbreviated on envelopes, but they should be spelled out elsewhere.

John F. Kennedy   105 B.C.   A.D. 319   112 Main St.

Use all capital letters and no periods for abbreviations that are pronounced letter by letter or as words. Exceptions are U.S. and Washington, D.C., which do use periods.

NAACP   NATO   PIN   NCAA   ACT   YMCA   UN   NBA

When addressing mail, use the United States Post Office abbreviations (two capital letters, no periods).

AZ (Arizona)   **IL** (Illinois)   **NV** (Nevada)   **TN** (Tennessee)   **VT** (Vermont)

Use abbreviations for some personal titles.

Sen. Carol Moseley-Braun   **Gen.** Colin Powell   **Rev.** Billy Graham   **Prof.** Rita Lopez

Abbreviate units of measure used with numerals in technical or scientific writing, but not in ordinary prose. These abbreviations stand for plural as well as singular units.

lb. pound	**kg** kilogram	**m** meter	**gal.** gallon	**tsp.** teaspoon
kg kilogram	**ft.** foot	**mm** millimeter	**qt.** quart	**l** liter
oz ounce	**in.** inch			

▶ **Exercise 1** **Underline the word or symbol in parentheses that best completes each sentence.**

The blacksnake Dad found on our camping trip was almost two (ft., feet) long.

1. Why do you think Sharon called the meeting for 6:30 (a.m.?, A.M.?)

2. Raoul's new apartment, 642 Burton (Court, Ct.), is in our old neighborhood.

3. To make hot chocolate, just add six (ounces, oz.) of boiling water to the contents of the package.

4. Hallie's aunt and uncle live in northern (Minnesota, MN) near the Canadian border.

5. Pravat opened the door and entered the offices of (General, Gen.) Williams.

6. LeShaun's bought four (gals., gallons) of gasoline for his moped.

Mechanics

7. Our class watched video about (N.A.T.O., NATO) peacekeeping forces around the world.

8. The president who officially ended reconstruction in the South after the Civil War was

   Rutherford (B, B.) Hayes.

9. Claudius was emperor of Rome from (41–54 a.d., A.D. 41–54.)

10. From my grandparents' farm, it is about eighty-five (kilometers, km) to downtown Cleveland.

11. Write this address on the envelope: Contest, P.O. Box 678, Anaheim, (CA, CA.) 92815.

12. May I borrow two (tsp., teaspoons) of ground ginger?

13. When Josh and I visited his mom in Phoenix, she took us to an (N.B.A., NBA) game.

14. Our 4-H Club was addressed by (Senator, Sen.) Sandra Walters.

15. The ribbon for the bookmark should be seven (inches, in) long.

16. Randy couldn't remember his (P.I.N., PIN), when we got to the bank.

17. A football field is forty-nine (meters, m) wide.

18. The Fourth of July fireworks display was scheduled to start at 10:00 (p.m., P.M.)

19. The computer store Amad was looking for was supposed to be at 5467 Sheridan (Ave.,

   Avenue.)

20. Maya is moving to Evanston, (IL, Illinois), in September.

▶ **Exercise 2** **If the abbreviation is given, write the word or words the abbreviation stands for. If words are given, write the abbreviation.**

NHL ____**National Hockey League**____   pound ____**lb.**____

1. tsp. _____

2. NV _____

3. National Association for the Advancement of Colored People _____

4. millimeter _____

5. before Christ _____

6. Gov. _____

7. qt. _____

8. AZ _____

9. ft. _____

10. Professor _____

Mechanics

Lesson 92
Numbers and Numerals

In general, spell out cardinal and ordinal numbers that can be written in one or two words. Spell out any number that occurs at the beginning of a sentence.

The National Football League has **thirty** teams.
Four hundred eighty-three people attended the concert last night.

In general, use numerals (numbers expressed in figures) to express numbers that would be written in more than two words. Extremely high numbers are often expressed as a numeral followed by the words *million* or *billion*.

The famous opera singer received more than **150,000** letters during her career.
The cost of the new bridges over the Missouri River is estimated at **$18 million**.

If one number in a sentence is in numerals, related numbers in the same sentence should also be in numerals.

Of the **9,463** spectators at the match, only **95** paid full price.

Use numerals to express decimals, percentages, and amounts of money involving both dollars and cents. Write out amounts of money that can be written in one or two words.

2.2 pounds	**$23.89**	**fifty-nine** cents
13 percent	**twenty-five thousand** dollars	

Use numerals to express the year and day in a date and to express the precise time with the abbreviations A.M. and P.M. Spell out expressions of time that are approximate or that do not use the abbreviations A.M. or P.M.

The Declaration of Independence was signed on **July 4, 1776**.
Around **ten** o'clock I'm going to the beach.

To express a century or when the word *century* is used, spell out the number. When a century or a decade is expressed as a single unit, use numerals followed by *-s*.

Rock and roll, which began in the fifties, is a **twentieth**-century development.
The **1790s** were known as a decade of revolution in Europe.

Use numerals for streets and avenues numbered above ten and for all house, apartment, and room numbers. Spell out numbered streets and avenues with numbers of ten or under.

Apartment **4B**	**789** East **119th** Street	**16** North **Third** Avenue

Use roman numerals to express line, act, and scene numbers in plays.

Macbeth sees a bloody dagger in Act **II**, Scene **i**.

Mechanics

▶ **Exercise 1** **Place a check (✔) beside each sentence that uses numbers and numerals correctly.**

_____   Tonya was very happy with her 2nd-place finish in the hurdles.

_____ **1.** The CD player that Gustavo wants to buy has a list price of $119.95.

_____ **2.** Kimane's great-grandfather was born on June first, 1899.

_____ **3.** The nineteen-thirties are known as the period of the Great Depression.

_____ **4.** My brother and his wife live at 433 East 72nd Street in New York City.

_____ **5.** The newly planted maple tree near the gate of the park is only 6 feet tall.

_____ **6.** The astronauts were greeted by 1,000s of people during the celebration of their return from space.

_____ **7.** Today at play practice we'll be rehearsing Act I, Scene iii.

_____ **8.** The woman was upset because she received a bill from the electric company for 6 cents.

_____ **9.** 9,890 excited fans attended the basketball game last Saturday night.

_____ **10.** Felipe's baby sister weighed six pounds, eleven ounces when she was born.

_____ **11.** 1 of you will have to hit a basket if we are going to win this game.

_____ **12.** The company built a new corporate headquarters next to the freeway for thirty-two million dollars.

_____ **13.** Two hundred sixty-five representatives voted in favor of the bill.

_____ **14.** My grandparents' farmhouse was built sometime in the middle of the 19th century.

_____ **15.** The address of the new firehouse is 1989 West 5th Avenue.

_____ **16.** I was the twenty-eighth person to try out for the school musical.

_____ **17.** The school Recycling Club collected two hundred twenty-five pounds of aluminum cans.

_____ **18.** Please read steps 7 and 8 to me on how to connect the VCR again.

_____ **19.** We gasped when the runner's time of ten point two five seconds was announced.

_____ **20.** More than sixty percent of the voters approved of the referendum in the last election.

_____ **21.** The U.S. Senate has 2 members from each state.

_____ **22.** The detective asked each suspect where he or she was at exactly nine P.M. on December 20, 1995.

_____ **23.** You can purchase a license for your dog in Room Twenty-Two on the second floor.

_____ **24.** Do you prefer the music of the 1960s or the 1990s?

_____ **25.** Five thousand two hundred eighty feet make up a mile.

Mechanics

✓ Unit 12 **Review**

▶ **Exercise 1** **Add all necessary punctuation marks. Cross out incorrect punctuation, abbreviations, and numbers using the delete (⅄) symbol. Write the correct form above the line.**

     One
⅄ of Tom Clancy's most popular novels⅄is <u>The Hunt for Red October</u>.

1. For our outing on Thursday, bring the following binoculars a notebook a pen or pencil and a sack lunch.

2. "Nature," my fathers favorite television show, begins at seven o'clock on Sunday and he is very disappointed if he misses it?

3. Barging through the crowd the king's herald shouted, Make way for the king!

4. Farm workers in that country make up about seventy-five percent of the population, or one hundred ten million people.

5. Act Two scene Two of the play is set in the main hall of a musty old French castle.

6. Fanning the embers Carrie tried to start a fire while Ericka who had planned the cookout took the hot dogs out of the cooler.

7. Juans sister-in-laws car had a flat tire near Fifty-Eighth Street.

8. Oh I never told you I was from Canada; in fact I lived above the Arctic Circle for a short time

9. Jara said, Robert Frost's poem Stopping By Woods on a Snowy Evening has a very quiet feeling.

10. Ms. Cathy Kepple will give her talk on the Perseid meteor showers at the planetarium not the observatory.

11. Two-thirds of the people present at the meeting approved of Mrs Hernandezs motion that the club spend $3,950.

12. Carter you will be going to the awards banquet won't you

13. The soldier died in June, 1945, but the letter was dated January 4 1946.

14. After the beautifully-prepared dinner we sang Happy Birthday to my mom.

15. The Ohio River flows from Pittsburgh Pennsylvania about 981 miles 1,578 km to the Mississippi River at Cairo Illinois.

Mechanics

Cumulative Review: Units 1–12

▶**Exercise 1** Underline the word in parentheses that best completes each sentence.

Akira has my Smashing Pumpkins CD; I loaned it (<u>to</u>, two) her yesterday.

1. I happily (accepted, excepted) the valentine card.

2. Lonnie has (all ready, already) gathered enough firewood for the night.

3. If we agree (all together, altogether) on this, then let's get the ball rolling.

4. Trent's bike is (beside, besides) the garage.

5. With a good deal of patience, Robin and Charley resolved the problem (between, among) them.

6. You can (choose, chose) between the sweater and the jacket.

7. Put this garbage bag (in, into) the dumpster.

8. (Its, It's) hard to imagine Lilly in a dress.

9. Karen decided to (lay, lie) down for a while before the rehearsal began.

10. I would like to (learn, teach) German so that Helmut and I can correspond in his native language.

11. (Leave, Let) the books on the shelf.

12. Don't (loose, lose) that ring.

13. (Raise, Rise) the TV antenna a little higher.

14. I want to (set, sit) by Trina at the assembly.

15. Is a chickadee smaller (than, then) a robin?

16. We heard that (their, they're) moving away.

17. Hercules was always (to, too) strong for the bad guys.

18. (Who's, Whose) jacket is this?

19. Where is (its, it's) boxtop?

20. Mr. White Feather told us the test will cover everything (accept, except) chapter six.

▶**Exercise 2** Draw a line under each prepositional phrase and write in the blank whether it is used as an adjective or adverb. Insert a comma if the sentence requires it.

_____ <u>From inside the doorway</u>, I heard the phone ringing.

_____ 1. All of my friends enjoyed the trip yesterday.

_____ 2. The house on the corner has been sold.

_____ 3. In front of the school, the choir is singing.

_____ 4. The song of whales sounds strangely beautiful.

_____ 5. Debra said she had enough of smog.

_____ 6. Because of the storm, we stayed inside.

_____ 7. The colors of the sunset were deep purple streaked with gold.

_____ 8. The kite flew over the electric wires.

_____ 9. The lightning crashed into the tree.

_____ 10. The dog from next door followed me home.

_____ 11. Across the lake I heard Camilla singing happily.

_____ 12. Melisa left the house before lunch.

_____ 13. The fence beyond the bushes needs painting.

_____ 14. Do you see the beautiful oriole among the leaves ?

_____ 15. On top of the mountains we saw the glittering snow.

_____ 16. The big book beneath the boxes looks very old.

_____ 17. I heard the baby birds cheeping inside their nest.

_____ 18. Jason and the Argonauts searched for the Golden Fleece.

_____ 19. You will find the swimming pool past the parking lot.

_____ 20. The breeze off the bay is invigorating.

▶ **Exercise 3** **Write *C* in the blank if the sentence is compound and *CC* if it is compound-complex.**

___CC___   I saw a blackbird chase a robin, but I'm sure the robin got away, although I didn't see it.

_____ 1. Will it snow tomorrow, or did you hear that it might rain?

_____ 2. My cat loves my dog, although that may seem strange to you; but my dog isn't very friendly to the cat.

_____ 3. Lord Byron is my favorite poet because he wrote beautiful, romantic verse; he also lived an exciting life before he died at the age of thirty-seven.

_____ 4. I've never seen a tornado, nor have I ever experienced a hurricane.

_____ 5. A Model T Ford was a great car; I, however, would have bought a Buick had I lived back then.

_____ 6. I've always wanted to learn ice-skating, but I doubt I have the talent to be very good at the sport.

_____ 7. The sunrise is beautiful, but last night's sunset was fantastic.

Mechanics

_____ 8. General Grant is remembered as a great military commander, but he should also be remembered as the president who first appointed a Native American (General Ely Samuel Parker) as head of the Bureau of Indian Affairs.

_____ 9. Rain makes you wet, sunshine makes you glad, and rainbows delight and thrill you.

_____ 10. Camilla loves classical music, but I am not so fond of it.

_____ 11. We heard the story when we were young, but I never believed it.

_____ 12. I painted the picture, and I sold it to Mrs. Smith because she wanted it so badly.

_____ 13. The tide went out, and the sailboats were all grounded because there wasn't enough water under their keels.

_____ 14. The old trolleys are fun to watch, but I prefer to ride buses.

▶ **Exercise 4** **Add punctuation marks where needed. Underline words or phrases that should be in italics.**

What is the name of that game you're playing?

1. The books title is The Clay Marble.

2. In January 1966 Montgomery Alabama had a record low temperature.

3. The tree house is full of birds this year Im surprised you haven't noticed.

4. My little brothers favorite television show is Sesame Street.

5. What in the world happened to Mr. Harriss new car?

6. "Don't tell me you don't like Much Ado About Nothing, Lisa said.

7. Mr. Chen said Raise your hand when you know the answer

8. The Wind in the Willows is an interesting book even for older readers.

9. Melissa loves roller coasters Ferris wheels and bumper cars.

10. Unlike Helen Jackson likes to swim laps.

11. Jeremy took his brother on the merry-go-round and Heather tried to break balloons with darts.

12. Her favorite movie as a child was Sleeping Beauty.

13. There will be a total eclipse of the sun on August 11 1999.

14. The Children's Hour is a short poem my mom reads often.

15. They drove all the way from Paris France to Naples Italy.

16. Oh, he was so disappointed about his mistakes, she said.

17. Did he really say What a nice book?

18. Bertie loves to swim his sister prefers bike riding

Vocabulary and Spelling

Unit 13: Vocabulary and Spelling

Lesson 93

Building Vocabulary: Learning from Context

Sometimes you can figure out the meaning of a word from its context—the words that surround the word. There are many context clues you can use to help you figure out the meaning of a word. The following chart describes five types of context clues:

TYPE OF CONTEXT CLUE	CLUE WORDS	EXAMPLE
Definition: The meaning of the unfamiliar word is stated in the sentence.	which means also known as in other words or	The anthropologist was interested in *ethnology*, **or** *a science that deals with the division of humans into races.*
Example: The meaning of the unfamiliar word is explained through examples or other illustrations.	for instance such as for example like	He was a *farrier*; **for example**, he *replaced shoes on horses.*
Comparison: The unfamiliar word is compared to a similar familiar word or phrase.	likewise also similarly as	There was a public *mania* for hula hoops; **likewise**, there was *excessive enthusiasm* for yo-yos.
Contrast: The unfamiliar word is the opposite of a familiar word or phrase.	however but on the contrary unlike	We were *tenacious* about the agenda; **however**, we were *flexible* about the meeting place.
Cause and Effect: The unfamiliar word describes a cause whose effects are familiar, or an effect whose causes are familiar.	therefore thus since because when as a result	Their white carpet was *immaculate*; **therefore**, *we took off our shoes before we stepped on it.*

▶ **Exercise 1** Determine the meaning of the italicized word in each sentence by examining the context. Write the meaning in the blank.

Relations between South Africa's peoples were based on *apartheid*, or racial segregation.

racial segregation

1. If his full name was to be on his *epitaph*, the tombstone would have to be extra wide.

_____

2. Our neighbor has *epicurean* tastes; for instance, he eats at the best and most expensive

restaurant in town at least once a week. _____

3. The woman is very *capricious*; as a result, we never know what to expect when we see her.

_____

4. Many poets write about the *transience*, or temporary nature, of life. _____

5. Of the two, the private was the *subordinate*; in other words, he was lower in rank than the

sergeant. _____

6. The couple loved to do the *rumba*; they also liked other Latin dances. _____

7. The business owners held a *clandestine* meeting because they didn't want their employees to

find out about it. _____

8. Because the woman was known as a *philanthropist*, the charity group approached her for a

donation. _____

9. Mr. Takashi was a *gregarious* person; however, his wife was painfully shy. _____

10. The riders on the bus had an instant *rapport*—they got along like long-lost friends.

_____

11. He always *monopolized* the conversation, just as he always took complete control of the

channel changer. _____

12. Her behavior at the board meeting was *obsequious*; for example, she actually offered to wash

the company president's car! _____

13. I've tried a lot of exotic fruits, but I've never tasted a *kumquat*. _____

14. His story was not *credible* at all; no one in our group believed him. _____

15. No matter where we walked, we could hardly see because the smoke from the fire was

ubiquitous. _____

16. Her voice was *mellifluous*, or rich and smooth. _____

17. We know a man who is a *hypochondriac*; in other words, he thinks he is sick when he really

isn't. _____

18. The little girl was *sullen* at first, but her face lit up when she saw the candy. _____

19. Because our mail carrier is such an *affable* person, it is difficult not to like her.

_____

20. The real estate agent *appraised* our house; that is, he told us how much he thought it was

worth. _____

Lesson 94
Building Vocabulary: Word Roots

You can figure out the meaning of a word by analyzing its parts. The main part of a word is its **root**. A root that is a complete word is called a **base word**. A root or base word, such as *think*, is often combined with a prefix (a word part attached to the beginning of the word), a suffix (a word part attached to the end of a word), or another root word to form a different word, such as *unthinkable*.

The root is the most important clue for finding a word's meaning. When unsure, think of other words that might share the same root. The meanings of the other words might give you clues to the meaning of the unfamiliar word. The following chart lists some common roots and words that share them:

ROOT	MEANING	EXAMPLE	MEANING
aqua	water	aquarium	tank of water
astro	stars	astronomer	one who studies stars
bio	life	biography	story of a person's life
cent	hundred	century	one hundred years
chron	time	chronological	arranged in order of time
geo	Earth	geology	study of Earth
nym	name	anonymous	with no name
scrib	write	inscribe	to write or mark on
viv	live	vivacious	full of life

▶ **Exercise 1** Circle the common root words in each set of three words. Write the meaning of the root word in the blank. Use a dictionary if necessary.

anthropologist   misanthrope   anthropomorphic   **human being**

1. thermometer   thermal   isotherm   _____

2. lithology   Lithopolis   monolith   _____

3. nautical   nautilus   astronaut   _____

4. cosmopolitan   microcosm   cosmonaut   _____

5. literal   illiterate   literary   _____

6. dynamite   dynasty   dynamo   _____

7. enumerate   number   numerous   _____

8. regent   regional   regimen   _____

9. consequence   sequential   sequel   _____

10. passport   deport   portfolio   _____

11. bicycle   cyclical   cyclone   _____

Vocabulary and Spelling

12.	paragraph	graphology	autograph	_____
13.	photography	photobiology	photon	_____
14.	theology	monotheism	theocracy	_____
15.	rotate	rotator	rotary	_____
16.	corpulent	corps	corporeal	_____
17.	partition	participate	partial	_____
18.	durable	obdurate	enduring	_____
19.	cartographer	cartoon	carton	_____
20.	lunatic	lunar	lunation	_____
21.	captain	decapitate	cape	_____
22.	sonorous	consonance	dissonant	_____
23.	diversity	reverse	versatile	_____
24.	solace	console	consolation	_____
25.	decathlon	December	decade	_____
26.	auditorium	audible	audition	_____
27.	mortician	mortify	immortal	_____
28.	generate	progeny	gender	_____
29.	assimilate	similarity	simulate	_____
30.	tenuous	distend	extensive	_____

▶ **Writing Link Write six sentences using at least ten words from Exercise 1.**

_____

_____

_____

_____

_____

_____

_____

_____

_____

_____

Lesson 95
Building Vocabulary: Prefixes and Suffixes

Prefixes and suffixes change the meaning of the root words to which they are attached. A **prefix** is a word part that is attached to the beginning of a word. Prefixes are important tools for building new words. Certain prefixes, such as *un-* and *in-*, can even reverse the meaning of a root word.

PREFIX	MEANING
co-	"together"
contra-	"opposed"
de-	"from" or "down"
dis-	"lack of" or "not"
il-, im-, in-, ir-	"not"
inter-	"among" or "between"
mis-	"wrong" or "bad"
pre-	"before"
re-	"again" or "back"
sub-	"under" or "below"

▶ **Exercise 1** Write a word with a prefix that could replace the word or words in italics.

_____**replay**_____ Classical music enthusiasts *play again* their favorite pieces.

_____ 1. The two actresses *starred together* in the television drama.

_____ 2. The writers *wrote again* the script five times before they were satisfied.

_____ 3. I think the director was *guided wrongly*.

_____ 4. The temperature must be *below zero* today!

_____ 5. Mrs. Lee was *informed wrongly* about the new laundry room policy.

_____ 6. The coach *did not agree* with the call.

_____ 7. I *recorded beforehand* the music I needed to present in class.

_____ 8. He knew that getting there on time was *not possible*.

_____ 9. Tanya and Paula were *workers together*.

_____ 10. She didn't follow directions, so the teacher asked her to *do it again*.

_____ 11. The contestants for the game show were *selected beforehand*.

_____ 12. Aristotle thought the question was *not appropriate*.

_____ 13. The museum director said the broken vase was *not replaceable*.

_____ 14. The threads of her sweater were tightly *woven together*.

Vocabulary and Spelling

In English, suffixes are more common than prefixes. A **suffix** is a word part that is attached to the end of a word. Like prefixes, suffixes create new words with new meanings. Many suffixes also change the part of speech of the original word. For example, when the suffix -*able* is added to the verb *forgive*, the new word *forgivable* is an adjective. With certain words, especially those ending in -*e*, the spelling of the original word may change slightly when a suffix is added.

SUFFIX	MEANING
-*ant, -ent*	"one who does an action"
-*dom*	"state" or "condition"
-*en*	"to become"
-*ful*	"full of"
-*ize*	"to become" or "to make"
-*less*	"without"
-*ly*	"in the way or manner mentioned"
-*ness*	"quality" or "state"
-*ous*	"full of"

▶ **Exercise 2 Write a word with a suffix that could replace the word or words in italics.**

_____diligently_____ Hector raked the leaves *in a diligent manner.*

_____ 1. An airbag could *make less* the impact of the crash.

_____ 2. Some of the sun's rays are *full of harm* to the skin.

_____ 3. The roads and highways are *full of use* for commuters.

_____ 4. *The state of being free* should not be taken for granted.

_____ 5. The *one who applied for the job* believed she had a good chance of being chosen for the job.

_____ 6. Melissa was *full of envy* of her sister's new sweater.

_____ 7. *The state of being happy* is something everyone searches for.

_____ 8. The scientist *made a theory* about life on other planets.

_____ 9. The sun glistened on the *quality of white* of the snow.

_____ 10. The missing puzzle piece seemed *to become material* out of nowhere.

_____ 11. The recipe said to let the sauce *become thick.*

_____ 12. The park in the spring is *full of beauty.*

_____ 13. Mitsuyo *in a patient manner* explained the problem to her younger sister.

_____ 14. The birds sang a tune that was *full of melody.*

Lesson 96
Basic Spelling Rules I

SPELLING *IE* AND *EI*

Put *i* before *e* except after *c*, or when sounded like $\bar{a}$, as in *neighbor* and *weigh*.

achi**e**ve   reli**e**ve   rec**ei**ve   dec**ei**ve   sl**ei**gh   v**ei**l

Exceptions to this rule include: *seize, leisure, weird, height, either, forfeit,* and *protein.*

SPELLING *-CEDE, -CEED,* AND *-SEDE*

Because *c* and *s* are often pronounced the same way, confusion arises in spelling words ending in *-cede, -ceed,* and *-sede.* Remember that in all words except four, the *sēd* sound is spelled *cede.* The only four exceptions are *supersede, exceed, proceed,* and *succeed.*

SPELLING UNSTRESSED VOWELS

The dictionary uses the schwa symbol (ə) to indicate an unstressed vowel sound. To help you spell a word with this sound, think of a related word in which the vowel sound is stressed. If you are unsure how to spell *final,* think of the word *finality.* Although the *a* in *final* is an unstressed vowel sound, the *a* in *finality* is not. You can hear the short *a* sound when you say *finality* aloud.

▶ **Exercise 1** **Find the misspelled word in each sentence. Rewrite the word correctly in the blank. Use a dictionary if necessary.**

__precede__   The high school band will preceed the fire engines in the holiday parade.

_____ 1. The Declaration of Independence expresses the beleifs of many Americans.

_____ 2. The hundred-degree heat was nearly intolerible.

_____ 3. The fantesy book was so interesting I could hardly put it down.

_____ 4. The preschool teacher's dedication was easily observible.

_____ 5. The dietitian showed us how to get enough protien in our meals.

_____ 6. Mrs. Robinson's beagle regulerly digs a hole under the fence to escape.

_____ 7. Spring has always been an insperation for persons to begin fitness programs.

_____ 8. Outer appearances are sometimes decieving.

_____ 9. The cloudless night sky seems to go on for infinety.

_____ 10. My grandfather thoroughly knows the histery of our town.

_____ 11. Some southern states seceeded from the Union before the Civil War.

_____ 12. The aorta is not a vien, but an artery.

_____ 13. May I have a reciept for the wool suit?

_____ **14.** The first thing the nurse does is take my height and wieght.

_____ **15.** His poems deal with fantasy rather than realety.

ADDING PREFIXES

Always keep the original spelling of the word when you add the prefix. If adding the prefix causes a double letter, keep both letters.

mis- + inform = misinform   *il-* + logical = illogical

SUFFIXES AND THE SILENT *E*

When adding a suffix that begins with a vowel or *y* to a word that ends with a silent *e*, usually drop the *e*.

excite + -*able* = excitable   shine + -*y* = shiny

However, when adding a suffix that begins with an *a* or an *o* to a word that ends with *ce* or *ge*, retain the *e* so the word will keep its soft *c* or *g* sound.

service + -*able* = serviceable   courage + -*ous* = courageous

When adding a suffix that begins with a vowel to a word that ends in *ee* or *oe*, keep the *e*.

agree + -*able* = agreeable   canoe + -*ing* = canoeing

When adding a suffix that begins with a consonant to a word that ends in silent *e*, keep the *e*.

bare + -*ly* = barely   place + -*ment* = placement

SUFFIXES AND THE FINAL *Y*

If a word ends in a consonant +*y*, change the *y* to *i* unless the suffix begins with an *i*. Keep the *y* in a word that ends in a vowel +*y*.

fry + -*ed* = fried   hurry + -*ing* = hurrying
stay + -*ing* = staying   joy + -*ous* = joyous

▶ **Exercise 2 Find the misspelled word in each sentence. Rewrite the word correctly in the blank. Use a dictionary if necessary.**

___palatable___   I think foods eaten raw, such as sushi, are just not palateable.

_____ **1.** The blacksmith is making horseshoes while the farrier is actually shoing horses.

_____ **2.** The new parents could barly keep their eyes open after 9:00 P.M.

_____ **3.** I have tryed several times to go ice-skating, but my ankles keep turning in and out.

_____ **4.** The shiney chrome on the classic cars gleamed in the sunlight.

_____ **5.** The aggressive pollsters were surveing people as they left the voting booths.

_____ **6.** The weather in coastal areas is very changable.

Lesson 97
Basic Spelling Rules II

DOUBLING THE FINAL CONSONANT

Double the final consonant in words that end in a consonant preceded by a single vowel if the word is one syllable, if it has an accent on the last syllable that remains there even after the suffix is added, or if it is a word made up of a prefix and a one-syllable word.

cap + -*ing* = capping   stop + -*age* = stoppage   concur + -*ent* = concurrent
compel + -*ing* = compelling   misstep + -*ed* = misstepped

Do not double the final consonant if the accent is not on the last syllable, or if the accent shifts when the suffix is added. Also do not double the final consonant if it is preceded by two vowels or by another consonant. If the word ends in a consonant and the suffix begins with a consonant, do not double the final consonant.

develop + -*ing* = developing   prefer + -*ence* = preference   rain + -*ing* = raining
remind + -*ed* = reminded   faith + -*less* = faithless

ADDING -*LY* AND -*NESS*

When adding -*ly* to a word that ends in a single *l*, keep the *l*, but when the word ends in a double *l*, drop one *l*. When adding -*ness* to a word that ends in *n*, keep the *n*.

ideal + -*ly* = ideally   full + -*ly* = fully   mean + -*ness* = meanness

FORMING COMPOUND WORDS

When joining a word that ends in a consonant to a word that begins with a consonant, keep both consonants.

snow + fall = snowfall   year + book = yearbook   hair + do = hairdo

▶ **Exercise 1** Find the misspelled word in each sentence. Rewrite the word correctly in the blank. Use a dictionary if necessary.

___enjoyed___   Many visitors to the state have enjoied seeing Mount Rushmore National Memorial.

_____   1. The likenesses of four U.S. presidents are carvved into Mount Rushmore's solid granite.

_____   2. Carving these figures was a physicaly challenging feat.

_____   3. A man named Gutzon Borglum began chiping away at the granite in 1927.

_____   4. He obviously had a keeness for sculpting on a large scale.

_____   5. Borglum's creation is considerabley larger than most other sculptures.

_____   6. This unusually large sculpture was not fullly finished when Borglum died.

Vocabulary and Spelling

Name _____ Class _____ Date _____

_____ 7. Borglum's son put the finishing touches on the sculpture by carving the rest of Theodore Roosevelt's likness.

_____ 8. South Dakota has many other entertainning places to visit.

GENERAL RULES FOR FORMING PLURALS

IF A WORD ENDS IN:	RULE	EXAMPLE
ch, s, sh, x, z	add -es	boxes
a consonant + y	change y to i and add -es	ladies
a vowel + y or o	add -s	radios
a consonant + o	add -es	potatoes
f or ff	add -s	reefs
lf	change f to v and add -es	calves
fe	change f to v and add -s	wives

SPECIAL RULES FOR PLURALS

To form the plural of proper names and one-word compound nouns, follow the general rules for plurals. To form the plural of hyphenated compound nouns or compound nouns of more than one word, make the most important word plural.

Sanchezes   newspapers   fathers-in-law   oil wells   attorneys general

Some nouns have unusual plural forms.

woman   women   mouse   mice

Some nouns have the same singular and plural forms.

sheep   deer   series

▶ **Exercise 2** **Write the plural form of each word.**

church **churches**

1. shelf _____
2. rodeo _____
3. branch _____
4. man _____
5. wallflower _____
6. roller coaster _____
7. Ramirez _____
8. life _____
9. baby _____

10. tomato _____
11. symphony _____
12. book report _____
13. passer-by _____
14. son-in-law _____
15. bush _____
16. blackberry _____
17. self _____
18. video _____

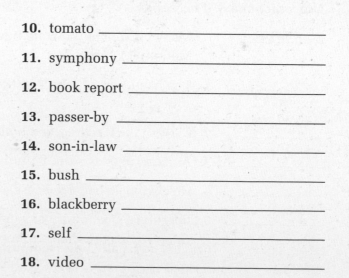

✓ Unit 13 Review: Building Vocabulary

▶ **Exercise 1** Write a definition for each italicized word using context clues, word roots, or a combination of the two. Use a dictionary if necessary.

I traced that ruler's *lineage* back to the Middle Ages. __line, ancestry_____

1. My Aunt Jane has become a *recluse;* for instance, she never goes out of her house. _____

   _____

2. The *incriminating* evidence against the suspect was overwhelming. _____

   _____

3. Some people have had *rhinoplasty* or other kinds of cosmetic surgery. _____

4. His performance was *mediocre* compared to the wonderfully talented actor who followed him.

   _____

5. There was much *jubilation* among the fans on the home team's side; however, the opposing

   side was marked by gloom and depression. _____

6. Mr. Jackson was *convalescing* in his home; the class sent him cards and flowers to hasten his

   recovery. _____

7. The pilot skillfully *manipulated* the controls in her effort to prevent the crash. _____

   _____

8. Our neighbors are the most *hospitable* people I've ever met; they make everyone feel welcome.

   _____

9. The presidents of the two companies regarded each other as *adversaries,* but many of their

   employees were friends. _____

10. The industrious *anthropologist* was studying the peoples of Ancient Egypt as well as the

    Native American cultures of the southwestern United States. _____

11. The jovial workers *perambulated,* or strolled, to lunch. _____

12. Because this customer had a reputation for being *parsimonious,* the waiter did not expect a tip.

    _____

13. The scientist took *aerial* photos of the formation from a small airplane. _____

14. After eating the huge holiday dinner, our appetites were more than *satiated.* _____

15. The cook sprinkled *marjoram* over the dish to add a hint of mint flavor. _____

Vocabulary and Spelling

16. The trees and bushes in the *arboretum* were thriving. _____

_____

17. The art collector favored *bucolic* scenes; her colleague, on the other hand, adored city settings.

_____

18. The five siblings were a *cohesive* group; they stuck together through the good times and the

bad. _____

19. The mechanic had a tendency to be *redundant;* for example, he told us what was wrong with

the car four times. _____

20. The program was specifically designed for *octogenarians,* or people in their eighties. _____

_____

▶ **Exercise 2** Write a word with a prefix or a suffix that has the same meaning as the italicized words.

__unsuited, or unsuitable__   That jacket is *not suited* for cold weather.

_____   **1.** Mia Greene is a *full of care* worker.

_____   **2.** The cat's heartbeat *became quick* when it spied the mouse
scampering across the floor.

_____   **3.** The theater goer's cough during the play's quietest moment was *not
voluntary.*

_____   **4.** The little girl's face was *full of spite* when she pulled her classmate's
hair.

_____   **5.** The food was *packaged beforehand* for your convenience.

_____   **6.** The cheap souvenirs in that store are *without worth.*

_____   **7.** The T-shirts I bought during the storewide sale were *not expensive.*

_____   **8.** The barbershop quartet drew crowds of people when they *made
harmony.*

_____   **9.** City officials decided to *make wide* Palm Street to allow for parking.

_____   **10.** The card player kept *dealing wrong* the cards.

_____   **11.** *The condition of being bored* can be easily overcome.

_____   **12.** Mr. Garcia recalls the days of his youth *in a fond manner.*

_____   **13.** The *ones who reside* on Whaley Avenue are unhappy about the new
mall being built behind them.

_____   **14.** A wave of *a lack of contentment* arose from the crowd of people.

_____   **15.** Will you please *distribute again* these pamphlets?

✔ Unit 13 **Review:** Basic Spelling Rules

▶ **Exercise 1** **Find the misspelled word in each sentence. Rewrite the word correctly in the blank. Use a dictionary if necessary.**

_____icing_____   The iceing on the cake was carefully done.

_____   **1.** The news about the earthquake was upseting.

_____   **2.** The intricate lace doilys added a touch of elegance to the room.

_____   **3.** The reignning champion had many adoring fans.

_____   **4.** There was no escapeing the fact that all of their belongings were lost in the fire.

_____   **5.** The enthusiastic volunteeres rallied around the candidate they supported.

_____   **6.** In the crisp autumn air, the leafs quietly fell from the trees.

_____   **7.** The roomes in the hospitals filled up quickly during the flood.

_____   **8.** Use your best judgment when crosssing a busy intersection.

_____   **9.** The new coat of paint on the house made a noticable improvement.

_____   **10.** The coach felt the championship slowly sliping away in the waning moments of the game.

_____   **11.** Congress has passed laws that are deterents to crime.

_____   **12.** It's hard to decide which of the steroes is the best value.

_____   **13.** The woman had poison ivy rashs on her arms and legs.

_____   **14.** The loseing team made a futile attempt to score a touchdown.

_____   **15.** Many writers prefer pens with eraseable ink.

_____   **16.** The swimer dove deep into the cool, clear water.

_____   **17.** The silence of the night envelopped the lone pedestrian.

_____   **18.** The new principal had defenite ideas about how a school should operate.

_____   **19.** He dirties the cuffes on his shirt when he writes on the chalkboard.

_____   **20.** Niether the cow nor the sheep seemed interested in the intruder.

_____   **21.** Have you ever ridden in a sliegh while the snow is falling?

_____   **22.** We were hoping the effects of the earthquake would not be catestrophic.

_____   **23.** The movie was truly aweful.

_____   **24.** The playful monkies climbed on the tree branches.

Vocabulary and Spelling

_____ **25.** Which of the gravies do you prefer for the mashed potatos?

_____ **26.** The anxious father cuped his hands to his mouth, calling out for his daughter in the crowd.

_____ **27.** The Jonesses decided to take a trip to the campgrounds this summer.

_____ **28.** The Victorian-era house was ornatly furnished.

_____ **29.** The recuring dream caused Tamika to toss and turn in her sleep.

_____ **30.** The astronauts experienced the sense of wieghtlessness for the first time.

_____ **31.** The actor playing Hamlet kept forgeting his lines.

_____ **32.** The tireless dog had not yet succeded in catching the agile cat.

_____ **33.** The television and newspaper reports had prejadiced the jurors.

_____ **34.** The first lady had an aristocratic, almost regel bearing about her.

_____ **35.** The hostages were traumitized by the day-long ordeal.

_____ **36.** Hungry and thirsty, the wolfs roamed the countryside in search of nourishment.

_____ **37.** The diplomat made formal introductions between the foriegn dignitaries.

_____ **38.** The gambler watched his winings dwindle to nothing.

_____ **39.** This movie was criticaly acclaimed nationwide.

_____ **40.** The car windows foged up in the freezing cold.

_____ **41.** South Dakota is realy a beautiful state.

_____ **42.** Aunt Jane enjoys siting in a rocker on the front porch.

_____ **43.** The spiralling staircase was the room's focal point.

_____ **44.** The strange formations resultted from the earth's movements many years ago.

_____ **45.** Tourists find Wind Cave National Park incredibley interesting.

Vocabulary and Spelling

▶ **Writing Link** **Write a paragraph using at least ten words from Exercise 1.**

_____

_____

_____

_____

_____

_____

_____

Composition

Unit 14: Composition

Lesson 98

The Writing Process: Prewriting

In the prewriting stage you choose your **topic**, or what you want to say; your **purpose**, or how to say it; and your **audience**, or to whom you want to say it.

Several methods can help you decide what your topic will be. Select a subject from the information generated through *freewriting* about anything that comes to mind; *collecting information* about things that interest you; *making a list* of events, experiences, people, ideas, or words that intrigue you; *asking general questions* that you would like to answer or explore. Make sure your topic is narrow, or specific, enough for you to cover thoroughly.

Next, think about your purpose for writing. Do you want to inform? Entertain? Persuade? Do you have more than one purpose?

Finally, think about your audience. Knowing your audience will help you decide what style, tone, and wording to use in your writing.

▶ **Exercise 1** Spend 10 minutes prewriting, using any of the techniques listed above.

_____

_____

_____

_____

_____

_____

_____

_____

_____

_____

_____

_____

_____

_____

Composition

▶ **Exercise 2** Identify five possible topics from your prewriting that you could write about.

_____

_____

_____

_____

_____

▶ **Exercise 3** Identify six specific topics that you might write about for each general topic listed. Circle the topic in each group that interests you the most. Write a statement that expresses the point you want to make about that topic. A topic has been selected as a sample.

School:

The grading system _____

Need for a larger gym _____

(**Peer-mediated conflict resolution**) _____

Graduation requirements _____

Spanish Club _____

Coach Danforth _____

I think the peer mediation program has helped students discover that conflicts can be resolved without violence.

1. Dating:

_____

_____

_____

2. Politics:

_____

_____

_____

3. Staying healthy:

_____

_____

_____

Composition

▶ **Exercise 4** Draw a line under the word or phrase that would be more appropriate to use in writing for each audience listed.

Letter to the president of the United States (Hey, Prez/<u>Dear Mr. President</u>)

1. Letter to a pen pal who speaks very little English (Toyota 4 × 4 /small truck)

2. Doctor's report to other doctors (arm bones/radius and ulna)

3. Short story for a group of second graders (oak tree/*Quercus alba*)

4. Letter to an older relative (Like, sure!/As if I didn't know that!)

5. Lab report for your biology teacher (monozygotic individuals/identical twins)

6. Description on a menu for restaurant customers (cooked/honey-roasted)

7. Petition sent to the mayor (a bunch of us high school students/we, the tenth graders of West Knox High School)

8. Letter to a possible employer (Later, dude/Cordially yours)

9. Application for a part-time job (greatly benefited/helped a lot)

10. Scientific report detailing seasonal changes (vernal equinox/first fall day)

11. Letter to the editor of the local newspaper (unwise/stupid)

12. Postcard to a close friend (if you get my drift/if you understand my meaning)

13. Caption for a photograph in a fashion magazine (sparkly, straight dress/sequined chemise)

14. Essay about a work of art for a general audience (coolest painting/most striking painting)

15. Poster designed to attract students to the school's tutoring program (Wanna' be a wise guy?/Have you heard about the school tutoring program?)

16. Instructions for doing an experiment (three milliliters/a small amount)

17. Description of the parts of a computer for noncomputer users (hard drive/the hard drive, or information storage area, of the computer)

18. Article in the school newspaper (paltry excuses/trivial excuses)

19. Note to a friend about a personal problem (bully/overbearing individual)

20. Sign warning passersby about danger (Do not enter!/It is not recommended that pedestrians go beyond this point.)

Composition

▶ **Exercise 5** Write a paragraph about the topic for each audience and purpose listed.

Topic: an interesting place to visit in your state

1. **Audience:** a family member **Purpose:** to entertain

_____

_____

_____

_____

_____

_____

2. **Audience:** neighbors **Purpose:** to inform

_____

_____

_____

_____

_____

_____

_____

_____

3. **Audience:** tourists **Purpose:** to persuade

_____

_____

_____

_____

_____

_____

_____

_____

Composition

Lesson 99
The Writing Process: Drafting

You can begin drafting after prewriting. **Drafting** means to put your sentences into paragraph form. Using the topic and purpose, you can develop a **theme**, the point you want to make in the piece. The theme should be stated in a **thesis statement** in the first paragraph. A paragraph consists of a **topic sentence**, which states a main idea related to the theme, and other sentences that support the main idea with details. Your audience, theme, and purpose will influence the **style**, or **voice**, of your writing, which gives it a particular "feel."

▶ **Exercise 1** Write a thesis statement for a paragraph using the topic and purpose provided. Use a complete sentence.

Topic: a sports event **Purpose:** to inform _The final game in the high school basketball tournament_

was a nail-biter.

1. **Topic:** safety **Purpose:** to persuade _____

_____

2. **Topic:** animals **Purpose:** to entertain _____

3. **Topic:** school rules **Purpose:** to persuade _____

_____

4. **Topic:** violence on television **Purpose:** to persuade _____

_____

5. **Topic:** fashions in clothing **Purpose:** to describe _____

_____

6. **Topic:** friendship **Purpose:** to describe _____

7. **Topic:** a complaint about a disappointing product **Purpose:** to persuade _____

_____

8. **Topic:** a person who has made the world a better place **Purpose:** to describe _____

9. **Topic:** a funny experience **Purpose:** to entertain _____

_____

10. **Topic:** immigration **Purpose:** to persuade _____

_____

Composition

Name _____ Class _____ Date _____

▶ **Exercise 2** For each item below, write three related sentences that provide details to support the stated topic sentence.

1. Families are an important part of our community. _____

_____

_____

_____

_____

2. Most students make the decision to stay in high school until they graduate. _____

_____

_____

_____

_____

3. Spring is the most beautiful season of the year. _____

_____

_____

_____

_____

4. High school is a time when you begin to discover who you really are. _____

_____

_____

_____

_____

5. The existence of slavery in the United States before the Civil War has had a long-lasting effect on

race relations in this country. _____

_____

_____

_____

_____

Composition

▶ **Exercise 3** Draft a short paragraph beginning with the thesis statement provided. Adopt a style and voice that is appropriate for the theme.

1. Our school is overflowing with students and desperately needs additional classrooms.

_____

_____

_____

_____

2. Pets! Some people can't live with 'em. I, on the other hand, can't live without 'em.

_____

_____

_____

_____

3. Recently I read a fascinating article about your African game preserve, and I would like to know

   more about it. _____

_____

_____

_____

_____

4. I believe I am well qualified for the position of bagger at the Safeway grocery store.

_____

_____

_____

_____

_____

5. If you like fun, friends, and snow, the Woolly Bears Ski Club wants you! _____

_____

_____

_____

_____

Composition

▶ **Exercise 4 Draft a brief paragraph on each theme. State the theme in a thesis statement, and include supporting sentences relating to the main idea.**

1. **Theme:** asking a teacher for a job recommendation

   _____

   _____

   _____

2. **Theme:** describing something beautiful that made a strong impression on you

   _____

   _____

   _____

   _____

3. **Theme:** restoring good feelings after a disagreement with another person

   _____

   _____

   _____

   _____

4. **Theme:** expressing an opinion on a community or national issue

   _____

   _____

   _____

   _____

5. **Theme:** informing an e-mail pen pal in another city about who you are

   _____

   _____

   _____

   _____

6. **Theme:** giving an account of an exciting or humorous experience

   _____

   _____

   _____

   _____

Composition

Lesson 100
The Writing Process: Revising

After you have completed your draft, take some time to **revise**, or improve, your writing: First, check for *meaning*. Does your thesis capture the point you intended to make? Did you include all the important details? Next, check for *unity*. Is the organization logical? Do the details you provided clearly support your thesis? Finally, check for *coherence*. Does the writing flow? Is each sentence clear?

▶ **Exercise 1** Revise the paragraph below for unity. Draw a line under the sentences that do not relate clearly to the main idea.

The Underground Railroad was the name for the escape network that allowed slaves in the pre-Civil-War South to travel north to freedom. It was not a road, nor was it underground. The first guides on the Underground Railroad were slaves. Houses, empty barns, and even caves were part of the network. So were attics, hidden rooms, and root cellars. The trails and paths connecting all these hiding places were also part of the Underground Railroad. Runaways often felt fearful and hopeless.

▶ **Exercise 2** Revise the paragraph below for coherence. Add words to make the sentences flow better, and clarify individual sentences as needed.

Most starfish have arms. A starfish loses an arm. It gradually regenerates it. First, the arm seals itself off at the break. Cells inside the stump divide quickly. As long as the central part of the starfish is not damaged, it can recover—even losing four out of five arms. _____

_____

_____

_____

_____

_____

_____

_____

_____

_____

Composition

▶ **Exercise 3** Draw a line under the thesis statement in the paragraph below. Replace it with a new thesis statement that clarifies the writer's theme.

Starfish are marine invertebrates. Sometimes sea waves roll rocks on top of the starfish, damaging an arm. In other cases, the starfish sheds an arm if it is attacked by a predator. The starfish sacrifices the arm as a way of escaping from the predator. As the new arm grows to full size, which takes several weeks, the other arms are used for feeding and moving.

_____

_____

_____

▶ **Exercise 4** Revise and rewrite the paragraph below.

The tadpole goes through a fascinating metamorphosis as it grows up, or change in shape. It also changes from an aquatic purely animal to one that can live on land as well. At first the tadpole has a small round body and a long tail. In its early development, it grows large feathery gills. The gills extract oxygen from the water. Inside the tadpole, however, lungs are developing, however. Once the tadpole can breathe air with these lungs. Gills are gradually absorbed by the body. The tadpole's back legs develop. When all four legs are present, the tail begins shrink. The tadpole now emerges from the water for longer and longer periods. Once the tail is gone, the young toad leaves. My little sister loves to catch tadpoles in a nearby creek. As an adult the toad it returns to the water only to breed.

_____

_____

_____

_____

_____

_____

_____

_____

_____

_____

_____

_____

_____

Composition

Lesson 101
The Writing Process: Editing

You are ready to **edit** your work after you have revised it. Look for correct word usage as you edit, and check for subject-verb agreement, correct verb tenses, clear pronoun references, run-on sentences, and sentence fragments. When editing, cross out words and write new words in the margins or spaces between the lines. Next, **proofread** your writing to correct spelling, punctuation, and capitalization errors. Use the following proofreading marks:

insert ∧	trẹdmill
delete ꟾ	developé
insert space # ∧	timẹcapsule
close up space ⌒	over‿achiever
capitalize ≡	hanukkah
make lowercase /	Ṣecretary
check spelling ⬭ sp	(zelous) sp
switch order ∽	red big
new paragraph ¶	. . . by 1965. The next year . . .

▶ **Exercise 1   Edit each sentence for clarity and correct grammar.**

In the past Mr. Arnez ~~runs~~ a car repair shop.
        ran

1. The man who won the lottery. He is from Scranton.

2. He be a featherweight boxer.

3. The woman that works at the bakery is my mother.

4. Lydia and Lynette is too of my best friends.

5. Yesterday's panel feature several college professor.

6. Shawna done made the honor role.

7. They want to use they free passes.

8. Scott the one who can skateboard the best.

Composition

9. Candy and flours are popular gifts on Valentine's Day.

10. Misty has became the star of the field hockey team.

▶ **Exercise 2** Edit the paragraph for clarity and correct grammar.

   The kiwi is a flightless bird from New Zealand. Their wings is only two inches long. Unlike most bird, the kiwi had a keen cents of smell, which it uses to find worms and insects. The kiwi once has the ability to fly. However, it lives on an island with few large predator. For the kiwi, flying were no longer an important means of finding food or escape predators.

▶ **Exercise 3** Proofread each sentence to correct spelling, punctuation, and capitalization.

   The Graph shows a increase in population growth.

1. Count basie who died in 1984, was a pianest, band leader, and composer.

2. Expresss the number using notation scientific.

3. An invertibrat is an animal without a back bone.

4. most rodents have constantly-growing teath.

5. The monguls completed their con quest of China in 1234 A.D.

6. The comunity center offers englsih coarses for immigrants.

7. Lena was talkingto Brad at her locker when denise walked by.

8. The tinny wings of the Humming bird beat about one hundred times a second.

9. Some peoples have greater perripheral vision than others?

10. Work usage refers to using the rightword in the right contaxt.

▶ **Exercise 4** Proofread the paragraph to correct spelling, punctuation, and capitalization.

   The Red Cross Bloodmobile will return for it's monthly visit this Saturday, Febuary 6, from 10 A.M. to 4 P.M. at the EastKnox Middle School. Doners of all blood types are needed at this time. Any one can donate bloood but a person must be at least 17 years old, weigh at least 105 pounds, and in be generaly good health.

Lesson 102
The Writing Process: Presenting

After completing a piece of writing, you may want to **present** or share your work with others. Consideration of this can occur as early as the prewriting stage. The nature of your material affects how and where you might present your writing.

An outlet for presenting your writing to a specific audience is called a **market**. As a tenth-grade student, several markets are available to you. These include school forums, such as newspapers and classroom presentations; community forums, such as newspapers and the newsletters of local organizations; and open-market forums, such as special-interest magazines, writing contests, and periodicals. The *Market Guide for Young Writers,* available in libraries, can give you many ideas for marketing your work.

To decide how to present your piece, first analyze it to pinpoint your audience; then search for an outlet serving that audience. Some markets, such as radio programs or speech contests, offer a chance for oral presentation. In some of these cases, visual aids may enhance your presentation.

▶ **Exercise 1** **Suggest an outlet or market for each piece of writing described below.**

Poem about your community _____local paper_____

1. A speech about the importance of the Fourtheenth Amendment _____

   _____

2. An opinion piece about whether a second high school should be built _____

   _____

3. An essay about how to achieve personal goals _____

4. Lyrics for a song _____

5. A set of ten original riddles _____

6. A one-page short story _____

7. A long, narrative poem about a typical day at your high school _____

   _____

8. An anecdotal essay about family life _____

9. A review of a current movie _____

10. A scary story with numerous sound effects _____

Composition

▶ **Exercise 2** **Suggest a visual aid that could increase the effectiveness of each presentation below.**

A discussion of Mayan ruins ___photos or slides of the ruins_____

1. An oral reading of a poem written in dialogue _____

2. A classroom presentation about recent trends in immigration _____

3. An original song presented at a school talent contest _____

4. A speech to the student body about your qualifications for student office _____

5. A presentation about foods from different parts of China _____

   _____

6. A speech to inspire the basketball team at a pep rally _____

   _____

7. A profile of your school for new students _____

   _____

8. A cable-television commercial to raise money for a new animal shelter _____

   _____

9. A presentation at a nature center about how to identify different shells _____

10. A research paper on how a combustion engine works _____

▶ **Exercise 3** **Develop an idea for a piece of writing intended for a specific audience or market. Then describe how and to whom you might present the piece, giving reasons for your decisions.**

Idea: _____

_____

_____

Intended audience: _____

_____

_____

Form of presentation: _____

_____

Reasons for choice of presentation: _____

_____

_____

Composition

Lesson 103
Outlining

Outlining is a method for organizing the information to be presented in a piece of writing. During prewriting you generate ideas; outlining gives you a way to structure those ideas before you begin drafting. One method for constructing an outline is to transfer pieces of information from your prewriting material to index cards. The cards can then be arranged by main topic and supporting details. When writing an outline, use roman numerals to indicate main topics. Use capital letters for subtopics. Under each topic, you can list details using regular numerals. (If you include details for a subtopic, always give at least two specifics.) An outline for an informational piece on cross-country skiing might look like this:

I. Background
  A. What is it?
    1. Traveling over snow in all kinds of terrain
    2. Skis are lighter and less expensive than in downhill skiing
  B. Is it difficult?
    1. Anyone can learn to ski in this way
    2. Safer than downhill skiing
  C. Benefits
    1. Develops the heart and lungs
    2. Develops muscles of entire body
    3. No need to travel to a ski resort
II. Equipment

▶ **Exercise 1** Evaluate the outline below. Write your comments on the writing lines that follow the outline.

  I. Small reptiles
    A. Turtles
  II. Large reptiles
    A. Crocodiles
      1. Largest is over 20 feet long
      2. Heavy armor plates cover body
      3. Carnivorous
    B. Lizards
      1. Closest relative is the snake
      2. Smaller; eat insects
    C. Alligators
      1. Resemble crocodiles but are in a separate family
      2. Closest living relative of dinosaur
      3. Most intelligent of all reptiles

_____

_____

Composition

_____

_____

▶ **Exercise 2** **Organize the following topics and details into an outline for a piece about Mount St. Helens. Create three main sections in the outline.**

Killed plants and animals within six miles

Considered a "young" volcano

People had time to leave the area

Last eruption before this century was in 1857

Recent eruption

Blew down forests twenty miles away

Warnings of the eruption

Cone of volcano was gone

Earthquakes for two months beforehand

History

Explosion in May 1980

Began as an avalanche of rock, snow, ice

Could be heard one hundred miles away

Created cloud of volcanic ash fifteen miles high

Ash cloud traveled all the way around the world

After the eruption

_____

_____

_____

_____

_____

_____

_____

_____

_____

_____

_____

_____

_____

_____

Lesson 104
Writing Effective Sentences

Use effective sentences to add interest and impact to your writing. As you create and combine sentences, keep the following strategies in mind. Vary the length of the sentences. Avoid using all long sentences or all short sentences. Also vary the structure of the sentences. Avoid using a single sentence pattern for all sentences. Use parallel construction for emphasis. Parallel construction enables you to deliberately repeat certain words, phrases, or sentence structures for effect. You can also use interruption for emphasis. A sudden break in thought can call attention to an important point or detail. Another way to emphasize is to use an unusual sentence pattern that stands out from all the other sentences. When writing a topic sentence, make it specific enough to arouse the reader's interest. Also, write the lead sentence of a piece in a way that will "hook" your readers so that they want to read on.

Use the **active voice** as much as possible. In a sentence in the active voice, the subject performs the action (*he or she speaks*). In a **passive-voice** sentence, the subject is acted upon (e.g., *he or she is spoken to*). Active verbs always make a stronger impression than passive verbs. Generally, only use passive for emphasis or when the "doer" of an action is not known (or when you do not want him or her to be known).

▶ **Exercise 1** **Rewrite the sentences below and add details to create more effective sentences.**

Long ago Persia invaded Greece with a gigantic army. The Greeks fought bravely to defend their freedom. Their heroism is an example to us all. **Although it happened long ago, the Greeks' heroic defense of their liberty against the invasion of the Persians and their gigantic army is still an example to us all.**

1. Badminton is a neglected racket sport in this country. The volleys are fast-paced. The slams can be sizzling. Drop shots can be extremely delicate.

   _____

   _____

2. The event was a baby-sitter's nightmare. It was one of the worst experiences of my life. I was responsible for my neighbor's two-year-old toddler. I almost lost him at the airport.

   _____

   _____

Composition

3. I watch all of the Winter Olympics. All the events are shown on television. Skiing, skating, and bobsledding are covered. I think the most exciting event is speed skating.

_____

_____

4. The Grand Canyon is beautiful. It is most beautiful at sunset. The sun's rays are red then. The sunlight brings out the reddish colors of the rock.

_____

_____

5. This is the beginning of my favorite science-fiction story. Imagine that you're all alone. There's a strange sound from the yard. You are amazed to see a flying saucer.

_____

_____

6. The song is very effective. It is sung by Paul Simon. The song is called "Diamonds on the Souls of Her Shoes." What stands out is vivid images.

_____

7. The dreariest time of year is February. The snow is dirty. Streets are gray. The trees are bare.

_____

8. Many high school basketball players want to play college ball. Some seek college scholarships. They must take the ACT. They must score at least a seventeen on the test.

_____

_____

9. People can find fashionable clothes at One More Time. This store sells lightly used clothes. The cost is one half to one third of the cost of new clothes. You can find designer labels.

_____

_____

10. Charles Dickens wrote *A Christmas Carol*. It is a short novel. The main character is a wealthy miser named Scrooge. He learns that human kindness is more important than money.

_____

_____

Composition

► **Exercise 2 Identify the strategy used to make the sentence or sentences below more effective.**

1. It was the best of times. It was the worst of times. _____

   _____

2. The desk is covered with books and papers, the rug is littered with games, and the bed is

   covered with clothes. And you say this room is "a little untidy"? _____

   _____

3. Some people believe that every woman expects candy and flowers from her sweetheart on

   Valentine's Day. I certainly do not. _____

   _____

4. This beautiful flute melody—listen, there it is again—always makes me feel a little sad.

   _____

5. During the day most owls sleep in the tops of trees. At night they hunt. _____

   _____

6. Do trees lose water through their leaves? To find out you can do the following experiment. You

   will need a twig with leaves, a beaker, cooking oil, and water. _____

   _____

7. Some people at the convention favored the incumbent, while others favored a dark horse

   candidate named Goodman. _____

   _____

8. Kerplop! A frog leaped into the pond. Then all was still again. _____

   _____

9. The fund-raising walk will be held on October 14. All types of people, including students,

   business people, and homemakers, are walking the ten-mile route to raise money to buy bread

   and flour for starving refugee groups in Ethiopia. _____

   _____

10. "Fish gotta swim, birds gotta fly." The seasoned Broadway star began to croon the tune that

    had made her famous. _____

   _____

Composition

▶ **Exercise 3** **Rewrite the sentence in active voice if appropriate. If passive voice is appropriate, explain why.**

1. Complimentary tickets will be distributed to choir members after the rehearsal. _____
   _____

2. After the game, Manuel was spoken to by the coach. _____
   _____

3. The votes were counted by midnight. _____
   _____

4. A good time was had by everyone who attended the picnic. _____
   _____

5. The song was sung with a full-throated voice and great feeling by Barbra Streisand.
   _____

   _____

6. Gold was discovered in this region around 1847. _____
   _____

7. Only one conclusion from this experiment can be drawn by us. _____
   _____

8. This painting, unlike the others, is painted in oil. _____
   _____

9. This film is believed by many students at our school to be the funniest film of the year.
   _____

   _____

10. All forty-one players were squeezed onto the risers for the team picture. _____
   _____

Lesson 105
Building Paragraphs

The supporting details in a paragraph can be arranged in different ways. **Chronological order** places events in the order in which they happened. **Spatial order** is the way objects appear. **Compare/contrast order** shows similarities and differences.

The first of the following paragraphs makes use of chronological order; the second, spatial order; and the third, compare/contrast order.

After parking the car, we walked to the top of a hill overlooking the Ohio River near Ripley, Ohio. There we saw the Rankin House, a famous stop on the Underground Railroad that helped fugitive slaves to escape. Gazing up at the second-floor window, I tried to imagine the lantern shining to inform runaway slaves that it was safe to cross the river.

On a table in the living room of the house are a wooden globe and John Rankin's Bible. Upstairs are the many hiding places, tiny wooden compartments where runaway slaves were hidden. Behind the house are a hundred steps, built by Rankin in 1828, that lead down to the Ohio River.

Looking south across the Ohio River, you can't help but think about the differences between Ohio and Kentucky in the years before the Civil War. Ohio was a free state, but Kentucky was a slave state. While Ohioans like John Rankin were helping slaves gain their freedom, just eleven miles south of the river, slaves were being sold at auction in Washington, Kentucky.

▶ **Exercise 1 Number the following sentences in chronological order.**

_____ First, open the door and climb in.

_____ Make sure the car is in park.

_____ When you're ready to go, put the car in gear—either *Drive* or *Reverse*.

_____ After making sure the door is closed, fasten your safety belt.

_____ Turn the key.

_____ Check the door to make sure it's closed.

_____ There's a safe way to start a car.

_____ Insert the key into the ignition.

_____ Then look carefully around you in all directions, and you're ready to drive off.

_____ Then let the car warm up for a short time, especially if it's cold out.

Composition

▶ **Exercise 2 Rewrite the paragraph in chronological order.**

After listening carefully to each person's description of the conflict, the mediator tries to get each person to find areas of agreement. To address this serious problem, our school has a peer mediation service. The peer mediator has to make it clear from the beginning that he or she is not taking sides. In peer mediation, student volunteers are trained to help other students resolve conflicts without resorting to violence. Building on points where the two people agree, the peer mediator tries to help them reach a solution that is acceptable to both. Some schools have a serious problem with fights and other kinds of violence. The mediator then asks each person to explain the problem from his or her point of view. Students who are having a problem meet together with a peer mediator.

_____

_____

_____

_____

_____

_____

_____

_____

_____

_____

_____

_____

_____

_____

_____

_____

_____

Composition

► **Exercise 3 Rewrite the paragraph in spatial order.**

  Past the campfire on the left was our family's tent. On the table was a bright red and white
checkered tablecloth and a candle, as in an Italian restaurant. Inside I could see our sleeping bags
and pillows all laid out for the night. High in the trees I thought I heard an owl hooting, and
somewhere in the distance I might have heard the lonesome cry of the whippoorwill. Beside the
table was a fire pit, with the burning logs crackling merrily. Sitting at the picnic table and looking
around our campsite, I was amazed at how comfortable we had made it. The dinner of spaghetti
and salad made my mouth water after a long day of hiking in the woods. Beyond the cozy clearing
of our campsite was the darkened forest, with its aromatic pine and fir trees.

_____

_____

_____

_____

_____

_____

_____

_____

_____

_____

_____

_____

_____

_____

_____

_____

_____

Composition

▶ **Exercise 4 Choose two topics below. Write one paragraph using the compare/contrast order and one paragraph using chronological order.**

your favorite relative   two of your best friends

what makes a vacation a really good one   dogs and cats as family pets

shopping for a new article of clothing   the most exciting sport to watch

Topic 1: _____

_____

_____

_____

_____

_____

_____

_____

_____

_____

Topic 2: _____

_____

_____

_____

_____

_____

_____

_____

_____

_____

_____

Composition

Lesson 106
Paragraph Ordering

Revising a first draft includes checking the **unity** and **coherence** of paragraphs. You need to make sure that each paragraph is unified, that it opens with a topic sentence (a sentence that states the main idea of the paragraph) and that the supporting details are related to the topic. To make sure the comparisons are clear, or coherent, you must check chronological details for proper order and compare/contrast details. Finally, you need to make sure that ideas are properly linked by transitions.

▶ **Exercise 1 Revise the following paragraphs for unity and coherence.**

Let's take a look at the place where everything begins and find out why the modern automobile engine is truly an engineering marvel. Ford, General Motors, and Chrysler are known as the Big Three United States auto manufacturers. It's an extremely complicated process, one that has been refined for more than a hundred years. Have you ever wondered what actually happens when a driver steps on the accelerator of a car? Dozens of different systems have to work properly—and work together—for that automobile to pull away from the curb or out of the driveway. Man, it's an amazing machine!

The piston goes through a four-stroke cycle, which serves to "combust," or burn, the fuel mixture and transfer its energy to the car's wheels. Each cylinder houses a moving arm called a piston, which fits very tightly against the walls of the cylinder. The four strokes are repeated as many as six thousand times a minute, and the piston can travel at speeds of three hundred miles per hour or more!

In the piston's first stroke, an inlet valve opens and the piston slides down the smooth walls of the cylinder, sucking in air and gasoline. Some cars and trucks use diesel fuel, but a diesel engine works in a different way. In the second stroke, the valve shuts and the piston moves upward to compress the fuel very tightly.

Next, the spark flares and the fuel explodes, pushing the piston down very fast. The pistons transfer the downward movement's energy to the crankshaft by means of connecting rods, and the crankshaft transfers the power to the wheels. If the crankshaft ever breaks or wears out, it's very expensive to replace. Mostly because it is very hard to reach. In the fourth stroke, the piston travels upward again, pushing the leftover hot gases out the exhaust valve.

Composition

While car engines vary in size and power, almost all are internal combustion engines that use the four-stroke cycle. Most are powered by a mixture of gasoline and air, which is ignited by a spark to release its considerable energy. Modern cars have from four to twelve cylinders. This controlled explosion, set off by an electrical spark from a component called the spark plug, takes place in a metal chamber called the cylinder.

▶ **Exercise 2 Rewrite the paragraphs using your revisions as a guide.**

_____

_____

_____

_____

_____

_____

_____

_____

_____

_____

_____

_____

_____

_____

_____

_____

_____

_____

_____

_____

_____

Composition

Lesson 107
Personal Letters

A **personal letter** is a letter to a friend or relative. You write letters to describe recent events in your life, to ask the recipient questions about his or her life, and to express your personal feelings, hopes, and desires. A personal letter can also be an invitation or a thank-you note. In every case, careful consideration of your audience is extremely important when writing personal letters. These letters are usually written in indented form. Each paragraph is indented, as well as each line in the heading and the signature line.

▶ **Exercise 1** Read the following personal letter. Answer each question.

> 7561 Knoxville Road
> Saddle River, New Jersey 07458
> January 12, 1995

Dear Shannon,
    Thanks for your letter. Being president of the Computer Club takes a lot of time. If I had known you were going to move to Dallas and that I would have to replace you, I might never have let myself be elected vice president!
    Well, the big news is that I finally bought a CD-ROM drive for my computer. I hate to say it, but you were right. It's fantastic! How did I ever live without one? I've already gotten a few games, and the graphics are unbelievable. Do you have any recommendations for multimedia encyclopedias? I want to get one. However, since they are expensive, I want to get advice from someone who knows something about them. Write back as soon as you can. Have you met any other computer nerds in Dallas? (Ha-ha, just kidding!)

> Your friend,
> *Courtney*

1. Why is Courtney writing to Shannon? _____

_____

2. Do you think Courtney and Shannon are good friends? Why? _____

_____

3. How is this a good example of a personal letter? _____

_____

_____

4. What might Shannon include in a response to Courtney's letter? _____

_____

_____

Composition

▶ **Exercise 2 Write a personal letter to a friend.**

_____

_____

_____

_____

_____

_____

_____

_____

_____

_____

_____

_____

_____

_____

_____

_____

_____

_____

_____

_____

_____

_____

_____

_____

_____

_____

Composition

Different situations call for different kinds of personal letters. You would probably use a different tone and style in writing to an adult relative than you would in writing to your best friend. Your letter to your relative would probably be more formal, while you might make use of slang or secret code words in your letter to your best friend.

You would also write differently to a favorite author, performer, or sports figure. In your letters to these people, you would probably want to describe why you admire the person and how he or she has influenced your life.

▶ **Exercise 3** **Write a letter to an adult relative asking for information for a school project on your family's personal history. Explain why you would like the information and what you are going to do with it.**

_____

_____

_____

_____

_____

_____

_____

_____

_____

_____

_____

_____

_____

_____

_____

_____

_____

_____

_____

_____

Composition

▶ **Exercise 4** Write a letter to an author, performer, or sports star whom you especially admire. Describe why you admire the person and how he or she has influenced your life.

_____

_____

_____

_____

_____

_____

_____

_____

_____

_____

_____

_____

_____

_____

_____

_____

_____

_____

_____

_____

_____

_____

_____

Composition

Lesson 108
Business Letters: Letters of Request or Complaint

A **letter of request** is a letter that asks for information or service. When you write a letter of request, always be clear and courteous. Explain what information you need and why you need it. Include any information the receiver may need to answer your request.

Business letters are usually written in block form or semiblock form. In block form, everything is lined up with the left margin. In semiblock form, the heading, complimentary close, and signature are placed on the right side of the page (see Exercise 1).

▶ **Exercise 1** Examine the body of the following letter. Do you think it is a good example of a letter of request? Why or why not? Write your critique below.

Dear Person in Charge of Research:
    I am a freshman at Glenville Hi School and am working on a project on family histry. Which is due next week, so I'm kind of like in a hurry. Do you have any information on the Guimond family in this area. We come from France. Please send me anything you have so I can use it in my project.

                          Sincerely,
                          Sarah Guimond

_____

_____

_____

_____

▶ **Exercise 2** Write a short letter requesting information on one of the following topics. Be sure to use proper business-letter format.

    information on a local service program you'd like to join
    information on the different guitar models a company sells
    information on how to obtain tickets to a sporting event
    information on which breeds of dogs would make appropriate pets for your family

_____

_____

_____

_____

_____

_____

Composition

A **letter of complaint** is a letter informing someone of a problem or concern and sometimes requests action. It should be clear, concise, and reasonable. Never let your anger get the best of you. Begin your letter by stating the problem and telling briefly how it happened. Then use supporting details as evidence of your problem. End the letter by explaining what you would like done about the matter. Always avoid insults and threats.

▶ **Exercise 3** **Read the following letter of complaint. Describe any problems and suggest how to correct them.**

1457 Piedmont Rd.
Lincoln, Nebraska 40521
March 20, 1996

La Créme Lotion
111 Corporate Dr.
Young America, MN 14444

Dear maker of stinky hand lotion,
   Something disgusting happened to me that you might want to know about because its all you fault. I bought a bottle of your La Creme hand lotion for $12.99 because your TV ads say that its the best. Well, your lying about that. It's not the best. More like the worst. the reason is it smells like rotten eggs—or worse, like there was something dead in there. I wouldn't put this stuff on a stray dog, not to mention my hands. Give me a refund or youll be sorry.

Not your friend,
Danielle Marshall

_____

_____

▶ **Exercise 4** **Revise and rewrite the above letter of complaint.**

_____

_____

_____

_____

_____

_____

_____

_____

_____

Composition

Lesson 109
Business Letters: Résumés and Cover Letters

A résumé is a summary of your work experience, school experience, talents, and interests. You use it to apply for a job or for admittance into a school or academic program. You want your résumé to be clear, concise, expressive, and informative. In describing your accomplishments, use action verbs (*won* the prize, *taught* the class). Because a résumé is a summary, it is not necessary to use complete sentences. However, you do want to use a consistent format, as in the following example.

Rebecca Chin
345 Boyle Street, Apt. 9
Concord, MA 01742
(508) 369-2120

Objective:	Part-time employment in a preschool or day-care center
Work Experience:	Counselor, Camp Rolling Hills, Lenox, MA, 1993, 1994
Responsibilities:	Cabin counselor for ten third-grade girls
Education:	Emerson High School, September 1994–present, 3.7 GPA
	Fox Middle School, September 1989–June 1993, 3.8 GPA
References:	Ruben Gonzalez, teacher, Emerson High School, (508) 567-1092
	Jean Robertson, Director, Camp Rolling Hills, (508) 444-9078

▶ **Exercise 1** **Answer the following questions.**

1. How might the headings (Objective, Work Experience, Responsibilities, etc.) be ordered if Rebecca were applying for a school program? Why? What else might she include if she were applying for a school program? _____

_____

_____

_____

2. The headings Rebecca used are not the only ones you can use on a résumé. What are some others? _____

3. If you were the manager of a day-care center and considering hiring Rebecca, would you be impressed by her résumé? Why or why not? _____

_____

_____

_____

_____

Composition

4. Whom should you use as references? Why is it a good idea to get permission before you use

someone as a reference? _____

_____

_____

▶ **Exercise 2** You are applying for one of the following:

      placement in an advanced school class
      a summer job as a camp counselor
      a job coaching children's sports
      a special off-campus study program

Freewrite for ten minutes about the information you would want in your résumé.

_____

_____

_____

_____

_____

_____

▶ **Exercise 3** Write your résumé.

_____

_____

_____

_____

_____

_____

_____

_____

_____

_____

_____

_____

Composition

A **cover letter** is a brief letter of introduction that usually accompanies a résumé. A cover letter states what you are applying for and where you can be contacted. It also refers the reader to your résumé for additional information. It may also briefly state why you are well suited for the position.

The following is an example of a well-formatted, concise cover letter. Note that the letter follows business-letter style and that it is directed to a specific person.

Rebecca Chin
345 Boyle Street, Apt. 9
Concord, MA 01742
April 13, 1996

Mr. Thomas Orlando
Director, Louisa May Alcott Preschool
14 Third Street
Concord, MA 01742

Dear Mr. Orlando:
I am an honors student at Emerson High and am interested in part-time after-school work in a preschool or day-care center. I am dedicated to helping young children learn and grow. I have a special interest in your preschool because of your focus on teaching French at an early age. I have taken three French courses and I plan to take the upper level course next year. Enclosed is a copy of my résumé I hope you find that my qualifications meet your needs. Please feel free to contact me if you have any questions. I hope to hear from you soon.

Sincerely,
Rebecca Chin

▶ **Exercise 4** **Write a cover letter to send with your résumé for the position you chose in Exercises 2 and 3.**

_____

_____

_____

_____

_____

_____

_____

_____

_____

Composition

_____

_____

_____

_____

_____

_____

_____

_____

_____

_____

_____

_____

_____

_____

_____

_____

_____

_____

_____

_____

_____

_____

_____

_____

When you have finished, exchange cover letters with a friend and critique each other's letters. Discuss suggested revisions and make any appropriate changes.

Composition

*I*ndex

Index

with nonessential elements, 15, 42–43, 255

for parenthetical elements, 15, 43, 257

in references, 15, 261

after salutations and closings in letters, 15, 263

in series, 15, 44, 253

in tag questions, 15, 263

with titles, 261

Common nouns, defined, 2, 49

Comparative degree, modifiers, 9–10, 199, 201, 203

Compare/contrast order, 18, 327

Comparison
of adjectives, 9–10, 199, 201
of adverbs, 9–10, 199, 201
double and incomplete, 10, 203
irregular, 10, 201

Complements, 3, 6, 57, 83, 85–86
direct objects, 6, 83
indirect objects, 6, 83
object, 6, 85
subject, 3, 6, 57, 86

Complete predicates, defined, 6, 77

Complete subjects, defined, 6, 77

Complex sentences, defined, 7, 105

Compound elements
adjectives, 279
numbers, hyphens in, 17, 279
predicates, 79, 103, 127
prepositions, 5, 67
sentences, 7, 103
subjects, 5, 79, 103, 127, 171

Compound-complex sentences, 7, 105

Concrete nouns, defined, 2, 48

Conjunctions, defined, 5, 69
conjunctive adverbs, 5, 71, 257
coordinating, 5, 69
correlative, 5, 69
list, 69, 71, 101
subordinating, 5, 69, 101

Context clues, 17, 291

Continual, continuous, 12

Conversations, punctuating, 15, 271

Coordinate adjectives, 253

Coordinating conjunctions, 5, 69

Correlative conjunctions, 5, 69

Could of, might of, must of, should of, would of, avoiding, 12, 222

D

Dangling modifiers, avoiding, 38–39, 209

Dashes, 15, 267

Dates, punctuating, 15, 283

Declarative sentences, defined, 8, 119

Degrees of comparison, 199, 201

Demonstrative pronouns, 54

Dependent (subordinate) clauses,
adjective, 7, 107, 109
adverb, 7, 111
essential, 109
nonessential, 109
noun, 7, 115
punctuating, 42, 109, 259
practice, 101–118

Diagraming
sentences with clauses, 133–134
simple sentences, 127
simple sentences with phrases, 129–130

Different from, not *different than,* 12, 223

Direct address, 15, 263

Direct objects, defined, 6, 83

Doesn't, don't, 12, 223

Double comparisons, avoiding, 10, 203

Double negatives, avoiding, 10, 207, 222

Drafting, 18, 311
style, voice, 311
theme, 311
thesis statement, 311
topic sentence and related sentences, 311

E

Each, agreement with, 171

Editing, 18, 317
proofreading marks, 317

Effect, affect, 11, 219

Either, agreement with, 69, 171

Ellipses, 15

Emigrate, immigrate, 12, 223

Emphatic verbs, defined, 4, 151

Except, accept, 11, 219

Exclamation points, 14, 119, 245
and quotation marks, 16, 273

Exclamatory sentences, defined, 8, 119

F

Farther, further, 12, 223

Fewer, less, 12, 223

Fragments, sentence, defined, 22–23, 121

Freewriting, 18, 307

Further, farther, 12, 223

Future tense, 3, 146, 149

Future perfect tense, 3, 147, 149

G

Gerund phrases, 7, 95

Gerunds, defined, 7, 95

Good, well, 12, 205

H

Had of, avoiding, 12

Hanged, hung, 12, 223

Hardly, in double negatives, 222

Helping (auxiliary) verbs, defined, 3, 59

Hung, hanged, 12, 223

Hyphens, rules, 16, 279

I

Illusion, allusion, 11

Immigrate, emigrate, 12, 223

Imperative mood, verbs, 4

Imperative sentences, defined, 8, 119

In, into, 12, 223

Incomplete comparisons, avoiding, 203

Indefinite pronouns, defined, 2, 54, 175
agreement with verb, 8, 175
as antecedents, 191
list, 8, 54, 175

Independent (main) clauses, 7, 101, 103, 105

Indicative mood, verbs, 4

Indirect objects, defined, 6, 83

Indirect quotations, 271

Infinitive phrases, 7, 97

Infinitives, defined, 7, 97
as adjectives, 7, 97
as adverbs, 7, 97
as nouns, 7, 97

Inquiry, letters of, 20, 337

Inside addresses in letters, 19–20, 337

Intensive pronouns, 2, 52

Interjections, 5, 71, 257

Interrogative pronouns, 2, 53
list, 53
who, whom, 185

Interrogative sentences, defined, 8, 119

Into, in, 12, 223

Intransitive verbs, defined, 3, 55